GHAZALI'S THEORY OF VIRTUE

STUDIES IN ISLAMIC PHILOSOPHY AND SCIENCE

Published under the auspices of
the Society for the Study of Islamic Philosophy and Science

Ghazali's Theory of Virtue

MOHAMED AHMED SHERIF

1975
State University of New York Press
ALBANY

Mohamed A. Sherif is an Assistant Professor of Philosophy, University of Tripoli, Tripoli, Libya

Ghazali's Theory of Virtue
First Edition
Published by the State University of New York Press
99 Washington Avenue, Albany, New York 12210

Printed in U.S.A.

Library of Congress Cataloging in Publication Data
Sherif, Mohamed A.
Ghazali's theory of virtue.
Bibliography: p.
1. al-Ghazālī, 1058-1111. 2. Virtue.
I. Title.
B753.G34S54 179'.9 71-38000
ISBN O-87395-206-5
ISBN O-87395-207-3 (microfiche)

To my brother Hammali

CONTENTS

LIST OF TABLES

TRANSLITERATION AND ABBREVIATIONS

TRANSLITERATION

Consonants

ء	=	ʼ (except when initial)		
ب	=	b	ط =	ṭ
ت	=	t	ظ =	ẓ
ث	=	th	ع =	ʻ
ج	=	j	غ =	gh
ح	=	ḥ	ف =	f
خ	=	kh	ق =	q
د	=	d	ك =	k
ذ	=	dh	ل =	l
ر	=	r	م =	m
ز	=	z	ن =	n
س	=	s	ه =	h
ش	=	sh	و =	w
ص	=	ṣ	ي =	y
ض	=	ḍ		

Short vowels

َ = a, ُ = u, ِ = i

Long vowels

ا = ā, ُو = ū, ِي = ī

ه is kept at the end of words, e.g., فضيلة = faḍīlah. All Arabic proper names are transliterated according to these rules with the exception of the following:

Ghazali = al-Ghazālī
Avicenna = Ibn Sīnā
Averroes = Ibn Rushd

ABBREVIATIONS

Two of Ghazali's works are of primary importance for this study. They are abbreviated as follows:

C = *Mīzān al-ʿAmal* ("Criterion of Action"). Cairo: Maṭbaʿat Kurdistān al-ʿIlmiyyah, 1328/1910.

R = *Iḥyāʾ ʿUlūm al-Dīn* ("The Revival of the Religious Sciences"). 15 vols. Cairo: Lajnat Nashr al-Thaqāfah al-Islāmiyyah, 1356/1937-1357/1938. The pagination is continuous throughout the fifteen volumes of this edition. I have only indicated the "Quarters" and "Books" proposed by Ghazali himself. Thus, *R*, IV. 6. = the sixth Book of Quarter four of the *Revival*.

Other works by Ghazali are cited in their short titles only, with no mention of author. Journals, encyclopedias, and general reference works that are cited more than once are also abbreviated. Full titles appear at the end of the bibliography.

Further information about these and other works of Ghazali is to be found in the bibliography.

ACKNOWLEDGMENTS

I wish to express my gratitude to my honored teacher, Professor Muhsin Mahdi, for his sympathetic guidance and painstaking assistance over a long period of study. It is a pleasant duty to acknowledge his numerous valuable suggestions concerning the methodology and organization of this work. He gave generously of his time, not only when he was a professor at the University of Chicago but also after he joined Harvard University. Professors Wilfred Madelung, Heshmat Moayyad, and Fazlur Rahman were all kind enough to read the original manuscript with great care and to offer detailed comments and criticism. Their help aided substantially in making this study possible. While gladly acknowledging my great indebtedness to all these scholars, I wish to point out that I alone am responsible for any defects.

This book is based on a Ph. D. dissertation. My graduate study was possible only through a generous scholarship from the University of Libya. My gratitude must also be expressed for a Ford Foundation International Studies grant which I received through the University of Chicago for the academic year 1969-70.

Dr. Hüseyn Atay was extremely kind in helping me to find manuscripts of Ghazali's works which were important for this study. While carrying out my research at Harvard University I received generous assistance from Harvard University College Library. This study owes a great deal to Mrs. Miriam Galston for her continuous criticism and comments. I also have to mention the great encouragement I received from my wife who endured patiently my indulgence in research.

Finally, this study owes more than I can state to a number of friends and colleagues. Without mentioning them by name. I wish to thank them all.

Chapter I / INTRODUCTION

The Unity in Ghazali's Thought

According to a tradition attributed to the prophet Muḥammad at the beginning of every hundred years God will send someone to revive the faith of the Islamic community.[1] In the history of Islam, Ghazali (Abū Ḥāmid Muḥammad b. Muḥammad, d. 505/1111) is considered the reformer (*mujaddid*) of the fifth century of the Islamic era, and he was himself of the opinion that he was favored by divine providence for this role.[2] The majority of Muslims agree that he is the Proof of Islam (*ḥujjat al-Islām*), and a large number of learned Muslims went so far as to consider him the greatest religious authority of Islam after the prophet Muḥammad. As a result of the great esteem accorded to him, Ghazali deeply influenced Islamic thought in particular and medieval thought in general.

Ghazali's accomplishments cover many diverse fields of learning: Islamic jurisprudence, dialectical theology, philosophy, and mysticism and because of his manifold interests students of Islamic thought differ sharply as to his greatest achievement. Some regard him as a dialectical theologian who put an end to philosophy in the Muslim East and even consider him its chief executioner.[3] Some regard him as a jurist, although

1. Abū Dāwūd, *Sunan* (Cairo: al-Maktabah al-Tijāriyyah, 1935), II, 424.

2. Ghazali, *al-Munqidh min al-Ḍalāl*, ed. by Jamīl Ṣalība and Kāmil 'Ayyād (5th ed.; Damascus: Maṭba'at al-Jāmi'ah al-Sūriyyah, 1956), p. 115. Ghazali was born in the town of Ṭūs in Khurāsān in 450/1058. He belonged to the Shāfi'ite school of law. For his biography and works see his own *Munqidh*; Tāj al-Dīn al-Subkī, *Ṭabaqāt al-Shāfi'iyyah al-Kubrā* (Cairo: al-Maṭba'ah al-Ḥusayniyyah, 1323/1905-1324/1906), IV, 101-182; al-Murtaḍā al-Zabīdī, *Itḥāf al-Sādah al-Muttaqīn bi Sharḥ Iḥyā' 'Ulūm al-Dīn* (al-Maṭba'ah al-Maymūniyyah, 1311/1912), I, 2-50; Duncan B. MacDonald, « The Life of al-Ghazali, with especial reference to his religious experiences and opinions, » *JAOS*, XX (1899), 71-132; *GAL*, I, 535-546; *GAL(S)*, I, 744-756.

3. For example, 'Alī Sāmī al-Nashshār, *Nash'at al-Fikr al-Falsafī fī al-Islām* (2d ed.; Alexandria, Egypt: Dār al Ma'ārif, 1965), p. 77; A. J. Arberry, *Revelation and Reason in Islam* (London: George Allen & Unwin, Ltd., 1965), p. 61.

others deny him this status on the grounds that his teachings violate the strictly established rules agreed upon by Muslim jurists. Others see Ghazali as a philosopher at heart who articulated his philosophy in Islamic terminology,[1] and many agree that he was a great champion of mysticism, pointing to his avowed pride in regarding himself a follower of the mystic path.

The diversity of attitudes toward Ghazali frequently results in considering him primarily a master of one or another field of learning. Consequently students of Islamic thought usually undertake to explain how one of these disciplines truly represents Ghazali's real doctrine, interpreting his writings in the other fields as supplementary and, therefore, as containing secondary and less significant views. These attitudes may attest to the richness of Ghazali's thought and his ability to contribute to many branches of learning in a substantial way but they offer only partial interpretations of Ghazalian thought.

The worst difficulty in any partial interpretation is that it cannot satisfactorily account for Ghazali's interest in contributing to many diverse fields, and to be aware of this crucial problem one need only turn to Ghazali's own intellectual autobiography, the *Deliverer from Error* (*al-Munqidh min al-Ḍalāl*), in which he relates his search for certainty. His inquiry into different sciences, he explains, was extensive and for the purpose of understanding their fundamental principles. He did not move haphazardly from field to field, but tried to discover the relationships among them. By examining his writings on all these subjects one can discern a movement which finally fulfilled Ghazali's quest for truth. Because the unity of his thought only emerges when we are aware of this movement. Ghazali's true teaching cannot be adequately understood by examining certain of his doctrines to the exclusion of the others.

On the other hand, by taking one central theme in Ghazali's writings it should be possible to explore the nature of this unity, and since such a theme should be representative of all the disciplines to which he contributed, I propose here a study of Ghazali's ethics. In all his works ethics appears as an important, if not always the central, issue. "He was

1. Taqiyy al-Dīn Aḥmad Ibn Taymiyyah, *Naqḍ al-Manṭiq*, ed. by Muḥammad 'Abd al-Razzāq Ḥamzah and Sulaymān b. 'Abd al-Raḥmān al-Ṣāni' (Cairo: Maṭba'at al-Sunnah al-Muḥammadiyyah, 1951), p. 56; *al-Radd 'Alā al-Mantiqiyyīn*, ed. by 'Abduṣ-Ṣamad Sharafud-Dīn al-Kutubī (Bombay: Qayyimah Press, 1949), p. 195; cf. al-Subkī, *Ṭabaqāt*, IV, 123, where he quotes the criticism of Abū 'Abd-Allāh al-Māzirī to the effect that Ghazali was never successful in theology because he was influenced by philosophy.

emphatically ethical in his attitude; he lays stress on the *value for us* of a piece of knowledge."[1] In his quest for truth in the *Deliverer*, Ghazali emphasizes that knowledge of any thing in any way must be evaluated in proportion to its usefulness in leading man to those moral states that make possible the attainment of ultimate happiness. Thus, ethics provides the link between knowledge and action and is the indispensable means for attaining man's highest end.

Ghazali's declaration that his search for the truth ended by adopting mysticism confirms the view that ethics is a central theme in his writings.[2] In his view, the ultimate end of mysticism is the vision of God in the hereafter, and he regards this as belonging to the knowledge of revelation (*'ilm al-mukāshafah*) which cannot be expressed or laid down in writing. What can be expressed, however, is the knowledge of devotional practice (*'ilm al-mu'āmalah*) which shows the novice how to reach the ultimate goal. This, in turn, comes about through refinement of the soul, which consists in purifying the soul of bad character traits and acquiring noble ones. The process of acquiring good character traits is continued by the novice until he attains love of God in this life which prepares him for the vision of God in the hereafter. Therefore, the core of Ghazali's mystical doctrine can ultimately be derived from his ethical teaching.

For these reasons, I propose to study the unity of Ghazali's ethical teaching as set forth in his principal writings. The objection may be raised that ethics comprises only part of Ghazali's understanding of the attainment of truth and happiness and that a complete account should include knowledge of revelation as well. However, I maintain that a coherent study is only possible through examining what Ghazali himself discussed and not through conjecturing about a subject which Ghazali omitted and, indeed, declared could not be expressed in writing. My inquiry, I believe, will raise the questions essential to any ethical teaching and will reveal the basic problems inherent in Ghazali's ethics.

The rest of this introduction will discuss Ghazali's principal works and the divisions of the sciences set forth in them, and will give a preliminary outline of the problematic elements of his ethics.

1. MacDonald, "Life of al-Ghazali," p. 120; cf. T. J. de Boer, "Ethics and Morality (Muslim)," *ERE*, V, 508.

2. *Munqidh*, pp. 95 ff.

The Place of Ethics in the Division of Sciences

Aside from his early manuals on jurisprudence (*fiqh*), the first work in which Ghazali speaks about ethics is the *Aims of the Philosophers* (*Maqāṣid al-Falāsifah*). This book was written some time after 484/1091-2 and before 486/1094, during the period of less than two years when he was studying philosophy in his spare time with the primary aim of understanding it.[1] He discusses briefly three of the sciences of the philosophers, namely, logic, physics, and metaphysics. His purpose is to give objective accounts of these philosophic disciplines without comment. The refutation of these sciences, he says, will be made in a subsequent work.[2]

Ghazali treats logic, metaphysics, and physics in this order. He prefaces his discussion of metaphysics with two introductory remarks. The first concerns the divisions of science. The science of wisdom *al-'ilm al-ḥikmī*) is divided into two parts. The first deals with man's actions and is called practical science; it aims at finding out the human activities conducive to man's well-being in this life as well as in the next. The second makes known the states of beings as they are, and is called theoretical science. Now practical science is, in turn, divided into three parts. One is the science of the governance of man's relations with other men; it culminates in political science. The second is the science of the governance of the household; it teaches the manner of living with one's wife, children, and servants, as well as all other domestic affairs. Finally, "the third practical science is ethics (*'ilm al-akhlāq*), which deals with the way man ought to act to be good and virtuous in his character and qualities."[3]

At the end of the *Aims*, Ghazali promises to refute certain philosophic sciences in the book entitled the *Incoherence of the Philosophers* (*Tahāfut*

1. *Munqidh*, pp. 69-70. Most of those who have written on Ghazali's works and their chronology agree on this date; cf. George F. Hourani. "The Chronology of Ghazali's Writings," *JAOS*, LXXX (1959), 227; L. Massignon, *Recueil de textes inédits concernant l'histoire de la mystique en pays d'Islam* (Paris: Librairie Orientaliste Paul Geuthner, 1929), p. 93; Maurice Bouyges. *Essai de chronologie des œuvres d'al-Ghazali* (Algazel), édité et mis à jour par Michel Allard (Beirut: Imprimerie Catholique, 1959), pp. 23-24; 'Abd al-Raḥmān Badawī, *Mu'allafāt al-Ghazālī* (Cairo: al-Majlis al-A'lā li-Ri'āyat al-Adāb wa al-Funūn wa al-'Ulūm al-Ijtimā'iyyah, 1961), pp. 53-63; W. Montgomery Watt, "The Authenticity of the Works Attributed to al-Ghazālī," *JRAS* (1952), p. 44.

2. Ghazali, *Maqāṣid al-Falāsifah*, ed. by Sulaymān Dunyā (Cairo: Dār al-Ma'ārif, 1961), pp. 31-32.

3. *Maqāṣid*, pp. 134-135.

al-Falāsifah), which appears to have been written about 488/1095.[1] In this latter book he argues against the philosophers' views on physics and metaphysics, but allows logic to stand as an unobjectionable science. He retains the divisions of science introduced in the *Aims*, but now he openly identifies his philosophic sources, the writings of Avicenna and al-Fārābī, who are, according to him, the best representatives of the Muslim philosophers, and the only ones who truly understood Aristotle, the master of Greek philosophy.[2] Ghazali's division of the sciences seems to be particularly influenced by Avicenna, who also divides practical science into the three parts mentioned by Ghazali in the *Aims*.[3] In the introduction to his major work, the *Healing* (*al-Shifā'*), Avicenna draws the same distinction between theoretical and practical sciences and then distinguishes the same three divisions of the practical sciences, namely, political science, household management, and ethics (*'ilm al-akhlāq*).[4] This division differs substantially from that of al-Fārābī in the *Enumeration of the Sciences* (*Iḥṣā' al-'Ulūm*) which does not mention an independent science of ethics but includes it in political science without mentioning it by name.[5] Ghazali prefers Avicenna's division in which ethics is a relatively independent practical science—independent, that is, from political science.[6]

The first statement of Ghazali on ethics is presented within a context which suggests that it is borrowed from the philosophers. A more personal and positive statement is found in two other works, which chronologically follow each other in the way that the *Aims* is followed by the *Incoherence*. They are the *Standard of knowledge* (*Mi'yār al-'ilm*), and the *Criterion of Action* (*Mīzān al-'Amal*).

1. *Maqāṣid*, p. 380; Hourani, "Chronology," p. 227; Massignon, *Recueil*, p. 93; Bouyges, *Essai*, p. 23; Watt, "Authenticity," p. 44; Badawī *Mu'allafāt*, p. 69.

2. Ghazali, *Tahāfut al-Falāsifah* ("Incoherence des philosophes"), ed. by Maurice Bouyges (Beirut: Imprimerie Catholique, 1927), p. 9; *Munqidh*, p. 73.

3. Avicenna, *Fī Aqsām al-'Ulūm al-'Aqliyyah* in *Tis' Rasā'il fī al-Ḥikmah wa al-Ṭabī'iyyāt* (Cairo: Amīn Hindiyyah, 1326/1908), pp. 105, 107-108. On the division of knowledge into theoretical and practical see also Aristotle *Metaphysics* 2. 1. 993b20-21; Abū Naṣr al-Fārābī, *Kitāb al-Millah wa Nuṣūṣ Ukhrā* ("Book of Religion and Related Texts"), ed. by Muhsin Mahdi (Beirut: Dār al-Mashriq, 1968), pp. 46-47.

4. Avicenna, *Shifā'*: *Introduction*, ed. by Ibrahīm Madkūr (U.A.R. Wizārat al-Ma'ārif al-'Umūmiyyah, 1952), pp. 12-14.

5. Abū Naṣr al-Fārābī, *Iḥṣā' al-'Ulūm*, ed. by 'Uthmān Amīn (2d ed.; Cairo; Dār al-Fikr al-'Arabī, 1949), pp. 102-103; *Millah*, pp. 69-70. Cf. Aristotle *Nicomachean Ethics* 1. 2. 1094a18-1094b10.

6. Cf. Muhsin Mahdi, *Ibn Khaldūn's Philosophy of History* (Chicago: University of Chicago Press, 1964), p. 7.

The *Standard* is an exposition of logic, appended to the *Incoherence.*[1] and perhaps written after the latter.[2] In it Ghazali argues that learned Muslims can accept Aristotelian logic without having to subscribe to other philosophic doctrines, and he endorses Avicenna's analysis of the status of nondemonstrative premises by drawing heavily on the sixth tract of the logic in Avicenna's *al-Ishārāt wa al-Tanbīhāt.* But he does not necessarily commit himself to Avicenna's specific ethical teachings. Rather, he adapts the analysis of ethical premises, by enlarging and blending them with Islamic theological concepts and thereby he elucidates their importance for strictly Islamic learning.[3]

In the *Criterion* Ghazali promises to apply these ethical premises to the knowledge and action which lead to ultimate happiness. His procedures in this book, he claims, go beyond mere blind imitation (*taqlīd*); if perfectly applied it can reach the level of demonstration according to the conditions stated in the *Standard.*[4] The exact date of the *Criterion* is rather difficult to establish and all that can be said on the basis of external and internal evidence is that this book was written sometime during the transitional period after Ghazali finished his study of philosophy and started his inquiry into mysticism. In any event, it is certain that the *Criterion* chronologically follows the *Standard.*[5]

The book is composed of thrity sections of unequal length, each of

1. *Tahāfut*, pp. 16-17, where the *Standard* is anticipated; Ghazali, *Mi'yār al-'Ilm*, ed. by Sulaymān Dunyā (Cairo: Dār al-Ma'ārif, 1964), p. 60, where it is stated that this book is appended to the *Incoherence.*

2. Hourani, "Chronology," p. 228; Bouyges, *Essai*, pp. 26-27; Badawī, *Mu'allafāt.* pp. 70-71; Watt, "Authenticity," p. 44.

3. *Mi'yār* ,pp. 193-198; cf. Michael. Marmura, "Ghazali on Ethical Premises," *The Philosophic Forum* (New Series), I (1969), 393-396; Avicenna, *al-Ishārāt wa al-Tanbīhāt*, ed. by Sulaymān Dunyā (Cairo: Dār al-Ma'ārif, 1958), I, 389-414.

4. *C*, p. 3.

5. *Mi'yār*, p. 348, where at the end of the book Ghazali promises to write the *Criterion of Actions*; *C*, p. 2, where he mentions that since he finished with the *Standard of Knowledge*, it is time now to write the *Criterion of Action*; cf. Hourani, "Chronology,' p. 228; Bouyges, *Essai*, pp. 28-29; Badawī, *Mu'allafāt*, pp. 79-81. However, Massignon, *Recueil*, p. 93, classifies the *Criterion* among the works belonging to the latter part of Ghazali's life, i.e. ,between 495-505. Influenced by Massignon, Hikmat Hachem, the translator of the *Criterion* into French, tried to prove that the *Criterion* was written after the *Deliverer*, i.e., after 500/1106; see his introduction to *Critère de l'action* (Paris: Librairie Orientale et Américaine, 1945), p. xv. W. Montgomery Watt, in his article "Authenticity," pp. 38-40, accepts this latter date of the *Criterion* and on the basis of this date rejects the work as unauthentic. For a further discussion on the authencitity of the *Criterion*, see Appendix I.

which is called an "exposition" (*bayān*).[1] Although there is no explicit division into chapters that cover groups of sections, some of these sections can still be considered key sections and they serve to divide the book into its larger parts. Of these we mention the following:

(1) Neglect of seeking happiness is folly.
(3) The way to happiness is knowledge and action.
(4) Refinement of the soul, its faculties, and its character qualities.
(14) The specific way of character training.
(15) Principal virtues.
(19) Excellence of reason, knowledge, and instruction.
(29) The sign of the first resting place of those who seek God.

It is evident from the title that the *Criterion* deals with "action" (*'amal*). Its aim is to discover the means of discerning and bringing about the "good action" which leads to happiness.[2] The book, therefore, is an inquiry into the kinds of knowledge and action which are relevant to man's highest end. Ghazali confirms the division of sciences and the view that ethics is a practical science, which were given in the *Aims*. After drawing a distinction between theoretical and practical knowledge in a way similar to that which he attributes to the philosophers in the *Aims*, he says:

> Practical science consists of three sciences: The science of the soul in respect to its qualities and character [ethics] . . . The science which deals with how man ought to conduct himself with his wife, children, servants, and slaves [household management] . . . The science of governing the people of the city and the region [politics].[3]

The significance of this statement is that here Ghazali adopts the philosophic (*Avicennan*) division of sciences as his own. More important, however, is the order which he introduces: the first of the three practical sciences, i.e., ethics, is the highest of the three, and the most important practical science.[4] Furthermore, Ghazali concludes this statement by declaring that ethics is conceived here as "the greater aim of this book [i.e., the *Criterion*]."[5] These statements occur in a book devoted to ethics and are not merely passing remarks in books dealing with other disciplines.

1. However, Esad Efendi MSS, 1759, lists thirty -two sections by dividing some of the sections into further divisions.

2. *C*, p. 3.

3. *C*, p. 54.

4. *C*, p. 55.

5. *C*, p. 54.

Ghazali repeats the assertion that ethics is a practical science in another part of the *Criterion*, emphasizing these same points again.[1]

Other statements in the *Criterion* serve to elaborate and modify Ghazali's attitude as presented thus far. In the *Criterion* he presents a psychological analysis of the soul which he attributes in the *Aims* and the *Incoherence* to the philosophic tradition. On the basis of this analysis, he discusses the virtues and explains how they lead to ultimate happiness. Since ultimate happiness, according to Ghazali, can only be realized in the hereafter, he brings in mysticism—that is, the discipline of character training—further to support the aim of ethics. In a section which deals with the difference between the rational and mystical approaches to knowledge and action, he shows that there is agreement between the two with regard to action (*jānib al-ʿamal muttafaq ʿalayh*), but that they differ with regard to knowledge.[2] The term "action" here apparently covers a wider sense of ethics and includes spiritual refinement as well as worship (*ʿibādah*).[3] In another part of the *Criterion*, Ghazali presents a different account according to which the sciences are divided into religious (*sharʿiyyah*) and rational (*ʿaqliyyah*), and he argues that these complement each other and are never contradictory.[4] Yet in the same section he divides the sciences acquired by the intellect into worldly (*dunyawiyyah*) and other-worldly (*ukhrawiyyah*), and, according to him, these oppose each other. "Good action" here is associated with the other-worldly sciences.[5] Thus, Ghazali's view of ethics in the *Criterion* starts as a philosophic view and then expands to include certain mystical and Islamic religious elements. It can be characterized as follows: (1) Ethics is independent of politics and is primarily concerned with the moral refinement of the individual. This confirms, of course, Ghazali's previous adoption of Avicenna's view of ethics as an independent practical science. (2) Ethics is a fundamental discipline which not only serves all other sciences but also is served by them.

This second characteristic is elaborated in the *Revival of the Religious Sciences* (*Iḥyāʾ ʿUlūm al-Dīn*), which is acknowledged by all students of Islamic thought to be Ghazali's *magnum opus*. Ghazali himself considered it

1. *C*, pp. 160-61.
2. *C*, p. 43.
3. *C*, pp. 48, 52.
4. *C*, p. 146.
5. *C*, pp. 147-148.

his greatest work and defended it in another book written for the sole purpose of answering objections raised about the *Revival*. He also composed two summaries of it, one in Arabic, and a longer one in Persian.[1] The work must have been written over a number of years. It seems that Ghazali started composing it after writing the Jerusalem Tract (*al-Risālah al-Qudsiyyah*), during his stay in Jerusalem[2] because the *Tract* is incorporated in the second book of the first part of the *Revival*, where Ghazali discusses the rules of the articles of faith: "Let us be satisfied therefrom with what we have written to the people of Jerusalem, which we called the *Jerusalem Tract Concerning the Articles of Faith*."[3] In the *Deliverer*, Ghazali says that he left Baghdad for Damascus in 488/1096; then, after spending about two years there he proceeded to Jerusalem.[4] Thus, Ghazali could not have reached Jerusalem before the beginning of 491 (December 9, 1097) and the *Revival* could not have been begun before 491/1098, or sometime during Ghazali's subsequent travels to Mecca and Madina and back to Khurāsān.[5]

The large number of existing manuscripts of this book, the still larger number of books written in its defense, and the commentaries on it, testify to its great influence on Islamic thought.[6] Our inquiry into Ghazali's attitude toward ethics in this vast and influential work must begin with a few introductory remarks. In the title, the term "religion" (*dīn*) was the subject of different and even opposing interpretations which, in turn, gave rise to different opinions concerning the "readers" for whom the *Revival* was written. While the choice of this ambiguous term may have been deliberate the reader can nevertheless find a precise definition of *dīn* in the work itself: "We mean by religion (*dīn*) the devotional practice (*mu'āmalah*) between man and his Lord." Therefore, "religious science" does not mean jurisprudence, theology, or Islamic traditional

1. The book he wrote in defense of the *Revival* is the *Dictation* (*Imlā'*), the summaries are the book of *al-Arba'īn*, and *The Alchemy of Happiness* (*Kīmiyā-yi Sa'ādat*).

2. This is clear from the text of *Qudsiyyah*, pp. 74-75.

3. *R*, I. 2. 180.

4. *Munqidh*, pp. 99-100.

5. Hourani, "Chronology," pp. 229-230. All the bibliographers of Ghazali regard the date of the *Revival* as belonging more or less to this period; cf. Bouyges, *Essai*, pp. 41-43; Massigonn, *Recueil*, p. 93; Badawī *Mu'allafāt*, pp. 98-125; *GAL*, I, 539; and *GAL*(*S*), I, 748.

6. Badawī, *Mu'allafāt*, pp. 100-122, where he lists 109 manuscritps of this book and the titles of books written about it. Cf. *GAL*, I, 539; *GAL*(*S*), I, 748. A ten-volume commentary on the *Revival* was composed by al-Zabīdī, *Itḥāf*.

learning in general, but a discipline whose central concern is how to establish and maintain a special spiritual relation with God. The *Revival* is not a religious book which shows Muslims how to perform religious rituals, although it does speak about them. Nevertheless, it is a work intended for all Muslims. It starts from things which are commonly known to the members of the Islamic community, but seeks to emphasize their spiritual significance so that some of them may become candidates for higher spiritual refinement, while the rest may enrich their ritualistic acts of worship and render them more spiritual. It is in this restricted sense that Ghazali considers the theme of the *Revival* the "science of the way to the hereafter" (*'ilm ṭarīq al-ākhirah*).[1]

The *Revival* is divided into four parts and each part consists of ten books, making a total of forty books, which are preceded by a preface. Some of the books are divided into an unequal number of chapters, which in turn are subdivided into sections. Others are not divided into chapters but only into sections.[2] As to the division into four parts, Ghazali explains in the preface that, in order to insure a wide circulation, he followed the external arrangement of the most popular books of his day. These dealt with jurisprudence, and were always divided into four parts, one for each part of the Islamic Law.[3] This, however, is only a secondary motive. The principal reason for the fourfold division is Ghazali's division of "the knowledge of the way to the hereafter" into the "science of devotional practice" (*'ilm al-mu'āmalah*) and the "science of revelation" (*'ilm al-mukāshafah*). The latter consists of knowledge alone, while the former covers knowledge as well as action in accordance with knowledge. Ghazali states openly that the purpose of the *Revival* is the explanation of the science of devotional practice and not the science of revelation, which it is not permissible to write down in books, even though it is the ultimate aim of the seekers of ultimate happiness and the end of the science of devotional practice. This science which is the subject of the *Revival* is, in turn, divided into external (*ẓāhir*) knowledge, namely, of the actions of the members of the body, and

1. *R*, pp. 3-5; IV. 9. 2810.

2. *R*, II. 10 and III. 1., for example, have no chapters.

3. *R*, 3-6; cf. Nabih Amin Faris, "Iḥyā' 'Ulūm al-Dīn of al-Ghazzālī," *Proceedings of the American Philosophical Society*, LXXI (1939), 15-19, where he gives examples of earlier medical doctors who followed the same practice. This article contains lists of the titles of the forty books of the *Revival*. For further analysis of this book see de Boer, "Ethics," pp. 508-509; G.H. Bousquet, *Iḥ'yā' 'Ouloum ed-Dīn ou Vivification des Sciences de la foi* (Paris: Librairie Besson, 1955).

internal (*bāṭin*) knowledge, namely of the inner deeps of the soul. The external knowledge is divided into acts of worship (*'ibādāt*), that is, acts of devotion directed to God alone, and customs (*'ādāt*), that is, types of actions directed toward one's fellow men; likewise internal knowledge is divided into destructive qualities of the soul (*muhlikāt*) and qualities leading to salvation (*munjiyāt*). Following these divisions, the *Revival* is divided into two major parts, the first dealing with the external and the second with the internal division, and each of these, in turn, is divided into two parts. The results are the four "quarters" bearing the names of the four divisions of the science of spiritual practice, respectively.[1]

Without entering now into a detailed discussion of the science of revelation or the science of spiritual practice, it can be said that in the "formal" sense defined in the preface to the *Revival*, they seem to correspond, broadly speaking, to theoretical and practical knowledge as presented in the *Criterion*.[2] Hence the entire *Revival* deals with practical and not theoretical knowledge. However, the *Revival* deals with practical knowledge of a certain kind. *'Amal*, which is the subject of the *Criterion* and *mu'āmalah*, which is the subject of the *Revival*, are both derived from the same verb root and their meanings are related. The former is a more general and loose form, whereas the latter is more defined and specific. While both works deal with actions as means to the ultimate happiness of the hereafter, the *Revival* offers a more elaborate discussion of the actions pertaining to the devotional practices which are mentioned briefly in the *Criterion*.

Ghazali's view of ethics is stated in the three books of the *Revival* (Quarter I, Book 1, Quarter III, Books 1 and 2), which preface the two major divisions of this work and which serve, therefore, as "introductions." The first, which is the first book of the first quarter of the *Revival*, is a general introduction to the entire work. This is the "Book of knowledge" (*kitāb al-'Ilm*). The second is an introduction designed especially for the first and second books of the third quarter, namely, the "Book of the Explanation of the Wonders of the Heart" (*kitāb Sharḥ 'Ajā'ib al-Qalb*) and the "Book of Training the Soul, Refining Character, and Treating the Diseases of the Heart" (*Kitāb Riyāḍat al-Nafs wa Tahdhīb al-Akhlāq wa Mu'ālajat Amrāḍ al-Qalb*).[3]

1. *R*, p. 5.
2. *C*, p. 54.
3. *R*, III. 1. 1349: "We must necessarily begin with two introductory books for the second half of the *Revival*. One deals with the *Explanation of the Wonders of the Heart*, and the other discusses the method of *Training the Soul* . . ."

In the "Book of knowledge," Ghazali explains that knowledge is praise-worthy in itself, and an excellent means to ultimate and eternal happiness. Knowledge of the way to the hereafter is only apprehended through the perfection of reason (*'aql*), which is man's noblest faculty.[1] Ghazali's main purpose in this general introduction of the *Revival* is to discuss the different types of knowledge to show which are commendable and which are blameworthy. In the second chapter of this book he quotes a prophetic tradition which says: "Seeking knowledge (*'ilm*) is a religious duty for every Muslim," and adds that, because of this tradition, as many as twenty Islamic disciplines professed to be that very "knowledge" which Muḥammad commanded the Muslims to seek. The theologians assumed that it was dialectical theology, the jurists jurisprudence, and so on. But Ghazali criticizes and rejects all these claims. For him, the only "knowledge" meant in the above prophetic tradition is that of devotional practice (*mu'āmalah*), because it is this knowledge which comprises belief in God, His Prophet, and all His creation, as well as carrying out religious duties and refraining from what is forbidden. It is only in this sense that knowledge is "a religious duty incumbent on every individual" (*farḍ 'ayn*).[2]

Ghazali then turns to the division of the sciences into religious (*shar'iyyah*) and non-religious (*ghayr shar'iyyah*). His choice of terminology here tacitly gives priority to the religious sciences before he even identifies what the non-religious sciences are. The non-religious sciences are divided into commendable, such as medicine and mathematics; forbidden, such as magic; and permissible, such as poetry and history. Although all the religious sciences are commendable, they may become mixed with something blameworthy and for this reason become blameworthy. Commendable religious sciences are divided into four parts, namely, fundamental principles (*uṣūl*), branches (*furū'*), preludes (*muqaddimāt*) and supplements (*mutammimāt*). The science of the fundamental principles is in turn divided into four parts, namely, the Koran, the prophetic tradition of Muḥammad, the consensus of the Islamic community, and the traditions of the Companions. The science of the branches is the knowledge of the true interpretation of these fundamental principles. It is divided into two kinds. The first, concerned with worldly affairs, is included in the manuals of jurisprudence. The other is concerned with other worldly things. The third of the religious sciences, the preludes,

1. *R*, I. 1. 23.
2. *R*, I. 1. 24-25.

provides instruments for the two religious sciences mentioned above, e.g., language and grammar as means of understanding the Koran. The fourth religious science, that of the supplements, such as the science of the Koran and of the principles of jurisprudence, deals with things that perfect or provide a full understanding of religious sciences.

Ghazali is particularly interested in the second religious science, i.e., the science of the branches; and within this science, he favors the part he calls the science of the hereafter over jurisprudence, which he regards an inferior worldly discipline. The science of the hereafter, according to Ghazali, is divided into two parts. The first is knowledge of revelation, through which one attains true and direct knowledge of God. The second is the science of devotional practice (*mu'āmalah*), which is the science of the states of the heart (*'ilm aḥwāl al-qalb*). It provides knowledge of noble and base character traits of the soul, which is the subject of the entire second half of the *Revival*, and knowledge of the "effects" of the states of the heart on the members of the body when practicing the acts of worship and the customs, which is the subject of the entire first half of the work. Ghazali then gives a partial list of virtues and vices which are made known by the science of devotional practice.[1]

In dividing the sciences in the "Book of knowledge," therefore, Ghazali considers ethics as part of a religious science—the science of devotional practice—whose aim is to seek the ultimate happiness of the hereafter. He distinguishes this science from the other religious sciences, especially jurisprudence which is primarily concerned with the external worldly affairs of men. Jurisprudence, in Ghazali's view, is relevant only in the second degree for the attainment of the ultimate happiness in the hereafter. Furthermore, the science of devotional practice is also distinguished from dialectical theology, which for Ghazali is permitted only for the sake of defending religion against the arguments of innovators; aside from the ability to refute innovators, theologians have the same knowledge or belief as the multitude. More significant, however, is the fact that in this (second) chapter of the "Book of knowledge," Ghazali discusses philosophy for the sake of judging whether it is commendable or blameworthy. He lists the four philosophic sciences he had listed in the *Aims* (mathematics, logic, metaphysics, and physics), placing those he finds acceptable within the province of dialectical theology. He does not list

1. *R*, I. 1. 28-36.

the practical philosophic sciences and consequently does not judge whether they are commendable or not.[1]

It is necessary now to compare Ghazali's view of ethics as embodied in the division of sciences just described with the view of ethics which emerges in the (more particular) introduction of the second half of the *Revival.* There Ghazali changes his terminology and divides the sciences which "reside in the heart' into rational (*'aqliyyah*) and religious (*shar-'iyyah*). By the former is meant the knowledge attained solely by the human intellect, and by the latter, the knowledge received from the prophets.[2] In this account Ghazali discusses the merits of both rational and religious sciences in an attempt to reconcile them. He states that rational sciences are not sufficient by themselves for achieving purification of the soul, although they are necessary for that. For this reason, they have to be complemented by the religious sciences. In the same manner, the religious sciences must be supported by the rational sciences. These two sciences are like food and medicine for man respectively; without them he cannot achieve his perfection, and no one who is in his right mind, according to Ghazali, should reject one or the other.[3]

This praise of both the religious and rational sciences is obviously intended to gain approval for the rational sciences. Aside from showing that religious science is in agreement with the rational and must be complemented by it, Ghazali does not present any subdivisons of the former, while he gives an elaborate analysis of the latter. Rational sciences, according to Ghazali, are divided into necessary or inborn (*ḍarūriyyah*) and acquired (*muktasabah*). Inasmuch as they are acquired, rational sciences are divided into worldly and otherworldly. The worldly rational sciences consist of medicine, mathematics, and the like. The otherworldly rational sciences comprise the science of the states of the heart (*'ilm aḥwāl al-qalb*), and the knowledge of God, His attributes, and creation. The relation between worldly and otherworldly sciences is one of opposition in the sense that the man who occupies himself with one of them departs from the other.[4] Thus, while Ghazali classifies ethics as a religious science in the general introduction of the *Revival,* he classifies it as a rational science in the more particular introduction to

1. *R,* I. 1. 38-39.
2. *R,* III. 1. 1372-1374.
3. *R,* III. 1. 1374.
4. *R,* III. 1. 1375.

the part concerned with the hidden or internal aspects of the soul. This classification corresponds to a similar one in the *Criterion*, in which Ghazali draws upon the philosophic view of ethics as a practical science.

In addition to these two views of ethics (as a religious and as a rational science), Ghazali adds a third view (already pointed to in the *Criterion*), namely, ethics as a mystical discipline. He takes up this subject in his discussion of the sources of knowledge. According to him, knowledge is either acquired through education and instruction, or occurs without acquisition. The former is called reflection (*i'tibār*). The latter is called inspiration (*ilhām*) when its source is not known (this is the knowledge of the mystic saints) and revelation (*waḥy*) when its source is known to man (this is the knowledge of the prophets).[1] Now, while men of wisdom occupy themselves with reflection and seek to acquire knowledge through inquiry beginning with observation of physical phenomena, the mystics engage only in the purification of their souls and the refinement of their character so that knowledge may shine in their hearts through inspiration. Therefore, ethics is the main or essential ingredient in the mystical approach to knowledge.[2]

Keeping these three views of ethics in mind, we shall now examine Ghazali's views in the principal works which come after the *Revival*.

The Treatise on Mystical Knowledge (*al-Risālah al-Laduniyyah*) is a shorter work which belongs to the latter period of Ghazali's writing and is considered to have been written sometime after the *Revival*.[3] The aim of this book is to explain what mystical knowledge is and prove the possibility of acquiring such knowledge.[4] Ghazali devotes a special section to the division of knowledge into religious and rational. "Most of the branches of religious knowledge are rational in the opinion of him who knows them and most of the branches of rational knowledge are religious in the eyes

1. *R*, III. 1. 1376.
2. *R*, III. 1. 1382.
3. Massignon, *Recueil*, p. 93; Bouyges, *Essai*, pp. 124-125, where he regards it unauthentic, then hesitates to take a clear stand toward it after a discovery of an early manuscript of this book which goes back to the sixth century; cf. Badawī, *Mu'allafāt*, p. 191, where he classifies it as an authentic work of Ghazali, and presents arguments for its authenticity on pp. 202-204; Watt, "Authenticity," p. 44, where he follows Asin Palacios in regarding this book unauthentic; cf. M. Smith, "Al-Risālat al-Laduniyyah by Abū Ḥāmid Muḥammad al-Ghazali," *JRAS* (1938), pp. 177-78.
4. Ghazali, *al-Risālah al-Laduniyyah* in *al-Jawāhir al-Ghazālī* (Cairo: Maṭba'at al-Sa'ādah, 1934), pp. 21-22; cf. *GAL*, I, 542, where under No. 40 the book is called *Fī Bayān al-'Ilm al-Ladunī*.

of him who knows them."[1] From the start, this division of knowledge is conciliatory in tone. Religious knowledge is divided into two parts. The first is concerned with the fundamental principles and includes knowledge of the essence of God and His attributes as well as knowledge of the states of prophets and of the rest of creation. According to Ghazali, this is theoretical knowledge The second part of religious knowledge is that of the branches (*furū'*); this is practical knowledge and comprises three kinds of obligations. The first is what is due to God., i.e., acts of worship; the second is what is due to one's fellow men, i.e., customs; and the third is what is due to one's own soul, i.e., ethics (*'ilm al-akhlāq*).

As for rational knowledge, Ghazali says that it is a difficult discipline. It is divided into three classes. The first class comprises mathematics and logic, and mathematics includes arithmetic, geometry, and music. The second class is physics, which includes medicine, minerology, and the rest of the natural sciences. The third and highest of the classes of rational knowledge, i.e., metaphysics, investigates existence and its divisions into necessary and contingent and reflects on the Creator, His essence, and attributes.[2] Thus, in this division of knowledge, Ghazali classifies ethics as a religious science. However, he also calls it specifically "ethics" and does not give it a different name as he does when classifying it among the religious sciences in the *Revival*. Furthermore, he explicitly applies the terms "theoretical" and "practical" to religious knowledge, indicating that ethics belongs to practical religious knowledge.

After thus dividing knowledge into religious and rational, Ghazali maintains that both divisions lead to a kind of knowledge which is a combination of both. This (i.e., the knowledge which is both religious *and* rational), he says, is the knowledge of the mystics.[3] Thus, ethics is indirectly incorporated in mysticism. In discussing the methods of acquiring knowledge, Ghazali offers the same view he expressed in the *Revival*: knowledge is acquired through human instruction and/or through divine teaching. Divine teaching is of two types—revelation and inspiration—and the latter follows upon the former, for revelation is the clear manifestation of the divine command, while inspiration is hinting at the command. The knowledge which is derived from inspiration is called knowledge from On High (*'ilm Ladunī*), i.e., mystical knowledge.

1. *Laduniyyah*, p. 27.
2. *Laduniyyah*, pp. 27-31.
3. *Laduniyyah*, pp. 31-32.

It is the knowledge attained when there is no longer an intermediary between the soul and the Creator.[1] In this book, mystical knowledge is higher than religious and rational knowledge. Therefore, although ethics is classified here as a religious science sharing some of the characteristics of rational sciences, it is ultimately incorporated in the domain of mysticism.

It is in *The Deliverer from Error* (*al-Munqidh min al-Ḍalāl*) that Ghazali explicitly classifies ethics as a mystical discipline. This book, whose authenticity has never been questioned, is Ghazali's intellectual autobiography. He must have written it after his return to Nīshāpūr in Dhū al-Qa'dah, 499/July, 1106. Thus, it is one of his last works. But although it is on the basis of this book that the dates of some of the earlier works have been established, we cannot tell how long before his death it was written.[2] In this book, Ghazali gives an analysis of different branches of knowledge which he says he had studied thoroughly for the purpose of attaining certainty. After presenting accounts of dialectical theology, philosophy, authoritative instruction (*ta'līm* of the Ismā'īlis), and mysticism, he concludes that certainty can only be found in mysticism. The first expression of Ghazali's attitude to ethics in this book occurs in his discussion of the various philosophic sciences. He enumerates six philosophic sciences: mathematics, logic, physics, metaphysics, politics, and ethics.[3] From this list it is clear that he considers ethics a philosophic discipline independent from politics:[4]

> As for ethics, all their [the philosophers'] discussion of it consists in defining the qualities and character of the soul, and enumerating the various genera and species of these qualities, and the method of moderating and controlling them. This they have borrowed from the teachings of the mystics . . . In their spiritual striving these mystics have learned about the virtues and vices of the soul and the defects in its actions, and what they have learned they clearly expressed. The philosophers have taken over this teaching and mingled it with their own disquisitions, furtively using them to sell their falsehood. Assuredly there was in the age of the philosophers, as indeed there is in every age, a group of those godly men, of whom God never denudes the world.[5]

1. *Laduniyyah*, p. 35.
2. Hourani, "Chronology," p. 322; Bouyges, *Essai*, p. 71; Massignon, *Recueil*, p. 93; Watt, "Authenticity," p. 44; Badawī, *Mu'allafāt*, p. 44.
3. *Munqidh*, p. 74.
4. *Munqidh*, pp. 80-81, where in his statement on politics, Ghazali distinguishes it from ethics. Politics, he says, is based on considerations of worldly and governmental advantage; the philosophers borrow it from the divine scripture revealed through the prophets.
5. *Munqidh*, p. 81.

This statement has been quoted in its entirety to indicate the many levels of Ghazali's argument. Philosophic ethics is acceptable in itself. What is bad is the philosophers' use of it to spread the false notions of their other disciplines. Ghazali does not credit the philosophers with originating their ethics, but regards it as a discipline which they borrowed from the mystics. It is significant here that ethics is not said to have been borrowed from the prophets (as is the case with politics), but from the mystics, and this emphasizes the fact that ethics deals with individual personal refinement of character. Since ethics has been incorporated by the philosophers in their disciplines, it presents two dangers. The first is that it may be rejected by men of slight intellect, who reject everything that comes from the philosophers. The second is that some weak people who accept philosophic ethics may gradually come to believe the falsehoods taught by the philosophers. It is, therefore, necessary to abstain from reading the books of the philosophers on account of the deception and dangers contained in them. It is in relation to the first danger that Ghazali mentions accusations made against himself by men of little insight on the ground that his books include statements taken from the works of the ancient philosophers (*al-awā'il*). The fact is, he answers, that some of these statements are the product of reflections which occurred to him independently while others come from the revealed scriptures, and in the case of the majority of these statements, the sense, though perhaps not the actual words, is found in the works of the mystics. But suppose, he adds, that these statements are found only in the books of the philosophers. "If they are reasonable in themselves and supported by proof, and if they do not contradict the Koran and the prophetic practice, then it is not necessary to abstain from using them."[1]

In this first statement on ethics in the *Deliverer* Ghazali views ethics, therefore, as originating in the teachings of mystics. The rest of the book only confirms this view. Thus, in a special section on mysticism, he maintains that the mystics' character qualities are so pure and refined that no one can add anything to improve them further.[2] This view of mysticism, however, does not imply a rejection of philosophic ethics, which is accepted on the assumption of its mystical origin, nor does it in any way cast doubt on ethics as a religious discipline.

1. *Munqidh*, pp. 82-83.
2. *Munqidh*, p. 101.

All the views on ethics which have been discussed in Ghazali's principal works seem to coexist on different levels of emphasis according to the aim for which each work was written.

The Problem

In the above brief account of Ghazali's views on ethics, only direct statements on ethics in his principal works have been considered, and particularly statements on the place he assigns to ethics in the several divisions of sciences. Nonetheless, from these preliminary remarks it is plain that ethics is central to Ghazali's entire thought. At the same time, this brief introduction raises the problem of the different and apparently contradictory elements present in his ethical doctrines. We can discern at least three different elements, namely, ethics as a practical philosophic science, as a religious science, and as a mystical discipline. In view of the statements we have examined above this problem cannot be eliminated by favoring one element and neglecting the others. On the other hand, to say that all three elements represent Ghazali's view of ethics raises the question as to how to resolve the differences and possible contradictions among them.[1]

Students of Ghazali have noticed this problem and some have even tried to suggest potential solutions for it. There are at least two attempts in this direction. The first assumes that Ghazali is inconsistent with himself. Inconsistency, however, can be acknowledged only in relation to minor points, not on the fundamental issues. For this reason, we shall not discuss this interpretation further.[2]

1. There are two studies of Ghazali's ethics which deserve mention here. The first is Zakī Mubārak's *al-Akhlāq 'ind al-Ghazālī* (Cairo: al-Maktabah al-Tijāriyyah al-Kubrā, n.d.) [The book was a Ph.D. thesis submitted to the Egyptian University on May 15, 1924.] In this study, ths author concerns himself, not with Ghazali's ethics as such, but primarily with the question whether Ghazali's ethics is directed to the well-being (power, economic interests, progress, etc.) of the political community. See, in particular, pp. 62, 92-93, 95, 96-98, 122-24. The second study is that of M. Umaruddin. In *The Ethical Philosophy of Al-Ghazzālī* he gives a detailed descriptive account of Ghazali's ethics, restating all its elements, but he does not raise or discuss any of the problems inherent in it.

2. The best representative of this attitude is 'Abd al-Ḥaqq Ibn Sab'īn (d. 669/1270) who maintains that Ghazali's thought is a mixture of contradiction and confusion. After mentioning that Ghazali appears to be a mystic, a philosopher, an Ash'arite theologian, a jurist, and a perplexed seeker who does not settle on one course, Ibn Sab'īn says that Ghazali is weak in his understanding of "ancient" sciences as well as mysticism. See 'Abd al-Raḥmān Badawī, *Rasā'il Ibn Sab'īn* (Cairo: al Dār al-Miṣriyyah li-al-Ṭibā'ah wa al-Nashr, 1965, p. 14, where he quotes from Ibn Sab'īn's *Budd al-'Ārif.*

The second and more important attempt to solve this problem is the assumption that Ghazali's thought developed through several stages during his lifetime, that the view he held during the last stage (just before his death) should be considered as his genuine and final view, and that the rest are earlier versions or abandoned ideas. This is an assumption which is popular among intellectual historians. It appeals to a number of the students of Ghazali because of the account of his intellectual life, which he presents in the *Deliverer*, namely, that towards the end of his life he decided in favor of mysticism. From this one might conclude that Ghazali viewed ethics primarily as a mystical discipline and, therefore, anything which is not mystical in his ethical system must be dismissed either as a position he later rejected, or (if it should be found in these last writings) as a forgery by some later writers.

While there are no representatives of this second attempt who have undertaken a complete study of the ethics of Ghazali, there are those who offer an explanation of his ethics which points in this direction. Montgomery Watt, for instance, considers some Ghazalian ideas as having been superseded by others and assumes that Ghazali rejected the earlier ideas. In commenting on the ethical theory presented by Ghazali in the *Criterion*, Watt says: "Since he became very critical of philosophical ethics, it is possible that, as his enthusiasm waned, he rejected much of what he had written in this work."[1] Furthermore, while discussing what he calls the closing phase of Ghazali's life, he argues against the opinion that Ghazali had then abandoned Ash'arism and become a neoplatonist. According to him:

> Works of a Neoplatonic character ascribed to al-Ghazali must be regarded as spurious. The only possible exception to this is, if it can be shown that a specific work was written between about 1091 and 1096, which is the time when his enthusiasm for philosophy was greatest. To this period belongs a work on ethics [i.e., the *Criterion*], mainly from the standpoint of Greek philosophy, which is genuine at least in part, but to which he never refers in his later books — presumably because he came to think about ethical questions more in traditional Islamic terms.[2]

According to this view, then, Ghazali's earlier theories can be dismissed as superseded, rejected by the author himself, or as a forgery by someone else. In this way the question of these three different elements of Ghazali's ethical theory is solved by selecting one of them and casting aside the

1. W. Montgomery Watt, "al-Ghazalī," *EI*², II, 1040.

2. W. Montgomery Watt, *Muslim Intellectual: A Study of al-Ghazali* (Edinburgh: Edinburgh University Press, 1963), p. 150.

others. But this solution itself poses certain difficulties. To begin with, we have seen in our examination of Ghazali's views on ethics in the *Deliverer* that he makes a strong case for mystical ethics, but does not in any way "reject" or "abandon" philosophic ethics, let alone Islamic religious ethics. The question of ethics as a philosophic science is of particular interest because many writers try to apply to philosophic ethics Ghazali's general position against the "authority" of philosophy as well as his refutation of certain physical and metaphysical doctrines. But from his discussion of philosophy, especially in the *Aims* and the *Incoherence*, it is clear that his opposition to philosophy does not extend to ethics. Furthermore, the position he expresses in the *Deliverer* is not essentially the last stage of Ghazali's development—one can find at least one other stage in which, according to some students of Islamic thought, he adopted a neoplatonic philosophic orientation while others say that a more traditional Islamic view dominated his thought.[1] In any case, the view that Ghazali expressed certain views and later abandoned them as he moved into a new or a different stage is not relevant to the problem of his ethics, because the three elements (i.e., philosophic, religious, and mystical) coexist in his later writings as well as his earlier ones. These three elements are not distributed in different works, but are all present in the same books, especially in Ghazali's two major works, the *Criterion* and the *Revival*. Therefore, any attempt to accept one element as genuine and reject the others fails to grasp the real problem of Ghazalian ethics.

Perhaps we can make a fresh start by asking the following question: Does Ghazali consider his view of ethics as philosophic, religious, and mystical at the same time? In other words, as a thinker who was aware of the differences among these three traditions, does he aim at developing a view of ethics in which all three elements are represented, if not integrated?

The answer to this question can be formulated into a positive hypothesis: that Ghazali's ethics includes philosophic, religious, and mystical elements, and that he purposely brings all of them together and blends them in such a way that they complement each other and form a whole,

1. Ibn Taymiyyah, *Muwāfaqāt Ṣaḥīḥ al-Ma'qūl li-Ṣarīḥ al-Manqūl*, ed. by Muḥammad Muḥy al-Dīn 'Abd al-Ḥamīd and Muḥammad Ḥāmid al-Faqī (2 vols.; Cairo: Maṭba'at al-Sunnah al-Muḥammadiyyah, 1951), I, 94, where he says that toward the end of his life Ghazali returned to the method of the "traditionalists" (*ahl al-ḥadīth*), and "died while he was studying the *Ṣaḥīḥ* of al-Bukhārī."

which is not merely the sum of the parts, but has its own characteristics as an ethical theory. Now, verifying this hypothesis is by no means easy, and the effort may very well end by raising questions that are as serious as the questions we raised about the solutions mentioned above. Let us, however, start by trying to avoid some immediate objections. First, when specifying the component elements of Ghazali's ethical theory, we do not deny the possible existence of other elements. However, we claim that these three elements are architectonic in the light of Ghazali's expressed views as well as of our own analysis of his ethical theory. Second, when we say that these elements are present in Ghazali's ethics, we do not mean that they are independent from each other in all cases; rather, Ghazali intentionally incorporates and synthesizes them in one ethical system. This means that each one of these elements had to undergo certain changes and modifications; only in such a way could Ghazali have constructed a "whole" out of different and sometimes contradictory elements. The task of the student is, therefore, to analyze this "whole," examine the parts, and find out how they fit together. The purpose in examining these elements is not primarily to find the original, either immediate or remote, sources to which they belong, even though we have frequently gone back to Ghazali's immediate sources and tried to determine how he uses them to serve his own purpose. Our method in examining the component parts of Ghazali's ethics is directed toward inquiring into each part, so as to see how it is related to the other parts in forming a new "whole." Throughout, we have been interested in finding out why these elements are chosen by Ghazali, why he orders them in this specific manner, why he constructs from them this particular ethics and not another, and finally, what end he has in mind in presenting his own ethics.

To conduct such an inquiry into Ghazali's ethical theory in its entirety is not only difficult, but hazardous as well. It is dangerous because the immense scope of Ghazali's ethics precludes any method which would give a direct and effective control of all its details and ensure a decisive test for our hypothesis. For this reason, we have chosen one aspect of Ghazali's ethical theory which is specific and at the same time central, in the sense that it pervades all the important characteristics of the theory and reflects the problems which are peculiar to a composite ethical theory. This aspect is virtue. Ghazali's ethics or moral theory, like most of the classical ethical theories, is an ethics of virtue. In his major ethical works, the *Criterion* and the *Revival*, Ghazali devotes a great deal of attention to the definition and analysis of virtues and vices, sometimes devoting an entire chapter or book to a single virtue or vice. Furthermore, virtue as presented by Ghazali in his ethical writings directs the attention of the student to the way in which the component parts of his ethics are ordered and arranged.

Thus, Ghazali's theory of virtue becomes the key to understanding his ethics. For example, after pointing out the aim of ethics in the *Criterion*, Ghazali first discusses virtues and vices which are common to philosophic ethics on the basis of an analysis of the soul which belongs to the philosophic tradition, then he mentions briefly some virtues which are particularly religious, and finally, points to some mystical virtues. In the *Revival*, we find a treatment of philosophic virtues at the beginning of the third quarter. This, according to Ghazali, is the natural beginning of ethics. The first half of the *Revival* consists of accounts of the external qualities of the members of the body in their relation to serving God (acts of worship) or in their relation with fellow human beings (customs). These qualities of the members of the body are the external effects of the internal and hidden character qualities of the soul which he introduces in the third quarter. Finally, the fourth quarter of the *Revival* consists of a discussion of a large number of mystical virtues. Thus, even without going into a detailed discussion of the reasons and motives, the starting point of the study of Ghazali's theory of virtue must be his treatment of the virtues which are commonly attributed to the philosophic tradition. And it is here that we shall begin our inquiry.

Chapter II / PHILOSOPHIC VIRTUES

In his two major ethical works, the *Criterion* and the *Revival*, Ghazali begins the discussion of virtue with what he calls the "mothers" (*ummahāt*) or principal virtues; the "mothers of character" (*ummahāt al-akhlāq*) refer to the same principal virtues.[1] These are listed as four: wisdom (*ḥikmah*), courage (*shajā'ah*), temperance (*'iffah*), and justice (*'adl*).[2] He derives them from an analysis of the soul and distinguishes them according to its faculties. These virtues and their psychological basis are identical with their counterparts in the Greek philosophic tradition especially in Plato and Aristole.[3] It is best, therefore, to determine the way in which Ghazali establishes, evaluates, and analyzes these virtues by examining them in relation to the philosophic tradition.

In its presentation of Ghazali's treatment of philosophic virtues, this chapter is divided into two major parts. The first part is concerned with the question of philosophic virtue in terms of its psychological basis, its genesis, its relation to character, and its equation with the doctrine of the mean. The second part is devoted to a discussion of the four principal virtues and their subdivisions.

General Characteristics

The Psychological Basis of Virtue

Ghazali regards the soul as different from the body in that the former is created and immortal, that is, it does not come to an end with the

1. *C*, p. 83; *R*, III. 2. 1442; cf. al-Rāghib al-Iṣfahānī, *al-Dharī'ah ilā Makārim al-Sharī'ah* (Cairo: Maṭba'at al-Waṭan, 1299/1882), p. 42.

2. *C*, p. 83; *R*, III. 2. 1442.

3. Plato *Republic* 4. 440-442, 10. 579-580; Aristotle *Nicomachean Ethics* 1. 13. 1102a27-35. Cf. Avicenna, *Fī 'ilm al-Akhlāq* in *Tis' Rasā'il fī al-Ḥikmah wa al-Ṭabī'iyyāt*, pp.

decay of the body. He explains that there are four terms used in relation to the soul: heart (*qalb*), soul or "self" (*nafs*), spirit (*rūḥ*), and intellect (*'aql*). Each of these has two meanings—one material, and the other spiritual. The spiritual meanings of these four terms refer to the same spiritual entity (*al-laṭīfah al-rūḥāniyyah*) but they denote different states (*aḥwāl*) of it. The soul in this sense is more important than the body and its members because the former is of divine origin, while the body is of base matter. The soul is, therefore, the essence of what is meant by "man"; it can only be known through intellect and by observing the activities which originate in it.[1] The only aspect of knowledge of the soul necessary for ethics is that of its states and activities. Knowledge of the "essence" of the soul belongs to a higher theoretical science which Ghazali calls the science of revelation (*'ilm al-mukāshafah*), the discussion of which is beyond the limits of ethics.[2]

To explain the activities of the soul, Ghazali gives an account of three powers or faculties (*quwā*) which belong to it and which he also calls "souls" (*nufūs*). These are: the vegetative (*al-nabātiyyah*), the animal (*al-ḥayawāniyyah*), and the human (*al-insāniyyah*). He takes special interest in the latter two because of their direct relevance to ethics. He explains the animal soul in the *Criterion* as having two faculties: the motive (*muḥarrikah*) and the perceptive (*mudrikah*). The motive faculty is of two kinds: either it is motive in so far as it gives an impluse, or in so far as it is active. In its active capacity, the motive faculty is a power which is distributed through the nerves and muscles; its function is to contract the muscles and pull the tendons and ligaments towards the starting point of the movement, or else to relax or stretch them so that they move away from the starting point. In so far as it provides the impulse, the motive faculty is the appetitive faculty (*al-quwwah al-nuzū'iyyah al-shawqiyyah*). When a desirable or repugnant image is imprinted on the

152-53; Abū 'Alī Aḥmad Miskawayh, *Tahdhīb al-Ahklāq* ("The Refinement of Character"), ed. by Constantine K. Zurayk (Beirut: American University of Beirut, 1968), pp. 27-28.

1. Ghazali and Muslim philosophers, like Avicenna, al-Kindī, Miskawayh, and others, follow Plato and Aristotle in their doctrines of the soul, except where these are irreconcilable with Islamic teachings, such as the pre-eternity of the soul. An exception to this is the position of Abū Bakr al-Rāzī, who accepts the doctrine of the pre-eternity of the soul in his *al-Qawl fī al-Nafs wa al-'Ālam* in *Opera Philosophica*, I, ed. by Paul Kraus (Cairo: University of Fu'ād I, 1939), p. 284. In regard to the question of the unity or plurality of the soul in man, Ghazali and most Muslim philosophers accepted and developed Aristotle's view of the functions and faculties of the soul; cf. *R*, III. 2. 1349.

2. *R*, III. 2. 1350; *C*, pp. 22, 36; cf. Aristotle *Nicomachean Ethics* 1. 13. 1102a1-2.

imagination, it arouses this motive faculty to move. This latter motive faculty, in turn, has two subdivisions which are crucial to virtue: one is called the faculty of desire or the concupiscent faculty (*shahwāniyyah*), which provokes a movement of the organs that brings one near to things imagined to be necessary or useful in the search for pleasure; the second is called the faculty of anger, or the irascible faculty (*al-ghaḍabiyyah*), which impels the subject to a movement of the limbs in order to repulse things imagined to be harmful or destructive, and thus to overcome them.

The perceptive faculty, which is the second principal faculty of the animal soul, can be divided into two parts: external sense and internal sense. Ghazali sees no reason for discussing the generally known five external senses in this context, whereas he deals in detail with the five internal ones. These are: the representative faculty (*khayāliyyah*), the retentive faculty (*ḥāfiẓah*), the estimative faculty (*wahmiyyah*), the recollective faculty (*dhākirah*), and lastly the faculty which is called "sensitive imagination" (*mutakhayyilah*) in relation to the animal soul and "rational imagination" (*mufakkirah*) in relation to the human soul.[1]

The animal soul exists in man as well, and Ghazali's detailed exposition of it reveals the importance of the concupiscent and irascible faculties in determining most of the human virtues. However, human virtues cannot be actualized without the introduction of the human soul, which in turn has two faculties: knowing or theoretical (*'ālimah*) and acting or practical (*'āmilah*). Both are called intellect (*'aql*), though equivocally. The practical faculty is the principle of movement of the human body, which directs it to individual actions after deliberation on whether they are in accordance with the rules defined by the theoretical faculty. The practical faculty must govern all the other subordinate faculties of the

1. *C*, pp. 23-26. This account of the faculties of the animal soul is a reproduction of Avicenna's account of the soul with some changes with respect to the order of such faculties and omitting the discussion of external senses; see particularly Avicenna, *al-Najāt* (2d ed.; Cairo: Muḥy al-Dīn Ṣabrī al-Kurdī, 1936), pp. 158-163; cf. F. Rahman, *Avicenna's Psychology* (London: Oxford University Press, 1952), pp. 25-31. Ghazali's discussion of the soul can be traced directly to that of Avicenna and indirectly to the Greek philosophic tradition, especially that of Aristotle. In addition to the above reference on Avicenna, see also his *Kitāb al-Nafs* (*al-Shifā'*: *Physics VI*) in *Avicenna's De Anima*, ed. by F. Rahman (London: Oxford University Press, 1959), pp. 40-45; *Aḥwāl al-Nafs*, ed. by Aḥmad Fu'ād al-Ahwānī (Cairo: 'Isā al-Bābī al-Ḥalabī, 1952), pp. 55-56. Cf. Aristotle, *Kitāb al-Nafs*, ed. by 'Abd al-Raḥmān Badawī (Cairo: Maktabat al-Nahḍah al-Miṣriyyah, 1954), pp. 30-31 (*De Anima* 2. 1. 412a27-2. 413a10) in the Arabic translation of Ḥunayn Ibn Isḥāq (see Bibliography). It must be remembered here that Ghazali considers Avicenna and al-Fārābī the best authorities on Greek philosophy; cf. *Tahāfut*, p. 40; *Munqidh*, p. 73.

body, lest passive dispositions arising from the body and derived from material things should develop in it. These passive dispositions are called bad character qualities (*akhlāq radī'ah*), i.e., vices. If, however, this faculty governs the other bodily faculties, it will acquire a positive disposition which is called virtue (*faḍīlah*) or good character quality (*khuluq ḥasan*).[1] The theoretical faculty, in contrast, has the function of perceiving the real nature of the intelligibles as they are abstracted from matter, place, and position. Therefore, the practical faculty is the one which determines ethical matters for man. The reason why ethics is attributed to this faculty is that the human soul is a single substance which is related to two planes—one higher and one lower than itself. It has special faculties which establish the relationship between itself and each plane: the practical faculty which the human soul possesses in relation to the lower plane, which is the body, and its control and management; and the theoretical faculty in relation to the higher plane, from which it passively receives and acquires intelligibles. It is as if the human soul has two faces—one turned towards the body, which it must govern, and the other turned towards the higher principles and angels because it receives knowledge from them.[2]

The faculties of the animal soul are dealt with in the *Revival* in the same manner as in the *Criterion*. However, in the *Revival* Ghazali calls them the "soldiers of the heart" (*junūd al-qalb*), because in this work he was generally unwilling to use philosophic terms, whereas in the *Criterion* the two faculties of the human soul, namely, the theoretical and the practical faculties, are called knowledge (*'ilm*) and will (*irādah*) respectively, Yet the "content" of the *Revival* on this point agrees with that of the *Criterion*, and both are in agreement with Avicenna's description of these faculties.[3]

This account of the faculties of the soul is derived, directly or indirectly, from the philosophic tradition. Ghazali does not draw upon the specifically religious tradition of Islam with respect to this question. He limits himself to quoting Koranic verses—verses which say no more

1. *C*, pp. 26-27; cf. Avicenna, *Najāt*, pp. 163-64; *Nafs*, pp. 45-47; cf. also F. Rahman, *Avicenna*, p. 32.

2. *C*, pp. 27-28; cf. Avicenna, *Nafs*, p. 47; *Najāt*, p. 164; cf. F. Rahman, *Avicenna*, p. 33.

3. Avicenna, *Nafs*, pp. 39-51, *Najāt*, pp. 158-65, *Aḥwāl*, pp. 55-56.

about the soul than that man should know his own.[1] Ghazali insists that knowledge of the soul is the foundation of religion,[2] but this assertion does not reveal the content of that knowledge. Since this question seems to be left open in the Islamic religious tradition, Ghazali introduces the philosophic analysis of the soul to provide the substance of that knowledge. He is aware of the relationship between the religious and philosophic traditions with regard to this issue, and states that his account of the faculties of the soul is that of the philosophers.[3] "Nothing of what we have mentioned need be denied on religious grounds, for all these things are observable facts whose habitual course has been provided by God."[4] Thus, he accepts the philosophic analysis of the soul and does not think that it is in conflict with Islamic religious teachings.[5] He regards it as a "natural" starting point to be developed beyond the strict philosophic limits.

1. Such as "And also in your souls: will ye not see?" (Koran 51:21); "We shall show them our signs on the horizons and in their own souls" (Koran 41:53); "And be ye not like those who forget God, and He made them forget their own souls" (Koran 59:19). All of these verses are quoted in *C*, p. 23; the last verse is also quoted in *R*, III. 2. 1349.

2. *R*, III. 1. 1348.

3. *Tahāfut*, pp. 297-303, where Ghazali gives the same account of the faculties of the soul he mentioned in the *Criterion*; cf. Averroes, *Tahāfut al-Tahāfut* (Incoherence de l'incoherence), ed. by Maurice Bouyges, Bibliotheca arabica scholasticorum, serie arabe, III (Beirut: Imprimerie Catholique, 1930), p. 546, where he comments on the account of the faculties of the soul: "All this is nothing but an account of the theory of the philosophers about these faculties, and his [Ghazali's] conception of them, only he followed Avicenna."

4. *Tahāfut*, p. 303.

5. This is clearly an answer to the charge that Ghazali did depart from the philosophic orientation, which is the attitude of Aḥmad Fu'ād al-Ahwānī. Cf. 'Abd al-Karīm al-'Uthmān, *al-Dirāsāt al-Nafsiyyah 'inda al-Muslimīn* (Cairo: Maktabat Wahbah, 1963), p. 7 of the Introduction, which is written by al-Ahwānī. Although the author of the book makes a detailed comparison between Ghazali and other Muslim thinkers, he seems to conclude that Ghazali abandoned this philosophic analysis of the soul after accepting it. However, Ghazali preserves this philosophic analysis of the soul in order to use it as a basis for a moral system which transcends blind imitation (*taqlīd*) and comes close to the level of demonstration. *C*, p. 3; cf. Fakhr al-Dīn al-Rāzī, *Kitāb al-Nafs wa al-Rūḥ*, ed. by Muḥammad Ṣaghīr Ḥasan al-Ma'ṣūmī (Islamabād, Pakistan: Islamic Research Institute, 1968), p. 3 where he introduces his book on the soul as "a book on ethics ordered according to the sure method of demonstration and not according to the persuasive method of preaching."

Virtue and Character

For Ghazali, both virtue (*faḍīlah*) and good character (*khuluq ḥasan*) denote the state in which bodily faculties are subordinated to the practical faculty of the human soul. This is the normal state, deviation from which produces vice and bad character. In the *Criterion*, Ghazali sums up the faculties which must be trained if good character is to be achieved. The deliberative faculty (*quwwat al-tafakkur*), when trained, will realize the virtue of wisdom; the concupiscent faculty will produce temperance; and the irascible will produce courage. When the latter two, which are faculties of the animal soul, are trained and have been subordinated to the first, the virtue of justice is achieved.[1] In the *Revival*, Ghazali provides examples and allegories explaining the relations among these three faculties and shows how they are trained. He calls the deliberative faculty "reason" or "intellect" (*ʻaql*) and the other two faculties "passion" (*hawā*). Passion and reason are in continuous conflict with each other. To achieve virtue, one has to follow reason. But the problem is how to distinguish between the motive which belongs to passion and that which belongs to reason. Following the philosophers, Ghazali argues that man should undertake actions which are more painful, since such actions are usually dictated by reason.[2] Still, he is not satisfied with this philosophic position and introduces divine aid as the only sure means for distinguishing between the motives of reason and of passion; and, furthermore, he advises that, whenever man is in doubt about which of the two motives is dictating his intention, he should pray to God for guidance.[3] This is the first of several amendments introduced by Ghazali to integrate philosophic virtues in his ethical system.

Once the question of which motive to follow is settled there remains the task of defining the kinds of action which are related to character. Ghazali accepts the philosophers' definition of character:

> Character is a stable state of the soul, one which causes it to perform its actions spontaneously and easily, without thought or deliberation. If this state is of the kind which causes good actions, i.e., those praised by intellect and religious law, the state is called good character, and vice versa.[4]

1. *C*, pp. 55-56; *R*, III. 1. 1350; *R*, III. 2. 1441.
2. *C*, p. 64; cf. Aristotle *Nicomachean Ethics* 2. 9. 1109b16.
3. *C*, p. 66.
4. *R*, III. 2. 1441; *C*, p. 71. The same definition of character is given by Miskawayh, *Tahdhīb*, p. 31; and by Avicenna, *Fī al-ʻAhd* in *Tisʻ Rasāʼil fī al-Ḥikmah wa al-Ṭabīʻiyyāt*.

Good character means training the three faculties, namely, the deliberative, concupiscent, and irascible faculties. Character is not identified with action, a faculty, or knowledge; rather it is the disposition of the soul from which actions emerge.[1] Character is inherent in the soul; it is permanent and not accidental or momentary. Hence a man who on the spur of the moment gives away a large sum of money is not really generous.[2] This description of character corresponds exactly to that of virtue, and Ghazali even uses "virtue" (*faḍīlah*) and character (*khuluq*) interchangeably. For example, the "character of generosity."[3]

Training the faculties of the soul does not entail uprooting or completely suppressing the faculties of the animal soul, which can only occur after death. It does, however, imply their subordination to the practical reasoning faculty so that the soul is directed towards the right goal, which is happiness.[4] On the basis of this idea, Ghazali makes a preliminary distinction between two general categories of virtues: excellence of mind (*jūdat al-dhihn*) and discernment (*tamyīz*), on the one hand, and good character on the other. In another passage of the *Criterion*, Ghazali makes the separation between theoretical and moral virtues even more explicit by asserting that virtue consists of theoretical and practical arts.[5] In this way, therefore, not virtue simply, but moral virtue, is identified with good character.

Ghazali's use of *faḍilah* and *khuluq* to mean the same thing does not reflect a confusion on his part in understanding the subject matter of virtue; rather, it stems from his deliberate intention to use the word *khuluq*, which in traditional Islamic moralist literature is used to mean virtue, as a synonym of *faḍīlah,* a term which is preferred by Muslim philosophers to indicate virtue as understood in the Greek philosophic tradition.[6] In this way Ghazali intends to resolve any misunderstanding

1. *C*, pp. 55, 57; *R*, III. 2 .1440-41.

2. *R*, III. 2. 1443.

3. *C*, p. 71. Ghazali uses *khuluq* to mean one aspect of character which denotes one virtue (or vice), and *akhlāq* to mean several aspects of character, virtues, or vices.

4. *C*, p. 68.

5. *C*, pp. 74, 76; Aristotle *Nicomachean Ethics* 2. 1. 1103a14-15.

6. Cf. Ibn Abī al-Dunyā, *Makārim al-Akhlāq* (Berlin, Staatsbibliothek, Prussischer Kulturbesitz MSS. 5388), fols. 2a-5b, for *khuluq*; for *faḍīlah*, cf. Miskawayh, *Tahdhīb*, pp. 19-24; Avicenna, *Akhlāq*, pp. 152-54; Jalinūs (Galen), *Mukhtaṣar Kitāb al-Akhlāq*, ed. by Paul Kraus in "Mukhtaṣar Kitāb al-Akhlāq", *Bulletin of the Faculty of Arts of the University of Egypt*, V (1937), 28. See particularly Aristotle *Akhlāq*, fol. 31a, where the translator of the *Nicomachean Ethics* renders "virtue' *faḍīlah.*

of virtue which can result from the difference of terminology between two disciplines of learning.

Origin of Virtue

In Ghazali's view, virtue can be acquired in three ways: habituation, learning, and divine generosity. The first two ways are fundamentally the same, since learning how to act virtuously is in fact a form of habituation; but Ghazali makes a slight distinction between the two. Habituation for him implies a positive attitude on the part of the agent in seeking to acquire virtue, whereas learning depends on an authority outside the agent that teaches him how to act virtuously even if he is not wholeheartedly seeking to attain such a state. As examples of such an authority, Ghazali mentions the father and the spiritual master (*shaykh*).[1] The third way of acquiring virtue, i.e., divine generosity, is realized when God bestows a gift of virtue on man at birth, as in the case of Jesus, John the Baptist, and other prophets. Thus, a man may be endowed with special ability through divine bounty to acquire virtue without habituation or training. Saints (*awliyā'*) are also considered by Ghazali as worthy recipients of this divine favor.[2] Ghazali holds that the virtue which is transmitted through divine favor is the most perfect of the three, even though the person who acquires virtue through all three ways at the same time will be the most virtuous man.[3] In this way, Ghazali modifies the philosophic concept of the origin of virtue. For Aristotle states that man possesses virtue not by nature but through habituation alone. According to him, nature permits the acquisition of virtue as well as its opposite. Contrary to this, Ghazali maintains that virtue can be acquired by nature (*bi aṭ-ṭab'*).[4] Ghazali, therefore, calls attention to the possibility of one's being born virtuous, a possibility that had been introduced by Islamic religious teachings both in the Koran and in the prophetic tradition. However, he adds that this is not the usual

1. *C*, p. 76.
2. *C*, pp. 76-77. According to the Koranic tradition, Jesus was reported to have spoken at the time of his birth and during early childhood. He spoke of divine things, life, and death. He also spoke of good character, such as being good to one's mother, religious obligations, and prayer. Koran 3:46; 19:24; 19:29-30.
3. *C*, p. 77.
4. *C*, p. 76. Cf. Aristotle *Nicomachean Ethics* 2. 1. 1103a19-15: "None of the moral virtues arises in us by nature, for nothing that exists by nature can form a habit contrary to nature."

way of possessing virtue for the majority of men. In any case, a man can be naturally favored with the inborn virute and nothing more can be said about this.

In discussing the acquisition of virtue that is not naturally bestowed, Ghazali emphasizes the importance of habituation, quoting a well-known prophetic tradition which says: "Every child is born with a natural disposition (*fiṭrah*); it is his parents who make him a Jew or a Christian or a Magian."[1] Ghazali rejects the view that character is an unchangeable natural quality on the ground that, if this were true, the teachings, advice, and even mission of all prophets would be in vain. Another basis for his rejection of unchangeable character is the fact that it is observable that animals can be trained to be domestic.[2] Moreover, Ghazali considers habit (*'ādah*) as the decisive factor in the acquisition of virtue by the majority of mankind, asserting that virtue is a habit, a good habit influenced by both reason and revelation.[3] The test of this habit is whether the agent finds it pleasing. According to Ghazali, habit can create almost a second nature. This he claims is visible in established vices that give joy to those who practice them, such as the joy of the gambler in his gambling, the swindler in his swindling, and the effeminate in his effeminacy.[4] He argues that if the soul can be habituated to acquire vices which are foreign to its essence, then it would be more proper to habituate the soul in virtues which are natural to it. Since the soul differs from the body in that it is of divine or spiritual origin, while the body is material, and because virtue means that the bodily faculties subordinated to the deliberative faculty, virtue is natural to the soul in the sense that it frees the soul from the control of the bodily faculties so that it can realize its divine spiritual nature. Vice affects it in a way opposite to this. Ghazali compares acquiring vice to eating clay (*ṭīn*), which is not "natural" to the body. By analogy, then, vice is

1. *C*, pp. 77-78. Although Ghazali quotes this tradition to emphasize habituation as a key factor in acquiring virtue, this tradition has more than one interpretation. In the Islamic tradition, the religion of Islam is considered to be in accordance with the natural disposition (*fiṭrah*) created in man by God. In this way the parents (i.e., habituation) corrupt the child's disposition by making him a Jew, a Christian, etc. Cf. Aḥmad b. Ḥanbal, *al-Musnad* (8 vols.; Cairo: Būlāq, n.d.), II, 481; Muslim b. al-Ḥajjāj, *Saḥīḥ* (16 vols.; Cairo: al-Maṭba'ah al-Amīriyyah, 1929), XVI, 210. In other reports, "this religion (*millah*)" is substituted for *fiṭrah*, referring directly to Islam; cf. Aḥmad b. Ḥanbal, *Musnad*, II, 253; Muslim b. al-Ḥajjāj, *Saḥīḥ*, XVI, 210.

2. *C*, p. 18; *R*, III. 2. 1445.

3. *C*, pp. 68-69.

4. *C*, pp. 69-70; *R*, III. 2. 1446-1450.

not "natural" to the soul, whereas acquiring virtue is compared to eating nutritious food.[1]

To acquire virtue, man must practice good deeds so that they become habits for him. The newly acquired good habit must be strengthened by performing good deeds continuously. Such practice and performance emphasize the importance of action (*'amal*) in acquiring and preserving virtue. In order to be just, for example, one must first behave in a just manner.[2] In his program for educating children, Ghazali maintains that if the child is habituated in goodness, he will grow up a virtuous man, but if habituated in vice, he will grow up to become an evil man.[3] Ghazali, therefore, equates virtue with good habit, while admitting the possibility of those born with virtue. In other words, while it is possible that a man may be divinely gifted with an inborn natural virtue, the ordinary way for man to acquire virtue is to acquire a good habit. For a good habit to be considered a virtue, it must be firmly established in the soul. It cannot come about by one good act, nor can it be destroyed by an occasional deviation. However, a single instance of deviation may incite others and finally destroy the virtue. By the same progress, a single good deed may initiate further good deeds and thus result in virtue. In addition to acquiring good habits and continuously acting accordingly, one must find virtuous acts pleasing and non-virtuous acts painful in order to be virtuous. The joy one has in acting according to virtue signifies whether one is truly virtuous or is feigning virtue but experiencing pain.[4]

Doctrine of the Mean

Although viewing the soul as healthy or sick was common in the Greek philosophic tradition, this same understanding can be traced independently to the Islamic tradition. The Koran, for example, uses the expression, "In their hearts is a disease, and God has increased their disease,"[5]

1. *R*, III. 2. 1451; cf. Avicenna, *'Ahd*, p. 146.

2. *C*, p. 71; *R*, III. 2. 1452-1453; cf. Aristotle *Nicomachean Ethics* 2. 4. 1105a17-18.

3. *R*, III. 2. 1474; cf. Avicenna, *'Ahd*, p. 145, where he says that habit is the source of both virtue and vice.

4. *C*, pp. 72-74; cf. Aristotle *Nicomachean Ethics* 2. 9. 1109b15; 2. 3. 1104b5.

5. Koran 2:10; also in twelve other verses, mostly meaning hypocrisy or bad character. An example of the latter is: "Be not too complaisant of speech, lest one in whose heart is a disease should be moved with desire." Koran 33:32.

to characterize those whose character is bad because they are hypocrites. Ghazali, therefore, does not have to reach beyond Islamic tradition to justify his acceptance of the doctrine of health and sickness of the soul which he compares with the health and sickness of the body. By means of these concepts Ghazali explains the doctrine of the mean as well as the necessity of character training.[1] For him, the health of the body is a state of equilibrium. The privation of this equilibrium constitutes sickness of the body. Treatment of a sick body consists of bringing the humors and parts of the body back to a natural balance by prescribing the opposite extreme. The physician of the soul (*al-shaykh*) follows the same procedure. When the soul is sick this means that it has deviated from the state of equilibrium. Following the extreme which is opposite to its sickness is the way to bring it back to the state of equilibrium. If the soul has, for instance, the bad character of meanness (*bukhl*), it should be treated with extravagance (*tabdhīr*) so that the equilibrium of liberality (*sakhā'*) will be reached. Equilibrium is the middle way between the two opposite character traits, each of which is an extreme. Good character (virtue), therefore, lies in this state of the middle way. The middle way, however, depends on states and circumstances, i.e., it is a relative mean.[2]

In the *Revival* Ghazali explains the mean (or the middle: *wasaṭ*) also as the furthest point from both extremes. To illustrate this, Ghazali gives the analogy of an ant which is placed in the middle of a hot ring on the ground; fleeing away from the heat of the ring around it, the ant finally settles in the center. If it dies, it will die in the center, because the center (or the middle) is the coolest place inside the ring. Man, surrounded by his desires, should emulate the experience of this ant by seeking the mean.[3] If a person can hit the mean and preserve the virtue of the middle way, his soul will in the end be able to depart completely from the body, cutting all relations with it. The result of this will be freedom from suffering and attainment of the pure joy of the beauty of truth.

It has been mentioned above that good character is acheived when the deliberative faculty of the human soul subordinates the irascible

1. *C*, pp. 77-79; *R*, III. 2. 1453-54, 1457-59. In a special section entitled "The signs of the diseases of souls and the signs of the returning of health to them," Ghazali states that all souls are sick and that it is difficult to know the sickness of the soul; even when it is known, it is difficult to stand the bitterness of the treatment, etc. (*R*, III. 2. 1457).

2. *C*, pp. 78, 82; *R*, III. 2 .1454.

3. *R*, III. 3. 1514, 1519-20.

and concupiscent faculties of the animal soul. Each of these two has to follow the middle way in order to attain good character. For instance, anger, which is the quality of the irascible faculty, can become a virtue, a mean between rashness (*tahawwur*) and cowardice (*jubn*). Character training leads to establishing or preserving the health of the soul by following the mean. If someone has the character of rashness, he can achieve the mean with respect to anger by training himself in the other extreme, i.e., cowardice. This method of curing vice was known to the philosophers, especially Aristotle, who advises the potential gentleman to consider his faults and to drag himself to the other extreme in order to hit the mean.[1]

Since deviation from the mean indicates that the soul is sick, Ghazali emphasizes the need for a physician of the soul, who teaches men how to hit the mean. This "teaching" of virtue may come through the parents or the spiritual leader who treats the soul of the novice. Ghazali gives a detailed account of how this spiritual leader (*shaykh*) treats the soul and restores equilibrium to it. He makes the novice practice the extreme which opposes his established vice, usually a lesser evil, taking into consideration the state of the novice, his circumstances and capability. To cure arrogance, for example, the *shaykh* makes the novice perform degrading activities, such as begging in the market place. It is obvious that the aim of the novice is different from that of Aristotle's gentleman; while the gentleman acquires virtue so as to obtain good moral character suited to living in the city, the novice acquires virtue for the sake of his own individual spiritual salvation.[2]

Ghazali's method of treating sick souls is not limited to special cases. Treatment of the soul continues constantly, curing it when it is sick, and when it is healthy maintaining it in this condition.[3] Furthermore, the term "sick soul" is a relative one according to one's position in the scale of salvation. A morally good man may still have to be treated as sick if he intends to seek higher levels.

The above discussion leads to the question of how to know the mean in order to attain it. Ghazali advises the person who wants to know the mean to look at the action which stems from bad character. If it

1. *R*, III. 2. 1453; cf. Aristotle *Nicomachean Ethics* 2. 9. 1109a30ff.

2. *R*, III. 2. 1455, 1456; C, p. 79.

3. *C*, p. 78; *R*, III. 2. 1456. Ghazali even shows that a vice may be treated by a lesser vice. He appeals to Islamic jurisprudence and cites the case of the person who cleans blood with urine, then cleans urine with water.

is easier for him to perform and he finds it pleasing, then he has acquired that bad character. In this case he must train himself in doing the opposite of that act so that he can come back to the mean.[1]

Ghazali also justifies the necessity of observing the mean on the basis of Islamic teachings. He quotes the Prophet's saying, "The best in all things is the mean."[2] He finds additional support from the Koran in the doctrine that liberality as a virtue lies in the middle between meanness and prodigality. "Make not thy hand tied [like a niggard's]to thy neck, nor stretch it forth to its utmost reach, so that you become blameworthy and destitute."[3] The same point is made even clearer in another verse, "Those who, when they spend, are not extravagant and not niggardly but hold a just [balance] between these [extremes]."[4] Following the mean in regard to appetite for food is a third example which shows Koranic support for the doctrine of the mean: "Eat and drink; but waste not excess, for God loveth not wasters."[5]

In his detailed discussion of baseness of worldly affairs in Book 6, Quarter III, of the *Revival*, Ghazali does not advocate rejecting such matters completely. Rather, the best way is the mean between the two extremes of defect and excess in worldly things.[6] In the *Criterion* he mentions three categories of people in relation to wealth: those who engage in worldly matters, paying no attention to the hereafter; those who engage in spiritual matters of the hereafter, paying no attention to this life, such as monks; and finally, those who follow the middle way or paying equal attention to the two worlds, and they are the truly virtuous.[7] Aristotle had acknowledged that the precise mean between two extremes is usually difficult to discover and attain with great exactness. "The intermediate state in all things is to be praised, but we must incline sometimes towards the excess, sometimes towards the deficiency, for so shall we most easily hit the mean and what is right."[8] Ghazali accepts this description, agreeing with Aristotle's view that since to hit

1. *C*, p. 81.
2. *R*, III. 2. 1459; C, p. 87.
3. Koran 17:29.
4. Koran 25:67.
5. Koran 7:31.
6. *R*, III. 6 .1757-58. This book deals with the disparagement of this life (*dhamm al-dunyā*).
7. *C*, pp. 187-88.
8. Aristotle *Nicomachean Ethics* 2. 9. 1109b24-28.

the mean is hard in the extreme, one must as a second best take the lesser of the evils. Indeed, it is no easy task to find the middle in everything. Hence, he who aims at the intermediate must first depart from what is more contrary to it.[1]

However, Ghazali goes beyond Aristotle to maintain that hitting the real mean is impossible. This he bases on the Koranic verse: "There is not one of you but shall pass through it [i.e., hell fire]. That is a fixed ordinance of the Lord. Then we shall rescue those who kept from evil, and leave the evil-doers crouching there."[2] He identifies the mean with the "straight path" (*aṣ-ṣirāṭ al-mustaqīm*) over which, according to Islamic teachings, every man must pass on the day of judgment. Since every man is destined to enter hell, the only hope for hitting the real mean is through divine guidance. Ghazali argues for this position on the basis of the Islamic religious tradition. He interprets a Koranic verse "Guide us on the straight path" which forms part of the first Koranic chapter (*sūrah*) which is recited in each section (*rak'ah*) of the Islamic daily prayer to mean praying for God to guide one to hit the mean.[3] Thus, while the philosophers believed that man could only reach the mean by his own effort, Ghazali introduces a new element to the philosophic view.[4] For him, an appeal to divine assistance, sought particularly during the performance of the prescribed prayers, is necessary to help man to hit the mean and, consequently, to acquire virtue. Therefore, he accepts the philosophic doctrine of the mean, justifies it on the basis of Islamic teachings, and finally modifies it by including prayer or appeal to divine guidance as a possible, if not the most efficient path to the achievement of the mean in moral habits.

This discussion of the doctrine of the mean concludes Ghazali's treatment of philosophic virtue in general. It is evident that Ghazali accepts the psychological basis of virtue and argues for it. He also accepts the basic characteristics of virtue acknowledged by the philosophic tradition. But he introduces certain changes such as the possibility of divinely

1. *R*, III. 2. 1459; cf. Aristotle *Nicomachean Ethics* 2. 9. 1109a24, 29-30, 33-35.

2. Koran 30:71-72, quoted in *C*, p. 86 and in *R*, III. 2 .1459.

3. Koran 1:6, quoted in *R*, III. 2. 1459-60. Since in the five daily prayers there are seventeen sections, this means that this Koranic verse is recited at least seventeen times by every devout Muslim. Ghazali interprets this as the minimum number of times one should appeal to God to guide him to reach the mean.

4. Cf. Aristotle *Nicomachean Ethics* 2. 6. 1106b32-33; Miskawayh, *Tahdhīb*, p. 25; Avicenna, *'Ahd*, p. 148.

bestowed inborn virtue, divine intervention to show man how to distinguish between good and bad deeds, and finally, the impossibility of fully observing the mean without appealing to divine guidance. Changes like these do not belong to the philosophic tradition, and Ghazali introduces them on the basis of religious teachings, particularly those of Islam.

The Four Principal Virtues

In the *Revival*, and more clearly in the *Criterion*, Ghazali begins his discussion of the virtues with a summary in which he introduces and defines every virtue. After this he examines them one by one in more detail.[1] According to him, there are only four principal virtues, which are based on the analysis of the faculties of the soul. The three principal virtues, namely, wisdom, courage, and temperance, correspond to the rational, irascible, and concupiscent faculties of the soul, respectively. The fourth principal virtue, i.e., justice, has the task of properly ordering these faculties in relation to one another. All other virtues enumerated by Ghazali are subordinated to these principal ones. They are assigned special places under each principal virtue on the basis of the role they are expected to play in the general hierarchy of virtues. In order to understand this hierarchy, it is necessary to present Table 1 (p. 76) which gives Ghazali's divisions and subdivisions of the principal virtues.[2]

The table shows that Ghazali's account of these virtues corresponds to that of the philosophers in general and the Muslim philosophers in particular. For example, the four principal Platonic virtues provide the framework for the rest.[3] The table also closely resembles that of Miskawayh, except that Miskawayh lists some subordinate virtues under justice and gives further subdivisions under liberality, and that Miskawayh disagrees as to the number, order, and location of several subordinate virtues. For example, Ghazali classifies magnificence and nobility under courage, while Miskawayh considers them as parts of liberality, which is, in turn, under temperance.[4] Ghazali's table also

1. *R*, III. 2. 1442-43; *C*, pp. 83-101.

2. This table of virtues is given both in the *Revival* (*R*, III. 2. 1443) and in the *Criterion* (*C*, pp. 92, 96-97). There are minor differences between the two accounts, particularly in relation to the order of virtues, their number, and the Arabic terms used for them. For further information about these two accounts, see Appendix II, p. 177.

3. Plato *Republic* 4. 442b-d.

4. Miskawayh, *Tahdhīb*, pp. 19-24. For a table of Miskawayh's virtues, see Appendix II, p. 179.

resembles that of Avicenna. Both agree in listing no virtues under justice, but they differ with respect to the number and location of the rest of the virtues. Avicenna lists only two virtues under temperance, namely liberality and contentment, reserving the larger number of his subordinate virtues for wisdom, while Ghazali does the opposite.[1]

There are also some resemblances between the virtues listed by Ghazali in this table and those enumerated by al-Fārābī and Ibn 'Adī, although these do not exhibit the unity of structure which is common to Ghazali, Avicenna, and Miskawayh.[2]

The close resemblance between classifications of these virtues made by Ghazali, and by the Muslim philosophers, reflects Ghazali's acceptance of philosophic virtues. This philosophic point of view can be more fully understood if we compare Ghazali's account of the virtues with that of the Greek philosophers, such as Aristotle, and the comparison will determine whether the Muslim philosophers introduced nonphilosophic views into their account. Aristotle does not organize his classification of virtues in the same way as Ghazali. Nevertheless, his enumeration of virtues, which includes the four Platonic virtues, is the basis of the lists of virtues presented by Muslim philosophers. In the *Nicomachean Ethics*, Aristotle divides virtues into moral and intellectual. The moral virtues are courage, temperance, liberality, magnificence, greatness of soul, proper pride, gentleness, truthfulness, wit, friendliness, righteous indignation, and justice. Modesty is a quasimoral virtue.[3] The major intellectual virtues are art, science, practical wisdom, theoretical wisdom, and intelligence. The minor intellectual virtues are excellence in deliberation, good understanding, and judgment.[4]

Examining the virtues presented by Muslim philosophers in the light of the Greek philosophic tradition, one sees changes and additions that

1, Avicenna, *Akhlāq*, pp. 152-54; *'Ahd*, p.p 143-45. For Avicenna's table of virtues, see Appendix II, p. 180.

2. Cf. al-Fārābī, *Fuṣūl al-Madanī* ("Aphorisms of the Statesman"), ed. by D. M. Dunlop (Cambridge: Cambridge University Press, 1961), pp. 113-14, 124, 131-33, where he deals with some of the virtues included in Ghazali's table without classifying them under the four principal virtues. Ibn 'Adī, a Jacobite Christian writing in Arabic, deals with many of these virtues without subordinating them to the four principal virtues in his *Tahdhīb al-Akhlāq*, ed. by Mar Severius Afram Barṣaum, in "Jahja ibn-'Adī's Treatise on Character-Training," *American Journal of Semitic Languages and Literatures*, XLV (1928-1929), 24-31.

3. Aristotle *Nicomachean Ethics* 2. 7. 1107b-5. 1. 1138b15.

4. Aristotle *Nicomachean Ethics* 6. 3. 1139b16-18; 9. 1142b-1143a24.

resulted when Muslim philosophers tried to reconcile Greek moral philosophy with the basic tenets of Islam. Miskawayh, for example, includes virtues with religious significance like worship (*'ibādah*) and abstinence (*wara'*).[1] Apart from virtues with religious significance, Muslim philosophers also include virtues such as modesty, which were not considered complete virtues by philosophers like Aristotle.[2] Changes like these, which will be treated in the following sections, are important for understanding Ghazali's account of the virtues, for in large measure they made possible his acceptance of these philosophic virtues. On the other hand, Ghazali did not accept completely the philosophic virtues as they are presented by the Muslim philosophers. He makes his own changes and modifications so that these virtues can be incorporated into his moral theory. By discussing Ghazali's treatment of each of the principal virtues and its important subdivisions, we hope to explain and substantiate the general remarks we have made about philosophic virtues.

Wisdom and its Subdivisions

Ghazali begins his discussion of virtues with wisdom, as does Miskawayh, whereas Aristotle began with courage rather than wisdom. The reason seems to be that wisdom, more than courage, is essential for individual salvation, and Ghazali considers this a higher end than those which are sought in political association.[3] In the *Criterion*, wisdom is *the* virtue of the human soul. Since the human soul has two faculties, theoretical and practical, there are two types of wisdom corresponding to the two faculties, namely: theoretical wisdom and practical wisdom.[4] Theoretical wisdom is concerned with the knowledge of God, His attributes, His angels, His prophets, and His revelation. This knowledge is true wisdom because the specific aim of theoretical wisdom is the knowledge of God and not simply knowledge per se. In the *Supreme Purpose* (*al-Maqṣad al-Asnā*), Ghazali defines wisdom as knowledge of the most excellent things through the best of sciences. But, he adds, the best knowledge is knowledge of

1. Miskawayh, *Tahdhīb*, p. 24: "honoring, glorifying, and obeying God (mighty and exalted is He), in revering His favorites: the angels, prophets, and *imāms*, and in following the commands of the religious laws. The fear of God (mighty and exalted is He) is the culmination and perfection of all these things."

2. Miskawayh, *Tahdhīb*, p. 20; Avicenna, *'Ahd*, p. 144; *Akhlāq*, p. 153.

3. *R*, III. 2. 1442; *C*, p. 84; Miskawayh, *Tahdhīb*, p. 19; Aristotle *Nicomachean Ethics* 2. 7. 1107b1.

4. *C*, pp. 83-84.

God, and the most excellent of things is God. Whoever knows all things but does not know God does not deserve to be called wise, whereas he who knows God is wise even if his knowledge of the rest of the "formal" sciences (*'ulūm rasmiyyah*) is defective.[1]

According to Ghazali, therefore, true wisdom is knowledge of God. But it is not the highest virtue. Unlike Aristotle, who considers the highest virtue as a form of the most perfect knowledge, [2] Ghazali regards wisdom, which is in his view the most perfect knowledge in this life, as important only insofar as it leads to the love of God. Love of God is higher than mere knowledge of Him, although it comes as a result of such knowledge. [3] The view that love of God and not the knowledge of Him is the highest virtue suggests a mystical understanding of virtue. Further discussion of this point would involve an assessment of the mystical influence in Ghazali's ethics and should therefore be postponed until we deal with Ghazali's view of mystical virtues.

Although theoretical wisdom is not the highest, it is higher than moral (i.e., practical) wisdom. Moral wisdom (*ḥikmah khuluqiyyah*), the virtue of the practical part of the human soul, is called wisdom only metaphorically. Ghazali defines it in the *Criterion* as

> a state and a virtue of the rational soul by which it governs the irascible and the concupiscent faculties. It consists of the knowledge of the rightness of actions. [4]

1. Ghazali, *al-Maqṣad al-Asnā Sharḥ Asmā' Allāh al-Ḥusnā* (Cairo: Maṭba'at al-Kulliyyāt al-Azhariyyah, n.d.), p. 77. This book of Ghazali, i.e., the *Supreme Purpose Concerning the Explanation of the Most Beautiful Names of God* (*al-Maqṣad al-Asnā Sharḥ Asmā' Allāh al-Ḥusnā*), was written sometime after the *Revival*, which it mentions. Although the subject of the book is the explanation of the divine attributes of God, each one of the ninety-nine attributes is concluded with a remark concerning its applicability to human beings. Ghazali defends this approach by quoting the prophetic tradition which says: "Emulate the virtues (literally: the character traits) of God (*takhallaqū bi-akhlāq Allāh*)" (*Maqṣad*, p. 97). This very point is emphasized in Chap. IV, Pt. I of this book, which deals with the question whether the perfection of man and his happiness lies in his emulation of the virtues of God (*Maqṣad*, p. 20). Because of this one expects to find a discussion of some virtues which are also applicable to God in an absolute sense. Indeed, the discussion of wisdom mentioned above occurs during an explanation of the divine attribute "Wise."

2. Aristotle *Nicomachean Ethics* 6. 3. 1139b16, where Aristotle classifies theoretical virtues as: art, scientific knowledge, practical wisdom, wisdom, and intelligence.

3. *R*, IV. 6. 2580.

4. *C*, p. 84. By calling practical wisdom moral, Ghazali seems to draw upon Avicenna who sometimes calls practical wisdom the wisdom of virtue (*al-ḥikmah al-faḍīliyyah*): cf. Avicenna, *Shifā'*: *Metaphysics*, Vol. II, ed. by Muḥammad Yūsuf Mūsā *et al* (Cairo: U.A.R. Wizārat al-Thaqāfah wa al-Irshād al-Qawmī, 1960), II, 455.

In the *Revival*, the same virtue, without being specified as moral, is defined as "a state of the soul by which it perceives right from wrong in all voluntary actions."[1] Thus defined, this virtue corresponds to the Aristotelian virtue "practical wisdom," defined as "a truth-attaining rational quality concerned with the action in relation to things that are good and bad for human beings."[2]

Like Aristotle's practical wisdom, Ghazali's virtue of moral wisdom is independent of theoretical wisdom but rational in that it engages in deliberation. This agreement ends, however, when Ghazali defines moral wisdom as itself a mean between two extremes, an excess which is deceit (*khibb*) and a defect which is stupidity (*bulh*). He defines the former as "a state in which man possesses cunning (*makr*) and trickery (*ḥīlah*) by letting the irascible and concupiscent faculties move toward the desired object in a way which exceeds what is necessary." Stupidity he defines as "a state of the soul which hinders the irascible and concupiscent faculties from reaching the necessary amount."[3]

Aristotle applies his doctrine of the mean to the individual moral virtues only and not to practical wisdom. Practical wisdom appears only in Book VI, chapter V of the *Nicomachean Ethics*, where no extremes of defect or excess are mentioned. Aristotle's discussion of this virtue assures us that it is a virtue which belongs to that part of the soul which forms opinion. This, in turn, excludes the view that practical wisdom is a mean between two extremes.[4]

Miskawayh and Avicenna describe practical wisdom as a mean between two extremes.[5] The latter gives the following explanation:

> By wisdom as a virtue (*al-ḥikmah al-faḍīliyyah*), which is the third of a triad comprising in addition temperance and courage, is not meant theoretical wisdom—for the mean is not demanded in the latter at all—but, rather, practical wisdom pertaining to worldly actions and behavior. For it is deception to concentrate on the knowledge of this wisdom, carefully guarding the ingenious ways whereby one can attain through it every benefit and avoid every harm.[6]

1. *R*, III. 2. 1442.

2. Aristotle *Nicomachean Ethics* 6. 5. 1140b4-7.

3. *C*, pp. 84-95. In a title of a section in *C* (p. 92), Ghazali mentions "wisdom" (*ḥikmah*) and its two vices: deceit and stupidity. By wisdom here we are to understand moral wisdom; the same approach is followed in the *Revival* with the exception that deceit is not mentioned; cf. *R*, III. 2. 1443.

4. Aristotle *Nicomachean Ethics* 6. 5. 1104b26.

5. Miskawayh, *Tahdhīb*, p. 26, where he considers wisdom (without qualifying it) a mean between impudence (*safah*) and stupidity (*bulh*).

6. Avicenna, *Shifā'*: *Metaphysics*, II, 455.

It seems that Ghazali only reproduces Avicenna's and Miskawayh's formulation of this virtue without concerning himself with its implications. For unlike the other philosophic virtues, practical wisdom is not developed further in Ghazali's ethical system and the subdivisions of practical wisdom receive only perfunctory treatment. Ghazali lists these as five virtues, namely, discretion (*ḥusn al-tadbīr*), excellence of discernment (*jūdat al-dhihn*), penetration of idea (*thaqābat al-ra'y*), correctness of opinion (*ṣawāb al-ẓann*), and awareness of subtle actions and of the hidden evils of the soul (*al-tafaṭṭun li daqā'iq al-a'mal wā khafāyā āfāt al-nufūs*). The last of these virtues is mentioned in the *Revival* only.[1] (The *Revival* merely recites the names of these virtues and the vices which oppose them; the explanation of the first four virtues and their opposite vices is to be found in the *Criterion*.) Ghazali's account reveals his dependence on the views of Miskawayh, Avicenna, and al-Fārābī[2] who reproduce, in part, the minor intellectual virtues which Aristotle considers to belong to practical wisdom.[3] Ghazali's discussion of the subdivisions of practical wisdom suggests that he does not consider them central to ethics. He mentions them without elaborating. Ghazali's definitions of these virtues can be easily traced to the Muslim philosophers, and to some degree even to Aristotle, and thus he shows his acceptance of these philosophic virtues as they are without extensive change, and at the same time his judgment that his ethical theory does not require more than a superficial knowledge of them.

Courage and its Subdivisions

When the practical faculty of the human soul acquires practical wisdom and subordinates the irascible faculty, the virtue of courage is attained. Ghazali defines it as a moderate state of the irascible faculty, the mean between cowardice (*jubn*) and recklessness (*tahawwur*). The latter, the extreme of excess, is the state in which man ventures upon risky matters, avoidance of which reason would dictate. Cowardice, the extreme of

1. *R*, III. 2. 1443; C, pp. 92-94.

2. Al-Fārābī, *Fuṣūl*, pp. 124, 129, 131-33 (where there is a close textual resemblance between al-Fārābī's accounts of these virtues and those of Ghazali); Miskawayh, *Tahdhīb*, p. 19; Avicenna, *'Ahd*, p. 143.

3. Aristotle *Nicomachean Ethics* 6. 9. 1142b1-11. 1143a24. For detailed accounts of the virtues subordinated to wisdom, see Appendix II.

defect, is a state in which the irascible faculty fails to move sufficiently, and as a result man does not act when he should.[1]

Courage is a virtue only when it is practiced in the right circumstances and in the right way and Ghazali quotes the Koranic verse: "Muḥammad is the Apostle of God; and those who are with him are strong against unbelievers, but merciful amongst each other."[2] Thus, neither strength nor mercy is commendable in itself. Circumstances determine when reason will determine that strength (*shiddah*) or mercy (*raḥmah*) is appropriate.[3] Ghazali illustrates the importance of circumstances by speaking of fear as an excellent, praiseworthy character trait, when it means fear of God.[4] Although the discussion of this kind of fear belongs to Ghazali's discussion of mystical ethics and, therefore, will be treated in detail in Chapter IV, the fact that he regards an extreme of defect capable of becoming a virtue reflects a sharp deviation from Aristotle's doctrine of courage. According to Aristotle, courage is a mean with respect to things which inspire confidence or fear. "The man who exceeds in fear is a coward, for he fears both what he ought not and as he ought not."[5] But fear of what? Aristotle lists a number of things considered terrible, death being "the most terrible of all things; for it is the end, and nothing is thought to be any longer either good or bad for the dead."[6] "Properly, then", Aristotle says, "he will be called brave who is fearless in face of a noble death."[7] Thus, he who faces death in battle is courageous, and courage has its locus in honor attained in battle. For Ghazali, the highest object of fear is God and His punishment in the hereafter, that is, fear of something beyond death. Therefore, Ghazali modifies the philosophic notion of courage and interprets it in terms of man's encounter

1. *C*, p. 85; *R*, III. 2. 1442. The Arabic term *shajāʻah* is used by Ghazali to mean "courage." This is the same term used by Muslim philosophers (such as al-Fārābī, *Fuṣūl*, p. 108; Avicenna, *ʻAhd*, p. 145; *Akhlāq*, p. 152; and Miskawayh, *Tahdhīb*, pp. 16, 27) as well as by the translators of the *Nicomachean Ethics*; cf. Aristotle, *Kitāb Arisṭū fī al Akhlāq* ("Nicomachean Ethics") (Rabat Bibliothèque Centrale MSS. 2508180), fol. 30b. Concerning the translation of *Nicomachean Ethics* into Arabic, consult A. J. Arberry, "The Nicomachean Ethics in Arabic, "*BSOAS*, XVII (1955), 1-9; and D.M. Dunlop, "The Nicomachean Ethics in Arabic, Books I-VI," *Oriens*, XV (1962), 18-34.

2. Koran 48:29.

3. *C*, pp. 85-86.

4. *R*, IV. 3. 2348ff.

5. Aristotle *Nicomachean Ethics* 3. 6. 1115a34-35; 7. 1116a10-13.

6. Aristotle *Nicomachean Ethics* 3. 6. 1115a26-27.

7. Aristotle *Nicomachean Ethics* 3. 6. 1115a32-34.

with God in the hereafter, rather than his encounter with death on the battlefield.

In *The Forty*, Ghazali repeats the definition of courage which he gave in the *Revival*, adding that "God loves courage."[1] Yet, courage is not one of the divine attributes. The closest thing to it in the *Supreme Purpose* is the attribute "Subduer" (*al-Qahhār*). The human parallel would be the man who overcomes his enemies. Since the real enemy of man is his passion, whoever subdues his passion will be able to subdue all his enemies. He who subjugates his desires during his lifetime will survive his physical death,[2] and Ghazali quotes the Koranic verse: "Think not of those who were slain in God's way as dead, nay, they live finding their sustenance in the presence of their Lord".[3] (This verse is usually explained as referring to the Muslims killed in the battle of Uḥūd.)[4] The idea of courage as an inner struggle exists in the Islamic religious tradition, and Ghazali stresses it at the expense of courage in the sense of military bravery, which Islamic tradition also extols. The Koran enjoins upon Muslims to have courage in their "strife" (*jihād*) and to show bravery on the battlefield[5] but Ghazali interprets the term *jihād* to mean struggle against the passions of the soul and the effort to purify it. He quotes a prophetic tradition which considers fighting in war a lesser struggle (*al-jihād al-aṣghar*), than striving against the passions of the soul (*al-jihād al-akbar*).[6] It is according to this view of *jihād* that Ghazali interprets the above mentioned Koranic verse to apply to those who win the struggle against their desires, and he proceeds similarly with regard to the martyrs (*shuhadā'*) to whom he denies their high traditional position. He even claims that, in the hereafter, martyrs will wish that they were learned men (*'ulamā'*).[7]

1. Ghazali, *Kitāb al-Arba'īn fī Uṣūl al-Dīn* (Cairo: Maktabat al-Jundī, 1383/1963), p. 167.
2. *Maqṣad*, p. 48.
3. Koran 3:169; cf. *Maqṣad*, p. 48.
4. Al-Ṭabarī, *Jāmi' al-Bayān 'an Ta'wīl al-Qur'ān*, ed. by Maḥmūd Muḥammad Shākir (Cairo: Dār al-Ma'ārif, n.d.), VII, 384ff.
5. Koran 4:95; 9:73; 9:81; 46:52, where *jihād* is mentioned in the sense of fighting. The Koran is firm in its stand against cowardice in combat. "If any do turn his back to them on such a day—unless it be in a stratagem of war, or to retreat to a troop [of his own]he draws on himself the wrath of God, and his shade is Hell" (Koran 8:16). See also Koran 8:15; 5:21.
6. *R*, III. 2. 1462-63; cf. al-Ḥāfiẓ al-'Irāqī, *al-Mughnī 'an Ḥaml al-Asfār fī Takhrīj mā fī al-Iḥyā' Min al-Akhbār* on the margin of *R*, p. 2606, where he says that the authenticity of this prophetic tradition is doubtful.
7. *R*, IV. 6. 2606.

In his program for educating children, Ghazali omits the training of warriors or fighting men; the short section about sports aims at building sound bodies without mentioning courage. Courage (*shajā'ah*) is only mentioned in connection with the attitude of a pupil who is beaten by a teacher. He should not, says Ghazali, ask the help of anyone, but be patient; and he should be told that this is the attitude of courageous men.[1] When giving an account of the prophet Muḥammad's noble character qualities, Ghazali devotes only a very small section to Muḥammad's virtue of courage in the sense of bravery on the battlefield. He says, "Muḥammad was the most gallant and the bravest of men,"[2] and the brevity of his treatment of bodily courage is another indication of Ghazali's determination to minimize the military aspect of this virtue.

Thus, Ghazali modifies both the philosophic and traditional Islamic understanding of the virtue of courage in the light of his own ethical theory. He examines courage in terms of a psychological analysis of anger and qualities related to it. The lack of emphasis on courage as bravery in battle reflects Ghazali's denial of the necessity of speaking about ethics in a political context. Likewise, whereas Miskawayh insists that virtue can be acquired only through association with others, and that "he who does not mingle with people and who does not live with them in cities cannot show temperance, courage (*najdah*), liberality, or justice,"[3] Ghazali argues that the only way for the soul to attain higher virtues and real salvation is to sever its connections with this world, be isolated from the rest of mankind, and live in seclusion.[4] This individualistic notion of character training necessarily causes courage to be understood as man's struggle against his animal soul.

Ghazali develops this view of courage further when he applies it to the virtues subordinated to it. His table shows that more virtues are subordinated to courage than to wisdom and he handles some of these virtues in the same way he handled the subdivision of wisdom. Subordinated to courage are: intrepidity (*najdah*), fortitude (*thabāt*), amiability (*mawaddah*), nobility (*nubl*), and manliness (*shahāmah*). Ghazali treats these virtues mainly by reproducing the philosophic accounts of them, especially those of the Muslim philosophers. His brief, indifferent sketch of them stems from the same attitude that underlies his psychological

1. *R*, III. 2. 1477.
2. *R*, II. 10. 1331.
3. Miskawayh, *Tahdhīb*, p. 29.
4. *R*, II. 2. 1467-68.

description of courage discussed above. Since the inquiry into these subordinate virtues only confirms, and does not add anything substantial to his view of courage, there is no need to examine them here. However, Ghazali's discussion of the rest of the subdivisions of courage, namely magnificence, greatness of soul, gentleness (suppression of anger is included in the discussion of gentleness), and correct evaluation of self seems to offer more than mere confirmation of his view of courage. It expands his view of courage to include ideas which not only help man in his "greater struggle" against the base passions of his soul, but also enable him to teach himself humility and even self-abasement. Thus it is important to investigate the virtues subordinate to courage.

"Magnificence" (*karam*) is classified as the first of the virtues subordinated to courage. Ghazali seems to follow Avicenna in listing magnificence under courage,[1] and although he does not explicitly explain why he does so, one possible reason may be that the element of greatness involved in magnificence implies "courage" in giving large sums of money for great things.[2]

Ghazali defines magnificence as spending gladly for things of high merit and great usefulness. It is the mean between vulgarity (*badhakh*), which is the extreme of excess, and paltriness (*nadhālah*), the extreme of defect.[3] The Arabic term *karam* (which is used here to mean magnificence) as well as those which Ghazali uses for the two extremes are those used by the translators of Aristotle's *Nicomachean Ethics*.[4] Furthermore, Ghazali uses the same Arabic term to denote a divine attribute of God, i.e., the "Magnificent" (*Karīm*) meaning the magnificent par excellence. He maintains that this term can be extended, with certain limitations, to apply to magnificent men as well.[5]

In both Aristotle and Ghazali, greatness and grandeur are what characterize the act of spending magnificently. Greatness seems to be required

1. *C*, p. 94; *R*, III. 2. 1443; cf. Avicenna, *Akhlāq*, p. 153. Concerning the order of virtues in the *Criterion* and in the *Revival*, consult Appendix II. See Appendix II also in regard to the subdivisions which are not discussed here, namely, intrepidity, endurance, fortitude, manliness, and nobility.

2. Cf. Miskawayh, *Tahdhīb*, p. 22. where he classifies magnificence under liberality; Aristotle *Nicomachean Ethics* 4. 1. 1119b20-2. 1123a23, where he discusses magnificence after liberality.

3. *C*, p. 94; *R*, III. 2. 1443, where only the mean and the two extremes are mentioned by name, but not their definitions; cf. Miskawayh, *Tahdhīb*, pp. 22.

4. Aristotle, *Ahklāq*, fol. 31a; cf. Aristotle *Nicomachean Ethics* 2. 7. 1107b18-19.

5. *Maqṣad*, p. 75.

in the person, the act, and the outcome of such an act. Aristotle says, "Magnificence is an attribute of expenditures of the kind which we call honorable; e.g., those connected with the gods—votive offerings, buildings, and sacrifices—and similarly with any form of religious worship and all those that are proper objects of public spirited ambition."[1] Ghazali agrees when enumerating the advantages of wealth and says it is also good to spend money for a public good, such as building mosques, bridges, hospitals, and the like.[2] Ghazali, however, disagrees with Aristotle, and consequently with the philosophers, about the evaluation of magnificence in the scale of virtues. It should be noted in this regard that in Aristotle the virtue of magnificence applies especially to religion and this implies that only a very powerful and wealthy man can offer sacrifices. No poor man and no obscure man can honor the gods properly because of his poverty and his obscurity. "Hence a poor man cannot be magnificent, since he has not the means with which to spend large sums fittingly."[3]

For Aristotle, therefore, the moral virtue in relation to the gods is magnificence.[4] Since he does not mention a special virtue called piety, the question of the inner reverence in prayers is never raised. Ghazali's procedure is exactly the opposite. He never suggests that a man who can afford to build a mosque is more decent in God's eyes than a simple man who is utterly poor. On the contrary, he considers poverty to be one of the higher virtues and better than having wealth and spending it for good causes. He names 'Abd al-Raḥmān b. 'Awf, one of the eminent companions of Muḥammad, as an example of a magnificent man and quotes a prophetic tradition which says that on the day of judgment the poor Muslim will enter paradise "running," while 'Abd al-Raḥmān will enter it "crawling."[5] In Ghazali's opinion, it is unlikely that a virtuous man would have sufficient wealth for magnificent spending since he will accumulate only enough money to satisfy his most basic needs. However, Ghazali identifies the ultimate end with individual salvation; this must be ranked higher than the virtues associated with public works.

1. Aristotle *Nicomachean Ethics* 4. 2. 1122b18-21.

2. *R*, III.7. 1769.

3. Aristotle *Nicomachean Ethics* 4. 2. 1122b26-28.

4. In the sense that magnificence is the only virtue in Aristotle's ethics which has anything to do with the gods. Cf. Aristotle *Nicomachean Ethics* 4. 3. 1124b14-15, where Aristotle compares the great souled man with Zeus.

5. *R*, III. 7. 1816; IV. 4. 2417-25.

Indeed, he realizes that magnificence may serve a great purpose for the community, but maintains that it is not essential for a man aiming at individual moral perfection and may even hinder his effort. Therefore, while accepting magnificence as a philosophic virtue, Ghazali values it less than the philosophers did, and subordinates it to virtues which may be considered as its opposite.

Another important virtue subordinate to courage is greatness of soul (*kibar an-nafs*). Ghazali defines it as a virtue which enables man to prepare himself for great deeds; while deserving these deeds he does not pay attention to them because he finds joy in the honor and greatness of his soul. Greatness of soul is a mean between vanity (*tabajjuḥ*) and smallness of soul (*ṣighar an-nafs*). The former means preparing the soul for great things without being worthy of them, while the latter expresses preparing the soul for inferior things.[1]

Unlike Miskawayh, Ghazali goes beyond this brief statement about greatness of soul to state that a person who achieves this virtue is moderately pleased by great honors accorded to him by learned men, but is not at all pleased by trivial honors or kinds of happiness which are brought about by fortune and chance.[2] In this respect Ghazali is closer to Aristotle who gives special attention to the discussion of greatness of soul. Aristotle however, seems to accord more importance to "the gifts of fortune," maintaining that they "make men more great-souled, because their possessors are honored by some people."[3] Although Ghazali admits that external goods are helpful in achieving virtues, he does not fully accept this Aristotelian view.[4] For Aristotle, a person is thought to be great-souled if he claims much and deserves much. Since it is honor above all else which great men claim and deserve, the great-souled man is primarily concerned with honor. Though Ghazali accepts the philosophic analysis of greatness of soul, his acceptance is qualified because honor is for him inferior to the goods of the hereafter. To claim honor is to forsake the realities of the world to come. It is

1. *R*, III. 2. 1443; *C*, p. 94. Ghazali here also uses the Arabic terms used by the translators of Aristotle's *Nicomachean Ethics*; cf. Aristotle *Akhlāq*, fol. 31a; cf. Aristotle *Nicomachean Ethics* 2. 7. 1107b21-25.

2. *C*, p. 94; cf. Miskawayh, *Tahdhīb*, p. 21.

3. Aristotle *Nicomachean Ethics* 4. 3. 1123a34-1125a35. Concerning this point, see particularly 1124a5-19: "Great honors accorded by persons of worth will afford him pleasure in a moderate degree . . . Honor rendered by common people and on trivial grounds he will utterly despise, for this is not what he merits."

4. *C*, p. 110.

with this in mind that Ghazali dedicates Book 8 of Quarter III of the *Revival* to "The Evils of Love of Fame and Dissimulation".[1]

To claim or seek honor is blameworthy, according to Ghazali, whereas possessing honor or fame without seeking it is not objectionable. Prophets, caliphs, and prominent learned men enjoy honor and are capable of guarding themselves against possible evils which may be caused by love of honor and fame. In order to avoid such evils, however, Ghazali advises that men should seek the virtue of obscurity (*khumūl*) and keep clear of honor and fame (*jāh*).[2] This is difficult and requires great effort since men by nature love to be honored and famous. Honors imply recognition of some kind of perfection in the person honored, such as knowledge, noble birth, skill in ruling, and the like. For Ghazali, all perfections for which men are honored are not really theirs because it is only God who has true perfection. Realizing this helps man to refrain from claiming honor and fame for perfections which are "in reality" not his, and although Ghazali admits that there is a minimum of honor which is not blameworthy and which is necessary for man's daily life with others, he is concerned that total preoccupation with satisfying others will result from seeking honor and, thus, will distract man from the way to the "nearness to God."[3] Since "nearness to God" is the final goal of character training, Ghazali suggests ways of curing love of honor and fame so that men's souls become free from attachment to perishable goods which hinder their salvation. One way is to engage in activities where the person thought to be perfect receives no honor and may even be blamed and disgraced. The best cure for seeking honor, however, is to isolate oneself from people and migrate to places where one is unknown.[4]

Although Aristotle agrees with Ghazali that the two extremes of this virtue are not thought to be actually vicious since they do no harm, he goes on to say that "smallness of soul is more opposed than vanity to greatness of soul."[5] The small-souled man, by considering himself

1. *R*, III. 8. 1836-1930 ("*Fī Dhamm al-Jāh wa al-Riyā'*").
2. *R*, III, 8. 1840.
3. *R*, III. 8. 1848-49, 1852-53.
4. *R*, III. 8. 1857, where Ghazali considers various ways of inviting blame and disgrace. Although he rejects and considers reprehensible doing anything which violates the religious law, he suggests practices which are permissible with certain qualifications, such as drinking non-intoxicants in a wine cup. Ghazali is aware of the objection which can be raised by the jurist, but for him the truly learned purify their souls in ways which are not easily judged by jurists.
5. Aristotle *Nicomachean Ethics* 4. 3. 1125a33-34.

inferior, may fail to fulfil his potentialities; whereas the vain man, although he may make himself ridiculous when he tries to act grandly, will not at least miss a chance of increasing his own nobility if circumstances afford him the occasion to do so. Ghazali's reaction to Aristotle's contention is simple: he is interested primarily in deeds that bring great goods in the hereafter, and these things seem to be accomplished most succesfully when men are obscure and engaged in activities which do not advertise greatness of soul. According to Aristotle, greatness of soul comprises all the rest of the virtues, presupposes them, and adorns them: "Greatness of soul seems therefore to be as it were a crowning ornament of the virtues; it enhances their greatness, and it cannot exist without them,"[1] and thus greatness of soul and justice seem to be the two peaks of Aristotle's *Ethics*, justice being concerned with social virtues, while greatness of soul emphasizes the perfection of the individual.

Since Ghazali is concerned with individual salvation, greatness of soul should appeal to him but it does not, because Aristotle deals only with wordly honor and is silent about immortal glory or great goods after death. In Aristotle the whole sphere of moral virtue is directed to what is perishable; it is only intellectual virtue which is concerned with the imperishable and immortal. For Ghazali, on the other hand, although morally virtuous actions are performed by one perishable being in relation to another, they are executed with a view to the divine reality of the hereafter. For this reason humility and obscurity serve the goal of Ghazali's character training better than greatness of soul and are therefore better fitted to crown the moral virtues. It is in this context that we can understand Ghazali's classification of greatness of soul as one of the virtues of courage, as well as his judgment that its extreme defect is a virtue which ranks higher than it.

According to Ghazali, one of the most important virtues subordinate to courage is "gentleness" (*ḥilm*), because it is related directly to anger which is the basic psychic quality of the irascible faculty. Furthermore, gentleness is one of those few virtues which also apply to God; thus, he speaks of the divine attribute "Gentle" (*Ḥalīm*).[2] Ghazali defines gentleness as restraining the soul from angry excitement. It is the mean between excessive anger or irascibility (*istishāṭah*) and spiritlessness

1. Aristotle *Nicomachean Ethics* 4. 3. 1124a1-3.
2. *Maqṣad*, p. 65.

(*infirāk*).[1] Gentleness thus defined is distinguished from what Ghazali calls "displaying gentleness" (*taḥallum*). This is a quality which also appears in the *Revival* as "suppression of anger" (*kaẓm al-ghayẓ*), which is a restraining of anger which is already excited. Ghazali classifies this quality as a virtue, but he considers it inferior to gentleness.[2]

In explaining the virtue of gentleness, Ghazali describes anger as a natural disposition. He equates anger with heat and describes it as blood boiling in the heart. It is a natural disposition which protects man against things which could destroy him. But this natural disposition has to be moderate if it is to be useful.[3] Because it is a natural disposition, Ghazali maintains that it cannot be completely eradicated as long as man lives and, thus, character training aims not at destroying but at controlling and refining it. Refining anger can best be accomplished by understanding its relation to man's desire for certain things. If the desired objects are necessary for man, such as food and shelter, and they are threatened by others, then one's anger is natural and proper and needs only to be moderated lest it bring bad consequences. But if the desired things are not necessary for man, like fame and wealth, then it is only through bad habit and ignorance that one's anger arises, and this kind of anger should be completely eradicated because it is not natural. A third possibility remains: if the desired things are necessary for some men and not for others, then those for whom these things are necessary will experience a natural anger when they lose them; yet, they should be moderate in their anger, especially since these desired things are not universally necessary.[4]

In dealing with anger, Ghazali keeps in mind the question of the mean and the two extremes. Yet he pays more attention to the extreme of excess, for he regards it as the more vicious. Indeed, when he uses

1. *C*, pp. 94-95; *R*, III. 2. 1443. The Arabic term *ḥilm* used by Ghazali to mean gentleness is the same term which is used by translators of the *Nicomachean Ethics* (Aristotle, *Akhlāq*, fols. 31a-31b). It is also used by Muslim philosophers (al-Fārābī, *Fuṣūl*, p. 113; Miskawayh, *Tahdhīb*, p. 22; Avicenna, *Akhlāq*, p. 154). Ghazali, however, does not use the term *infirāk* in the *Revival*. This term is used in the *Criterion* to denote the extreme of defect of this virtue. Indeed the terms used for the two extremes are not used by Muslim philosophers and seem to reflect Ghazali's own choice of terms.

2. *C*, p. 131; *R*, III. 5. 1663; cf. al-Rāghib al-Iṣfahānī, *Dharī'ah*, pp. 131-32, where he makes the same distinction; Avicenna, *Akhlāq*, p. 154 where he lists suppression of anger, together with qualities such as forgiveness, forbearance, and fortitude, as synonymous with gentleness.

3. *R*, III. 5. 1647-48; *C*, p. 132; cf. Miskawayh, *Tahdhīb*, pp. 193-94.

4. *R*, III. 5. 1651-52.

the term anger (*ghaḍab*) without any qualification, he usually means excessive anger, i.e., irascibility.[1] This emphasis on the dangers of irascibility suggests that Ghazali regards gentleness as a virtue which inclines to the side of spiritlessness. In his view, the gentle-tempered man is not the "gentleman" of the Aristotelian polis; rather, he is a man who not only forgives those who wrong him, but also behaves nicely toward them.[2] In order to attain the virtue of gentleness, man must avoid the things which usually give rise to excessive anger, such as false pride, boasting, love of wealth, and love of fame—in other words, qualities which are related to association with others. Even if these things are avoided, one must still guard against excessive anger by meditating on his position as a created thing in relation to God. He should fear God's punishment and continuously appeal to Him for assistance in controlling his anger by reciting the formula: "God protect me from the damned Satan."[3] Thus, while accepting gentleness as a philosophic virtue, Ghazali modifies it to suit the character training of the man who seeks individual salvation.

The last of the subdivisions of courage which show how Ghazali modifies and amends philosophic virtues is the virtue of "correct evaluation of self" (*waqār*). For him, correct evaluation is behaving toward one's soul in proportion to its merit. In the *Criterion*, he regards correct evaluation as the mean between arrogance (*kibr*) and humility (*tawāḍu'*);[4] whereas in the *Revival* he lists the extremes of this virtue as arrogance and baseness (*khasāsah*).[5] When defining the extremes in the *Criterion*, however, Ghazali only mentions arrogance and baseness. He defines the former as putting the soul higher than it deserves and the latter as lowering the soul below what it deserves, commenting that if this lowering "is in the right way, it is called commendable humility".[6] This change of emphasis in the *Criterion* is important in preparing for the detailed discussion of the virtue of humility in the *Revival*. Aside from mentioning and briefly defining the virtue of correct evaluation of self, Ghazali seems to have little to say about it. Muslim philosophers such as

1. *R*, III. 5. 1690. This is reflected throughout this book and even present in part of its title which reads: "On Rebuking Anger" (*Fī Dhamm al-Ghaḍab*).

2. *R*, III. 5. 1670-73.

3. *R*, III. 5. 1659.

4. *C*, p. 95.

5. *R*, III. 2. 1443.

6. *C*, p. 96.

al-Fārābī and Avicenna do not even mention it as a virtue; instead, they classify humility as one of the virtues.[1] Although Miskawayh and Ibn 'Adī consider correct evaluation of self as a virtue, their definition of it emphasizes aspects different from those described by Ghazali.[2]

Although Aristotle does not mention this virtue, Ghazali's view of it can be understood in terms of the qualities of the Aristotelian gentleman.[3] A difficulty, however, arises when one tries to trace humility as well to Aristotelian ethics, for this quality is completely incompatible with Aristotle's notion of the gentleman, who must be, among other things, a great-souled man and humility is the vice which stands as the defect of greatness of soul. When he introduces humility into his ethical system, Ghazali is in agreement with most of the well-known Muslim philosophers; al-Fārābi, for example, considers humility as a virtue which is the mean between arrogance and baseness, and Avicenna regards it as a subdivision of wisdom which restrains the soul from arrogance.[4] Thus, earlier Muslim philosophers had already departed from the Aristotelian position by considering humility as a virtue. This was due, not only to the influence of Christianity and Islam, but also to the spirit of Hellenistic thought, especially that of the Stoics.[5] Ghazali's attitude toward humility seems to be more positive than that of the Muslim philosophers. For while some of those philosophers only briefly mention this virtue, and others like Miskawayh completely ignore it, Ghazali discusses it at length and regards it as "the principal virtue of pious men."[6] His view of humility, therefore, is a valuable illustration of his qualified acceptance of the philosophic virtues.

Ghazali's table of virtues in the *Criterion* and the *Revival* does not include humility; in one case he even explained it as a vice of defect.

1. Al-Fārābī, *Fuṣūl*, p. 113; Avicenna, *Akhlāq*, p. 153; *'Ahd*, p. 144.

2. Miskawayh, *Tahdhīb*, p. 21, where he classifies correct evaluation of self under liberality, which is itself a subdivision of temperance, defining it as "tranquility and stability of the soul during the agitations which accompany the pursuit of desires." Ibn 'Adī, *Tahdhīb*, pp. 27-28, where correct evaluation of self is equated with good manners of speech and respectful conduct in discourse with others.

3. Aristotle *Nicomachean Ethics* 4. 3. 1125a14-15; "Other traits generally attributed to the great-souled man are a slow gait, a deep voice, and a deliberate utterance."

4. al-Fārābī, *Fuṣūl*, p. 113; Avicenna, *'Ahd*, p. 144; *Akhlāq*, p. 153.

5. Fehme Jadaane, *L'Influence du stoicisme sur la pensée musulmane* (Beirut: Dār al-Mashriq, 1968), pp. 189-234; cf. Ibn 'Adī, *Tahdhīb*, p. 28 where he classifies humility as a virtue.

6. *R*, III. 9. 1953 (*at-tawāḍu' wa huwa ra's akhlāq al-muttaqīn*).

He now introduces it in a subtle fashion which suggests that he is aware of its special relation to the rest of the philosophic virtues. He presents it as the defect of correct evaluation of self in the *Criterion* and then discusses it as the excess of correct evaluation of self in the *Revival*. Then he replaces correct evaluation of self, which had been originally introduced as the mean between arrogance and baseness, with humility as the mean between these two extremes.[1] Although Ghazali maintains that humility is an inferior attitude and that a learned man should not trade positions with a shoemaker, some of his examples of humble men show that a humble master cannot be distinguished from slaves when he is with them.[2] Indeed, Ghazali identifies the humble person as the one who intentionally gives up some of what he deserves,[3] and in this way, humility implies self-abasement. This meaning is implicit in the verb root from which the Arabic term for this virtue is derived,[4] and humility for Ghazali is a virtue which reflects man's knowledge of himself and of his Creator. In realizing his true position in this universe, man can only be humble and can never be arrogant. It is for the purpose of achieving humility, Ghazali says, that Islamic prayer includes prostration.[5]

Ghazali seems to value humility more highly than some other moral virtues when he lists it as an essential quality of the student of higher learning.[6] It is obvious that Ghazali's great interest in humility stems from his desire to make all virtue serve as a means for the individual spiritual salvation of man and he modifies and changes the philosophic concept of this virtue because he considers the purpose of character refinement to lie beyond the mere political association with others. This purpose must consider that there lies beyond this life another one in which man can attain an ultimate happiness if he prepares himself for it . This purpose is different from what the pious men in the religious community called paradise and it is higher. To describe this ultimate happiness will raise several questions which have not yet been touched

1. *R*, III. 9. 1993.

2. *R*, III. 9. 1993-96. The example given refers to 'Abd al-Raḥmān b. 'Awf, one of the companions of the Prophet; cf. *R*, II. 10. 1332-34, where Ghazali devotes a special section to the examples of Muḥammad's humility.

3. *R*, III. 6. 1993; cf. al-Rāghib al-Iṣfahānī, *Dharī'ah*, p. 111.

4. Edward William Lane, *Arabic-English Lexicon* (Bk. I, 8 Pts.; London: Williams and Norgate, 1863-1893), I, 8. 3055; cf. al-Rāghib al-Iṣfahānī, *Dharī'ah*, p. 111.

5. *R*, III. 6. 1979.

6. *C*, p. 151.

in this study and it must be postponed to the concluding chapter. However, one thing can be made clear here: only through the "greater struggle" against the passions of the soul can man attain ultimate happiness.

Temperance and its Subdivisions

Definition

The third principal virtue is temperance which is the virtue of the concupiscent faculty. When the activity of this faculty is controlled, that is, when it readily follows the guidance of reason and does not independently pursue its own desires, the virtue of temperance is achieved.[1]

As the mean in regard to desire and appetite, it is not different from the Aristotelian concept of temperance; for, while Aristotle uses temperance in relation to sensual pleasures, he does not mean all pleasures of all senses, but only the pleasures of touch and taste.[2] "It is actually enjoying the object that is pleasant, and this is done solely through the sense of touch; alike in eating and drinking and in what are called the pleasures of sex."[3] Although Ghazali also mentions pleasures in general, he too discusses temperance primarily in relation to the desire for food and sex.

According to Ghazali, temperance is the mean between two vices, namely, self-indulgence (*sharah*) and insensibility (*khumūd ash-shahwah*). The former is the extreme of excess, that is, the concupiscent faculty exceeding the right limits set by reason. The later is the extreme of defect which occurs when the concupiscent faculty fails to desire what reason recommends. He says that most men err on the side of excess, especially in relation to the requirements of the desires for food and sex—a view which Aristotle also shares.[4] For both Ghazali and the philosophers, temperance is associated with the lowest desires, and for this reason it is considered the most apparent, and, therefore, the most basic virtue. But while the philosophers discuss the desire for food and sex in relation to temperance only briefly, Ghazali deals with them in detail, emphasizing that desire for food and sex is the starting point of all character

1. *C*, pp. 82, 87-88; *R*, III. 2. 1443.
2. Aristotle, *Nicomachean Ethics*, 2. 6. 1107b4-5-10. 1118b24.
3. Aristotle, *Nicomachean Ethics*, 2. 10. 1118b26.
4. *C*, p. 88; *R*, III. 2. 1442; cf. Aristotle, *Nicomachean Ethics*, 2. 6. 1107b7-8.

training.[1] He makes both desires the subject of the third book of the third quarter of the *Revival*, entitled: "The Breaking of the Two Desires" (*Kasr ash-Shahwatayn*); this immediately follows the book on "Training the Soul," where the general characteristics of virtue are given.[2] The same subject is dealt with in the first and second books of the second quarter of the *Revival* as well as in the *Criterion*;[3] we must examine Ghazali's views on these two desires to understand his view of temperance.

Food

For Ghazali, the desire for food (*shahwat al-baṭn*, literally, the desire of the stomach) is the most destructive desire in man if it is not controlled. It is the source of all desires which drive man to reprehensible and vile deeds.[4] To control the desire for food, however, does not mean abstaining completely from eating. Man desires food to preserve his body and to carry out such important activities as acquiring knowledge and performing good deeds but he must be moderate if food is to be beneficial for him. Man should eat so as to avoid the pain of hunger, without making himself suffer the pains of overindulgence. He should be in a state in which he, as Ghazali puts it, "forgets his stomach" (*yansā baṭnah*), meaning that he is not disturbed either by the pains of hunger, or by those of excessive eating.[5] Since the requirements of self-preservation preclude dispensing with physical satisfactions entirely, man will derive the greatest benefit by observing the mean in regard to them. Ghazali, therefore, holds to the doctrine of the mean in establishing temperance with respect to food. Yet he warns that this state belongs only to the one who has reached the mean in all character qualities. Before reaching this stage man has to train himself toward the defect lest he fall into excess in satisfying his desire for food.[6] This emphasis on inclining toward one of the two extremes in order to reach the mean is a method generally recognized by the philosophers, and we have mentioned earlier that Ghazali recommends this method. However his emphasis on the

1. *R*, III. 3. 1490; cf. Aristotle, *Nicomachean Ethics*, 2, 10. 1118ff; Avicenna, *'Ahd*, p. 145; Miskawayh, *Tahdhīb*, pp. 90, 27.

2. *R*, III. 3. 1490-1539.

3. *R*, II. 1. 654-84: "The Manners of Eating"; *R*, II. 2. 687-758: "The Manners of Marriage"; *C*, pp. 122-29.

4. *R*, III. 3. 1490.

5, *R*, III. 3. 1519; *C*, p. 123,

6. *R*, III. 3. 1519-20.

necessity of inclining toward the defect in regard to eating seems to go beyond merely restating this method of reaching the mean. This becomes clear in Ghazali's analysis of persons who can observe the mean with respect to food. They are of two kinds, namely, the sincere man (*ṣiddīq*), a person who has achieved a high degree of moral training, and the deluded man (*maghrūr*), a man who only thinks that he is sincere. But Ghazali says it is difficult even for the sincere man to know that he is truly sincere, and thus all men, except prophets, should incline toward defect when seeking to satisfy the desires of their stomachs. This position is defended at length in both the *Criterion* and the *Revival*[1] but the equation of temperance with hunger is more evident in the latter work, where Ghazali goes so far as to speak of the excellence and merit of hunger (*faḍīlat al-jū'*).[2]

Intentionally suffering hunger is explained by Ghazali as the highest of several levels on which the individual can train himself in the amount of food he should eat. Ghazali decides what these levels are on the basis of the following prophetic tradition:

> It suffices the "son of Adam" [man] to eat few morsels (*luqaymāt*) in order to keep his backbone erect; but if it is necessary [that he should eat more], then one third [of the capacity of his stomach] is for food, one third for beverages, and one third for breathing.[3]

Now, *luqaymāt* (few morsels), means less than ten mouthfuls. This, according to Ghazali, is the equivalent of one seventh of the capacity of the stomach, and the amount of food eaten by those who reached the highest level of temperance. Men of this type eat only the amount

1. *C*, pp. 121, 124-25; *R*, III. 3. 1491ff; cf. *R*, II. 10.1309-18, where Ghazali gives an account of Muḥammad's character, showing that he was moderate in regard to food.

2. *R*, III. 3. 1491-95. This is the title of a section which occupies more than three quarters of the part devoted to the discussion of the desire for food in Book 3 of Quarter III of the *Revival*. In order to show the merit of hunger, Ghazali quotes several prophetic traditions and sayings of the Companions and learned men, but no Koranic verses (cf. al-Ḥāfiz al-'Irāqī, *Mughnī*, pp. 1491-95, where he shows that only seven out of the twenty-one prophetic traditions quoted by Ghazali in this section are acceptable, while the rest are either weak or unsound). In addition, Ghazali lists ten beneficial aspects of hunger in order to make it attractive. These are:

(1) clarity of mind, kindling of talent, and acute discernment; (2) sensitivity and purity of heart; (3) humility, which leads to submissiveness to God; (4) reminding one of God's punishment; (5) subordinating all evil desires; (6) less sleep, which means more time for worship; (7) making worship easier; (8) keeping the body healthy; (9) reducing the need for worldly goods; and (10) encouraging charity.

3. *R*, III. 3. 1493. 1496, 1507; *C*, p. 125.

necessary for their subsistence, and there are some who have trained themselves to be satisfied with the equivalent of a chickpea a day.[1] The second level of temperance is to eat what comes to one-third of the capacity of the stomach. Although this is the largest indulgence permitted to those who aim at refining their character, Ghazali allows a third level of temperance in which one may eat up to two-thirds of the capacity of the stomach. This he considers the limit of temperance and what exceeds it is intemperance (*isrāf*).[2]

Because men's appetites differ according to their particular circumstances and the kind of work they are engaged in, Ghazali maintains that the underlying principle is that man should eat whenever he is "truly" hungry, that is, he should eat the amount which does not hinder him from carrying out his good activities, and he should not be misled by a false desire for food.[3] In order to guard against overindulgence of this desire, Ghazali enumerates in detail several measures concerning the amount of food to be taken and the length of time which should lapse before one eats the specified amount. In doing this he always favors the most extreme cases of defect, e.g., the highest level with regard to the time span is to suffer hunger intentionally for three days or more; the lowest level is to eat one meal during a whole day; more than this is excess. This reflects Ghazali's zeal in emphasizing the virtue of the defect in relation to the desire for food.[4]

Immoderation in eating is only discussed as it concerns the amount of food a person should consume, for it is generally agreed that immoderation in the kinds of food consumed is difficult to control.[5] Ghazali enumerates several types of food common at his time, giving preference to the toughest kinds. "Those who seek the way to the hereafter should abstain from every kind of food which is desirable to them."[6] Furthermore, under the influence of the Islamic law, Ghazali maintains that there are types of food which should not be eaten at all, and there is no question of moderation concerning them: intoxicating drink (*muskir*) the flesh of swine, and any food which is harmful or not legally ac-

1. *C*, p. 184; *R*, III. 3. 1507.
2. *C*, p. 125. where he regads the second level the lower limit; *R*, III. 3. 1508, where he adds the other lower level.
3. *R*, III. 3. 1508; *C*, p. 125.
4. *R*, III. 3. 1509-1510.
5. Aristotle *Nicomachean Ethics* 2. 11. 1118b22-23.
6. *R*, III. 3. 1511.

quired.[1] Ghazali refuses to recommend moderation with regard to these things because it implies a deviation from the Islamic religious law. This attitude differs from that of earlier Muslim philosophers who "interpreted" some of the requirements of the religious law when they could not easily reconcile them with some aspects of the philosophic tradition. Abū Bakr al-Rāzī and Avicenna, for example, allow intoxicating drink in certain circumstances as long as it is not used to excess.[2]

Ghazali's view of temperance in relation to the desire for food, therefore, is based on the philosophic concept of moderation in terms of observing the mean between self-indulgence and insensibility. It is commonly known that the philosophic concept of temperance prefers the extreme of defect to the extreme of excess, but for Ghazali, however, this is not enough. He considers the practice of deliberately suffering hunger to be praiseworthy. Since this attitude is linked to what he calls "severing relations with this world," Ghazali seems to have some support for his attitude in Islamic teachings, especially since Islam requires every Muslim to practice fasting (*sawm*) during the daytime for the length of one month a year. But Islamic tradition does not support what Ghazali considers the higher levels of abstinence. The source for such higher levels seems to be found in the practices of a few men who devote their lives entirely to spiritual and moral refinement.

Sex

Sex for Ghazali is the second important desire after that of food, and unless this desire is controlled, it can lead to great evils. He considers sex, or, as he calls it, the desire of the generative organ (*shahwat al-farj*), a natural desire which aims at preserving the human species, just as food preserves the body.[3] Ghazali uses the term *nikāḥ*, which primarily

1. *R*, III. 3. 1506; *C*, p. 125; cf. *R*. II, 4. 555, 817, 818, 828.

2. Abū Bakr al-Rāzī, *al-Ṭibb al-Rūḥānī* in *Opera Philosophica*, pp. 72-74, where he devotes a special chapter to "On Drunkenness," in which he concludes that "sometimes, of course, drink is a necessity so as to dispel anxiety, and in other situations requiring excessive cheerfulness, courage, impetuosity, and recklessness." In his *al-Sīrah al-Falsafiyyah* in *Opera Philosophica*, p. 110, he relates about himself as follows. "As for my habits of eating, drinking, and amusement, those who have frequently observed me so engaged may be amazed that I have never erred on the side of excessive indulgence." Cf. Avicenna, *Akhlāq*, p. 155, where he says: "As for intoxicating drink, man should abstain from it for the sake of pleasure; only for the sake of healing (*tashaffiyan*), curing (*tadāwiyan*), and keeping strength can he take it." Ghazali criticizes this view in his *Munqidh*, p. 113, as one of the bad effects of philosophy.

3. *C*, pp. 122, 126; *R*, III, 3. 1525.

means marriage, for sexual intercourse, thereby suggesting that sex is acceptable only within the legal relation between a man and a woman.[1] Thus it is only within marriage that the question of the mean in regard to satisfying carnal pleasures can arise. Outside marriage any sexual relation is considered forbidden and is consequantly rejected by Ghazali.

Within its accepted form, sexual intercourse can be commendable or reprehensible. It is commendable when man seeks to have offspring so as to preserve the species, thereby pleasing God.[2] It is also commendable when it is practiced for the sake of moderately satisfying the desire for sex. This helps man to guard against possible acts of fornication and cures him from diseases which might otherwise affect the body. Unlike other Muslim philosophers such as Abū Bakr al-Rāzī, Ghazali does not associate the health of the body with complete suppression of sexual desire; he argues that attempts to control sexual desire completely cannot succeed, since even when men through piety effectively control all the external aspects of this desire, they cannot control their thoughts (*khawāṭir*) about it. Since such thoughts then affect men when engaged in worship and learning, the best way to put an end to all the complications which may result from the influence of sexual desire is to satisfy it moderately.[3]

The fact that sexual intercourse is acceptable in marriage does not mean that man may be inordinately concerned with sexual enjoyment and even take special kinds of food to strengthen this desire. Such an attitude reflects enslavement to passion and may incite man to transgress the religious law and commit fornication. Sexual desire must therefore be satisfied under the guidance, not only of the religious law, but of

1. *R*, II. 2. 687-758; *C*, p. 126.

2. *C*, pp. 126-27; *R*, II. 2. 694-97. Begetting offspring, according to Ghazali, is important also because it gives man a chance to have a pious child who will pray for his salvation; cf. Avicenna, *Shifā'*: *Metaphysics*, II, 448.

3. *R*, II. 2. 700; Abū Bakr al-Rāzī, *Ṭibb*, p. 25: "frequent use of the sexual organ enlarges the testicles and attracts to them much blood, with the result that more and more sperm is generated in them; so the sexual desire and yearning to indulge augments and increases over again. Contrariwise, when one diminishes or refrains from intercourse, the body retains that original freshness . . . with the result that the period of growth and development is extended. It therefore behooves the intelligent man to rein and restrain himself." Rāzī discusses the desire for sex in a special chapter of his *Ṭibb*, p. 75, in which he makes the following argument. "This particular pleasure [of sex] is in any case the most proper and right of all pleasures to be cast away. This is because it is not necessary for the continuance of life, like eating and drinking . . . its excessive and immoderate indulgence destroys and demolishes the structure of the body."

reason as well.[1] A more dangerous kind of enslavement to sexual desire can be seen in the case of passionate lovers (*'ushshāq*) who are ignorant of what is meant by sexual desire and transgress even the bounds of animality in their lack of self-control. Not content to gratify their sexual inclination by normal means, they seek to increase desire and hence sink to a lower level of slavery. Such men not only exhibit an animal subservience to instinct, but they also compel intellect to serve instinct and thus reverse the proper order in which the lower serves the higher.[2]

Ghazali's opposition to excessive sexual indulgence stems primarily from his conviction that such overindulgence distracts the soul and turns it away from its proper tasks, which are worship and learning.[3] The extreme of defect, on the other hand, is the vice of failing to satisfy sexual desire which deprives man of having offspring, of experiencing sexual pleasure himself, and of providing sexual enjoyment to his partner in marriage.[4] The mean between these two extremes is temperance. Since the extreme of excess predominates, Ghazali prescribes ways which help man to guard against it. The most important of these is to suffer hunger intentionally so as to weaken the urge for sexual intercourse; next, to engage in something which turns one's attention from this desire. The ultimate solution is marriage, which enables man to satisfy the urgent demands of his desire.

Although Ghazali discusses at length the advantages of marriage and considers it the ultimate solution for the desire of sex, he points out some problems related to marriage which make some men prefer celibacy. The first and most serious difficulty which marriage can cause is the hardship involved in providing for a family. These may drive the man without independent means to seek illegal earnings.[5] The second difficulty is the failure to provide what is due to women and inability to forbear their bad temper. The third harm is that wife and children may preoccupy the man and divert him from seeking ultimate happiness to seeking worldly success.[6]

1. *R*, II. 3. 1526-28; *C*, pp. 127-29.

2. *R*, III. 3. 1527; *C*, p. 129; cf. Abū Bakr al-Rāzī, *Ṭibb*, p. 39. In his discussion of passionate love (*'ishq*) Ghazali seems to be influenced by Rāzī, *Ṭibb*, p. 35.

3. *C*, p. 186.

4. *R*, III. 3. 1532.

5. *R*, II. 2. 705-710.

6. *R*, II. 2. 711.

This third difficulty reflects the principal source of Ghazali's reservations about marriage and satisfying sexual desire, that is, his preoccupation with the necessity of freeing one's soul from everything except "good deeds which lead to ultimate happiness." This is incompatible with mundane things such as marriage and sexual intercourse.[1]

Discussion of Temperance Extended

In dealing with temperance as to food and sex, Ghazali accepts the basic philosophic view of this virtue and then enlarges it by discussing these two desires in great detail. Thus he introduces certain modifications of temperance. For example, with respect to the desire for food, he virtually identifies temperance with the extreme of defect. However, although this brings about some changes in the characteristics of temperance as understood by the philosophers, Ghazali still preserves its basic philosophic nature in that it is the virtue of the concupiscent faculty of the animal soul. However, aside from his detailed discussion of temperance as applied to food and sex, Ghazali also uses temperance to cover things outside the concupiscent faculty, such as the irascible instincts and sometimes all the irrational parts of the soul. This wider usage of temperance will be clear if we examine other meanings of the Arabic term for it.

The Arabic term for temperance used by Ghazali is *'iffah.* It is the term which the Muslim philosophers as well as the translators from Greek used to render *sophrosyne.*[2] Ghazali also uses *'iffah* in a general sense, meaning much more than mere training of the concupiscent faculty. In this, he seems to be influenced by the Arabic lexicons, the Koran, and the prophetic tradition. According to Arabic lexicons, *'iffah* is a noun derived from the verb root *'affa,* whose basic meaning is to abstain from what is unlawful or what is base, and thus it comes to be identified with abstention from doing anything which should not

1. *Munqidh,* pp. 100-101, where Ghazali relates that he had to leave his family behind when he decided on his journey to Syria. Later, the summons of his children was among the reasons for his return.

2. Aristotle *Akhlāq,* fol. 31a; Abū Bakr al-Rāzī, *Ṭibb,* p. 91; *Sīrah,* p. 110; al-Fārābī, *Fuṣūl,* p. 108, where he says that "the ethical virtues are the virtues of the appetitive part, such as temperance (*'iffah*)"; Avicenna, *'Ahd,* p. 145, where he says that "temperance (*'iffah*) is a mean between self-indulgence and insensibility of desire"; *Akhlāq,* pp. 152-53; Miskawayh, *Tahdhīb,* pp. 16, 20, 27.

be done.[1] The term *'iffah* does not occur in the Koran; what occurs are two verbal derivatives of the verb root, *'affa*. One of these is used three times as an imperative (*falyasta'fif*) commanding the wealthy to practice abstinence.[2] The other derivative (*ta'affuf*) occurs only once and means general continence.[3] In the prophetic tradition, the term *'iffah* occurs six times. In three instances it is used to mean general continence.[4] The other three usages mean temperance (in the sense of Ghazali) as to food and sex.[5]

Influenced by these usages of the term *'iffah*, Ghazali's concept of temperance is enlarged to include an abstinence and restraint not limited to objects of the concupiscent faculty alone. In applying temperance to all faculties of the soul and all organs of the body, Ghazali extends its meaning beyond that accepted by the philosophic tradition. He states that to restrain the requirements of the appetites (*shahawāt*) and anger (*ghaḍab*) is temperance,[6] and this wider sense of temperance consists primarily in refusing control by the appetites. Restraint which excludes what is forbidden by the religious law, Ghazali calls abstinence (*wara'*); and he calls it piety (*taqwā*) when such religious restraint grows stronger and rejects what is not explicitly forbidden so that actual prohibitions will be obeyed. Finally, the highest form of restraint, according to Ghazali, is to refrain from anything in this world which does not directly aim at ultimate happiness.[7] This ascent of temperance from simple restraint of desire to the exclusion of everything which is

1. Jamāl al-Dīn Muḥammad Ibn Manzūr, *Lisān al-'Arab* (20 vols.; Cairo: Būlāq, 1308/1901), XI, 158; Muḥammad Ibn Ya'qūb al-Fīrūzābādī, *al-Qāmūs al-Muḥīt* (4 vols., 3d ed.; Cairo: Būlāq, 1344/1925), III, 176-77; Lane, *Arabic-English Lexicon*, I. 5. 2088.

2. Koran 4:5; 24:33; 24:60.

3. Koran 2:273: "The ignorant man counts them wealthy because of their continence (*ta'affuf*)."

4. Aḥmad b. Ḥanbal, *Musnad*, I, 389, 434, 443.

5. Muḥammad Ibn Yazīd Ibn Mājah, *Sunan*, ed. by Muḥammad Fu'ād 'Abd al-Bāqī (2 vols.; Cairo: Dār Iḥyā' al-Kutub al-'Arabiyyah, 1952-1953), II, 817, 1308; Aḥmad Ibn Ḥanbal, *Musnad*, II, 177.

6. *R*, IV. 2. 2248-49; *C*, pp. 134-36, where Ghazali maintains that a man who restrains the animal faculties is not truly temperate (*'afīf*) unless his temperance is accompanied by abstinence (*'iffah*) on the part of the hand, tongue (speech), hearing, and eyesight.

7. *R*, IV. 3. 2341-48; I. 1. 32-33; II. 3. 820-27. Ghazali repeats these different levels of "restraint" in different Quarters of the *Revival* to emphasize their hierarchy. Cf. *C*, p. 109, where he maintains that abstinence (*wara'*) is the perfection of temperance (*'iffah*).

not necessary for the ultimate end of spiritual salvation, shows how Ghazali broadens the meaning of temperance, not only to include Islamic religious restraint, but also a high ideal of religious asceticism.

Subdivisions of Temperance

Our next task is to examine the virtues subordinated to temperance and this is especially important because temperance contains the largest number of subdivisions. Ghazali enumerates eighteen virtues as belonging to temperance, many of which other Muslim philosophers subordinated to the other three principal virtues. In spite of the large number and the fact that he does not organize them as most Muslim philosophers did, Ghazali seems to agree with them in his definition and explanation of most of these virtues. The differences to be noticed are basically two: (1) Ghazali minimizes the social significance of some of thsee virtues and modifies them to fit a morality primarily directed to individual spiritual salvation. This is clear especially with regard to virtues of joy (*inbisāṭ*), cheerfulness (*ẓarf*), and wit (*ṭalāqah* or *laṭāfah*); (2) With regard to all the virtues subordinated to temperance, Ghazali makes the mean incline toward the defect and sometimes to be almost identified with it. Aside from this, Ghazali's account of these virtues intentionally reproduces the Muslim philosophers' version of them and this suggests that he does not have a special use for such virtues in his moral system. An exception to this statement may be found in Ghazali's discussion of four of these virtues—modesty, shame, liberality, and contentment.

Modesty and Shame

Ghazali starts his list of the divisions of temperance in the *Criterion* with the "virtue of modesty" (*ḥayā'*), followed by a related "virtue" he calls "shame" (*khajal*).[1] In the *Revival*, however, he begins his list with liberality, followed by modesty, and does not name shame as a virtue, although he mentions its conditions when dealing with modesty in detail.[2] To so emphasize the importance of modesty seems to reflect

1. *C*, p. 96; cf. Aristotle *Akhlāq*, fol. 31a, where the translators of the *Nicomachean Ethics* use the term *ḥayā'* to render "modesty." Cf. Aristotle *Nicomachean Ethics* 2. 7. 1108a30-35. For Ghazali's account of the rest of the subdivisions of temperance, see Appendix II.

2. *R*, III. 2. 1443; III. 8. 1911-12.

the Islamic view of virtue presented by Muslim traditionalists like Ibn Abī al-Dunyā, who devotes the first chapter of his book, *Noble Qualities of Character* (*Makārim al-Akhlāq*) to the discussion of modesty, and explains his procedure with an Islamic traditional saying which names a number of noble qualities of character, but describes modesty as "the chief of them all."[1] Ghazali's unqualified acceptance of modesty as a virtue is in agreement with most of the Muslim philosophers, especially al-Fārābī, Avicenna, and Miskawayh,[2] and a departure from Aristotle, who maintains that "modesty should not be described as a virtue, for it is more like a feeling than a state of character."[3] According to Ghazali, modesty is "self-restraint of the soul out of fear of committing shameless deeds."[4] This is what Ghazali considers modesty, which applies universally and is commendable for everyone. In addition Ghazali recognizes shame in a qualified sense as "weakness of the soul because of excess of modesty,"[5] which is praiseworthy for young people and women only. In carefully distinguishing shame from proper modesty, Ghazali emphasizes the need to regard modesty a real virtue, situated between shamelessness (*waqāḥah*), the extreme of excess, and effeminacy (*khunūthah*), the extreme of defect.[6] Just as some Muslim philosophers consider "shame" the extreme of defect of modesty, for Ghazali effeminacy appears as an extreme which is beyond "shame." Therefore, in relation to effeminacy, shame is a relatively praiseworthy state. For Ghazali, the extreme of excess is more opposed to modesty than that of defect. A shameless man both commits a bad deed and is disgraced.[7]

Although Ghazali's distinction between modesty and shame can be regarded as a way of meeting Aristotle's objection to modesty as a virtue by directing the criticism to shame rather than modesty, Aristotle's

1. Ibn Abī al-Dunyā, *Makārim*, fols. 8a-11b.

2. Al-Fārābī, *Fuṣūl*, pp. 113-14; Avicenna, *'Ahd*, p. 144; Miskawayh, *Tahdhīb*, p. 20. Ibn 'Adī mentions modesty as part of the virtue of correct evaluation of self (*wa min qibal al-waqār al-ḥayā'*), *Tahdhīb*, p. 26. This seems to indicate that he does not regard modesty an independent virtue.

3. Aristotle *Nicomachean Ethics* 4. 9. 1128b10-11.

4. *C*, p. 97; *R*, III. 8. 1911; cf. Miskawayh, *Tahdhīb*, p. 20: "Modesty is self-restraint of the soul for fear of committing bad deeds, and carefulness to avoid blame and justified insult." Cf. al-Rāghib al-Iṣfahānī, *Dharī'ah*, p. 106.

5. *C*, p. 97; cf. *R*, III. 8. 1912.

6. *C*, p. 97.

7. *R*, III. 8. 1911; al-Fārābī, *Fuṣūl*, p. 114, "Modesty is a mean between impudence, and bashfulness and shame."

position seems to be irreconcilable with Ghazali's. For Aristotle, modesty is a kind of fear of dishonor which is a praiseworthy feeling among people who are restrained by shame; but no one would praise an older person for being prone to the sense of disgrace, since we would think he should not do anything that needs to cause this sense. He concludes that modesty can never be a virtue because the virtues are not subject to the qualification of feeling disgrace. "It is for voluntary actions that shame is felt, and the good man will never voluntarily do bad actions."[1] In spite of this, Aristotle admits in another work, the *Rhetoric*, that, among other things, men feel shame in the presence of good men.[2] This hint points in the direction of Ghazali's view of modesty, because, in his opinion, man has to be modest with a view to others. Ghazali, however, goes beyond Aristotle to state that true modesty is shame before God.[3] This implies that God is omiscient or that He knows what is going on in man better than man does. Thus, any person who truly "knows" God will be ashamed and modest before Him.[4] Although Aristotle is completely silent about modesty with a view to God or the gods, Plato identifies it with divine fear.[5] It is this Platonic tradition and not that of Aristotle which the Muslim philosophers follow in regarding modesty as a virtue. Ghazali, on the other hand, seems to be motivated by the Islamic religious teachings in his view of modesty. He goes beyond the Platonic position and regards modesty as a virtue related to God which men should emulate. He supports his view with the tradition of the Prophet: "God feels shame (*yastaḥī*) to punish a gray-haired Muslim."[6] In this way Ghazali establishes modesty as an important virtue.

Liberality

"Liberality" (*sakhā'*) is another division of temperance which is important in connection with the question of Wealth (*māl*). Since there is no doubt that liberality is a virtue, Ghazali concentrates in his inquiry on

1. Aristotle *Nicomachean Ethics* 4. 9. 1128b11-29.
2. Aristotle *Rhetoric* 2. 6. 1384b24-25.
3. *C*, pp. 97-98; *R*, III. 8. 1912.
4. *C*, pp. 97-98. where Ghazali quotes the Koran 96:14.
5. Plato *Laws* 2. 671d: " . . . that divine fear which received the name of modesty and the sense of shame."
6. *C*, p. 97; *R*, III. 8. 1912 The tradition of the Prophet is this: *inna Allāha yastaḥī min dhī shaybatin fī al-Islām an yu'adhdhibahu.* It is also quoted in the same context by al-Rāghib al-Iṣfahānī, *Dharī'ah*, p. 106.

the acquisition, preservation, and expenditure of wealth. He defines liberality in the *Criterion* as "a mean between prodigality (*tabdhīr*) and meanness (*taqtīr*). It is giving easily and refraining from acquiring things in the wrong way."[1] This definition emphasizes both giving and taking in regard to liberality. In the *Revival*, however, liberality is associated with giving only: the virtue of a man who possesses wealth.[2] The shift of emphasis to giving alone in the *Revival* accords with the philosophic description of liberality, especially in Avicenna and Miskawayh, who define liberality only in terms of giving.[3] In the *Criterion*, however, it is Aristotle's account which Ghazali prefers, since Aristotle praises the liberal man "with regard to the giving and taking of wealth, and especially in respect of giving."[4]

An integral part of Ghazali's attitude toward liberality is his insistence on evaluating the sources from which the liberal man acquires his wealth, so as to determine to what extent the liberal man occupies himself with the task of accumulating wealth. Ghazali discusses wealth in all four Quarters of the *Revival* and devotes a special section to it in the *Criterion*, and thus indicates its importance to moral refinement.[5] He enumerates the many advantages of wealth in relation to worldly well-being as well as to ultimate happiness. Besides securing good things for himself, the man who possesses wealth can also give to those who are in need and contribute to public goods.[6] These advantages, however, should be measured against the potentially harmful consequences of wealth. A man who possesses wealth may be influenced to satisfy his desires in an excessive way, and thus become immoderate. But the most harmful and serious consequence of wealth, in Ghazali's view, is the effort and time which man spends in keeping and increasing his possessions. Thus preoccupation

1. *C*, p. 98. Ghazali uses two Arabic terms for liberality, namely *sakhā'* and *jūd*, and considers them synonymous. (*R*, III. 7. 1809). But he frequently uses *sakhā'*, which is the term preferred by the translators of Aristotle's *Nicomachean Ethics* to render liberality; cf. Aristotle *Akhlāq*, fol. 31a; Aristotle *Nicomachean Ethics* 2. 7. 1107b7-8. This term is also used in the same context by Muslim philosophers such as al -Fārābī, *Fuṣūl*, p. 113; Avicenna, *'Ahd*, p. 145; *Akhlāq*, p. 153; and Miskawayh, *Tahdhīb*, pp. 20, 22.

2. *R*, III. 7. 1781.

3. Avicenna, *Akhlāq*, p. 153; Miskawayh, *Tahdhīb*, p. 20.

4. Aristotle, *Nicomachean Ethics*, 4. 1. 1119b25-26.

5. *R*, I. 5, which deals with "alms-tax" (*zakāt*); *R*, II. 3 (entitled "Manners of Earning and Livelihood"); *R*, III. 7 (on "The Evils of Avarice and of Love of Wealth"); and, finally, *R*, IV. 4 ("On Poverty and Asceticism"). *C*, pp. 178-92.

6. *R*, III. 7. 1768-69.

with wealth may completely distract man from truly purifying his soul in order to attain ultimate happiness.[1]

Because man has basic bodily needs, and because he must possess something to satisfy such needs, the question which arises in relation to wealth is not whether to possess it or not, but rather to determine the amount which it is proper to acquire and the time for which it can be decently possessed. In answering this question, Ghazali describes the needs of man. Food, dress, dwelling, and the like are necessary for the continuation of man's life, and there can be minimum, maximum, and intermediate satisfaction of them. In his discussion, Ghazali clearly prefers the minimum satisfaction of all of these needs for the shortest time; this is for him the right way for those who are engaged in moral refinement.[2]

Acquiring wealth for necessities in a minimal way hardly generates any possessions which may become the instruments of liberality. Ghazali is aware of this problem and frequently raises the question whether one should acquire more wealth than one needs in order to give it to others. This question is important, particularly since Ghazali maintains that in caring for worldly things one should be controlled by satisfying his real basic needs only, and whatever exceeds that is riches (*ghinā*). In a special chapter entitled "the evils of richness and the goodness of poverty," Ghazali maintains that "poverty (*faqr*) is more excellent than riches."[3] His attitude toward acquiring wealth and keeping it ends therefore in preferring poverty and considering it one of the virtues most conducive to individual salvation.[4]

After indicating the superiority of poverty, Ghazali prescribes special conditions for giving away wealth to others. In addition to the religious alms-tax, one can dispense charity (*ṣadaqah*), e.g., voluntarily give to the needy, or give wealth to rich and noble people in the form of hospitality, gift, or aid. This practice helps one win new friends and learn the virtue of liberality. A man can also pay others to attend to his worldly activities so that he can have time for worship and learning. Finally, wealth may be spent in building mosques and hospitals, and in other projects for the common good.[5]

1. *R*, III. 7. 1769-71.
2. *C*, pp. 183-86.
3. *R*, III. 7. 1816. In this chapter Ghazali quotes a long passage from al-Muḥāsibī in support of preferring poverty; cf. *R*, III. 7. 1816-32.
4. *R*, IV. 4. 2399-2442.
5. *R*, I. 5. 408-417; III. 7. 1768-69.

Seen in the context of his overall view of wealth, Ghazali's ideal definition of liberality is "giving without expecting anything in return." This idealized virtue, he admits, can be fully actualized by God alone.[1] Yet Ghazali maintains that the term liberality can be applied to man if he gives for the sake of God or otherworldly rewards, or so as to practice the virtue of liberality and free himself from the vice of meanness. But no one can be called liberal if he gives for the sake of a worldly reward, even if this reward is praise, gratitude, or helping others. In this Ghazali differs substantially from Aristotle, who, in spite of his insistence that the liberal man gives for the sake of the virtue of liberality, concedes that things such as praise, gratitude, honor, and aiding the needy are some of the incentives for giving liberally.[2] For Ghazali, the truly liberal man gives for the sake of God only. The highest form of liberality, according to Ghazali, is giving wealth while still in need of it: this is called altruism (*īthār*). Therefore, in observing the mean in regard to giving wealth, the liberal man is only permitted to err in the direction of prodigality, the extreme of excess.[3] Both Ghazali and Aristotle have a certain dislike for meanness because it implies enslavement of the soul and because it is less curable than prodigality. Ghazali, however, shows a special interest in meanness; he devotes the seventh book of Quarter II of the *Revival* to discussing the evils of meanness (*bukhl*) and of love of wealth. For him, a man who loves wealth as such is so mean that he can hardly be cured. It seems that the chief reason for Ghazali's concern with meanness is that this is a vice which makes man strongly attached to worldly things; and this, in turn, hinders the refinement of his soul which is necessary for attaining happiness in the hereafter. In contrast, liberality gives man the freedom needed for the most noble end.[4]

Thus Ghazali accepts liberality as a virtue and considers it good for everyone, especially for the "multitude" who are concerned with wealth. For the "few," however, who are engaged in more advanced stages of moral training, liberality is not the highest virtue in regard to wealth. Ghazali points out four veils which stand between the novice, who is

1. *R*, III. 7. 1809; *Maqṣad*, p. 48, where he states that man can only be liberal in a qualified sense.

2. Aristotle *Nicomachean Ethics* 4. 1. 1120a11-23.

3. *R*, III. 7. 1803; *C*, p. 96; cf. *Tahdhīb*, p. 22; Aristotle *Nicomachean Ethics* 4. 1. 1121b13-17.

4. *R*, III. 7. 1810-14.

starting his spiritual refinement, and God. The first of these veils is wealth and "the novice must relinquish all wealth except for what is most necessary for his needs."[1] Since these needs are meager, this means that the novice who follows the right way in relation to wealth will eventually have no means for liberality and, indeed, no use for it.

Contentment

Unlike liberality, "contentment" (*qanāʿah*) is a virtue which deals, in the first place, with acquiring and possessing wealth; or, as Ghazali says, it is man's virtue when he lacks wealth.[2] He defines it in the *Criterion* as good management of means of livelihood in the right way.[3] This definition corresponds to the concept of contentment in Miskawayh and Avicenna[4] but, while these two emphasize moderation, Ghazali leaves "the right way" undecided so that it can be easily incorporated into his view in the *Revival* where he joins contentment with the virtue of poverty. A contented man is satisfied with the amount of wealth which provides him with the minimum of his basic needs for the period of one day or at most one month. Such a man gives away what is beyond his needs and never occupies himself with keeping money for the future, because he has complete trust in God as the source of sustenance.[5]

Exceeding what is necessary brings about the evils of greed (*ḥirṣ*) and covetousness (*ṭamaʿ*), which are both the extremes of excess of this virtue. Ghazali does not mention the extreme of defect but Avicenna defines contentment as a mean between greed and carelessness in acquiring necessities.[6] Ghazali's silence about the deficiency of contentment here anticipates his subsequent inclusion of poverty and asceticism as important qualities for salvation.

The discussion of these four virtues belonging to temperance shows how Ghazali modifies the philosophic concept of this princiapl virtue. It strengthens the view that he modifies temperance by closely identifying it with the extreme of defect, and in this discussion quasimoral

1. *R*, III. 2. 1482.
2. *R*, III. 7. 1780.
3. *C*, pp. 98-99.
4. Miskawayh, *Tahdhīb*, p. 20: "Contentment is moderation in food, drink, and adornment"; Avicenna, *Akhlāq*, p. 153.
5. *R*, III. 7. 1771, 1776-78.
6. Avicenna, *ʿAhd*, p. 145.

virtues in the philsoophic tradition are given the full status of virtue, and even considered higher virtues, e.g., modesty. The significance of temperance in Ghazali's view, however, remains the purification of the soul through abstinence from everything which is not necessarily related to the attainment of ultimate happiness. Since ultimate happiness lies in the hereafter, temperance means minimal participation in worldly affairs. In this way, it is not moderation which prepares man for his end; rather, it is self-restraint in a literal sense. All these changes and modifications which we have noticed in the course of Ghazali's discussion of temperance and some of its important subdivisions seem to aim at this more comprehensive view of temperance.

Justice

The fourth principal virtue is justice. It is a state in which the concupiscent and the irascible faculties are subordinated to the rational faculty. By equating justice with the order and harmony of these three faculties, Ghazali considers it not only "a virtue" but also the "whole of the virtues." It is the perfection of all other virtues because it is only achieved when each of the other faculties realizes its respective virtue.[1] Ghazali maintains that justice in this sense does not have two extremes as do the other virtues. Rather, the only vice which opposes it is injustice (*jawr*), because order is only opposed by disorder. This kind of justice Ghazali calls justice in relation to the character traits of the soul (*al-'adl fī akhlāq al-nafs*).[2] In addition, there are two other kinds of justice, namely, political justice and justice in relation to transactions.[3] Political justice is the ordering of the parts of the polis in a manner that corresponds to the order of the faculties of the soul.[4] Since political justice in this sense is identified with order, it also has but one vice. In the *Supreme Purpose*, Ghazali adds to political justice the notion of distributive justice, emphasizing that distribution of goods in the city can only be just when the ruler takes into consideration the functions of the different classes of the city as well as the natural order of things.[5]

1. *C*, pp. 90-91; *R*, III. 2. 1442; *Maqṣad*, p. 62; cf. Aristotle *Nicomachean Ethics* 5. 1. 1130a9-11; Plato *Republic* 4. 443c-44a; Avicenna, *'Ahd*, p. 149.

2. *C*, pp. 90. 92; *R*, III. 2. 1442.

3. *C*, p. 91. Ghazali's idea of justice in relation to transaction corresponds to Aristotle's concept of distributive justice (*Nicomachean Ethics* 5. 2. 1130b30-1131a5).

4. *C*, p. 91. Political justice as presented here reflects particularly Plato's position, especially in the *Republic*; cf. Plato *Republic* 4. 443a-35b.

5. *Maqṣad*, pp. 62-63.

Only justice in transactions is presented as a mean between two vices, namely, doing injustice (*ghubn*) and suffering injustice (*taghābun*).[1] In the *Revival*, he mentions money as a means of establishing justice in transactions.[2]

It is remarkable that Ghazali pays more attention to the first of the three kinds of justice he mentions, i.e., justice in respect to character traits. It is true that he speaks about the religious law and the need to observe it,[3] but justice for him is important because it is the virtue of the soul which is a sign of individual perfection, not because it has a social function. Justice brings about a harmony among the faculties of the soul, preparing the individual for superior virtues. Because of this view of justice, Ghazali does not list any virtues under justice, unlike some Muslim philosophers, such as Miskawayh.[4] This brief description is all that Ghazali has to say about justice. He devotes more space to other virtues and thus he shows his disagreement with the philosophic tradition in which justice, especially in its social context, occupies a high position.

Conclusion

Ghazali's treatment of philosophic virtues reflects, to begin with, his acquaintance with philosophic ethics. His account of these virtues corresponds directly to that of the Muslim philosophers, such as Avicenna, Miskawayh, and al-Fārābī; and indirectly to the Greek philosophic tradition of Plato and Aristotle. What emerges from this discussion is that Ghazali accepts the philosophical virtues in general: he accepts the psychological basis of virtue, its division into four principal virtues, the definitions of some of these and many of their subdivisions, equating virtue with good habit, and identifying it as a mean between two vices. Ghazali justifies his approval of these virtues by their usefulness for the attainment of happiness in general, and on the basis of Islamic religious

1. *C*, p. 91, cf. Aristotle *Nicomachean Ethics* 5. 5. 1133b31-34; "It is plain that just action is intermediate between acting unjustly and being unjustly treated; for the one is to have too much and the other to have too little. Justice is a kind of mean, but not in the same way as the other virtues, but because it relates to an intermediate amount, while injustice relates to the extremes"; cf. Miskawayh, *Tahdhīb*, p. 28; Avicenna, *'Ahd*, p. 145.
2. *R*, III. 6. 1754; cf Aristotle *Nicomachean Ethics* 5. 5. 1133b18-21.
3. *R*, III. 2. 1442; *Maqṣad*, p. 62.
4. Miskawayh, *Tahdhīb*, pp. 23-24.

teachings in particular. For example, he shows how Islam calls for training the soul in good habits, and how it teaches man to observe the mean in all his activities. In cases when he does not find a convincing "Islamic" argument for some of the characteristics of virtue, he is satisfied with showing that at least there is no "Islamic" argument against them, as, for example, the analysis of the soul into certain faculties.

These efforts to justify philosophic virtues reflect Ghazali's eagerness to show that the right attitude toward philosophic virtue is to consider them initially acceptable. This attitude differs from that of the Islamic traditionalists, who reject such virtues altogether. But Ghazali's acceptance of the philosophic virtues in general does not put him in the camp of the philosophers either. He has his own conditions for accepting these virtues, introducing specific changes in some of them, and adding other elements to those which he modifies. Thus, for example, while acknowledging the necessity of habituation in acquiring virtue, he maintains that it is possible that man be virtuous by nature, a possibility which is denied by the philosophers. Furthermore, he accepts and justifies the doctrine of the mean, and then insists that no man can hit and observe the true mean without appealing for divine assistance. The best way to examine how Ghazali modifies and changes philosophic virtues, however, is to inquire into his treatment of the four principal virtues and their subdivisions. It has been shown above that in regard to some virtues—for instance, all the subdivisions of wisdom and most of the subdivisions of courage and temperance—Ghazali does not go beyond a mere very brief reproduction of the accounts of the philosophers. This method reflects his view that while these virtues are acceptable as they are, they do not play a major role in his ethical theory. In contrast, his discussion of wisdom (in its theoretical sense) shows that, for him, the highest virtue is not a more genuine form of knowledge, as is the case with Aristotle, but an "emotion" produced by such knowledge, namely, "love of God." His discussion of courage, on the other hand, equates it with man's struggle with his base passions, not his struggle in the battlefield. More important, however, is the fact that in dealing with courage and some of its subdivisions, e.g., greatness of soul and magnificence, Ghazali identifies virtue with the extreme of defect, and in this he differs sharply from the common philosophic view of these virtues. The method of going to one of the extremes instead of the mean in acquiring virtue is illustrated best in Ghazali's treatment of temperance and some of its subdivisions, such as liberality and contentment.

Ghazali also modifies the treatment of philosophic virtues by paying attention to some of them at the expense of others. For example, he deals with temperance in great detail, while explaining the virtue of justice only summarily. Furthermore, he considers some quasiphilosophic virtues, such as modesty, not only full, but also important virtues. Although other Muslim philosophers added to the list of virtues in Aristotle such virtues as abstinence (*wara'*) and worship (*'ibādah*), Ghazali does not pay great attention to these added virtues within the context of his treatment of philosophic virtues, nor does he elaborate on them.

The question which must now be raised is, what is the purpose of all these changes and modifications? In order to be able to answer this question, one must first acknowledge that in spite of the changes and modifications, the philosophic virtues are accepted in principle. His modifications are designed to prepare these virtues for a role that is different from the one they serve in philosophic ethical theory, and which they will have to assume in a wider ethical system which will include other nonphilosophic elements. Ghazali sees in philosophic virtues a "natural" starting point (natural in the sense that man arrives at it by unaided reason) which can serve as a basis for a further organization of virtue.

In order to substantiate this general proposition, it is necessary to refer to Ghazali's description of the four principal virtues as "the true principles of religion (*uṣūl al-dīn*)."[1] Resorting to religious teachings in an attempt to reconcile philosophic and religious ethics is a practice known to some Muslim philosophers.[2] Avicenna, for example, concludes his account of philosophic virtues by stating that the characterization of each of these virtues is the responsibility of the "masters of religions (*arbāb al-milal*)."[3] Ghazali, however, maintains that all these virtues have been dealt with in detail by the Islamic religious teachings, and that they can be sought in the prophet Muḥammad's conduct and way of life.[4] Hence, according to him, further inquiry into these "philosophic" virtues should take into consideration an investigation of

1. *C*, p. 109.
2. R. Walzer and H.A.R. Gibb, "Akhlāḳ," *EI*² I, 326; cf. Miskawayh, *Tahdhīb*, pp. 1, 35, 170, 196-97.
3. Avicenna, *'Ahd*, p. 144.
4. *C*, pp. 81, 102.

Islamic moral teachings. In Ghazali's view, Muḥammad is the only man who perfectly attained the four principal virtues. Man's success in attaining ultimate happiness is, therefore, determined by the extent to which he achieves the virtues of the prophet Muḥammad.

TABLE I

GHAZALI'S CLASSIFICATION OF PHILOSOPHIC VIRTUES

WISDOM	COURAGE	TEMPERANCE	JUSTICE
Discretion	Magnificence	Modesty	......
Excellence of discernment	Intrepidity	Shame	......
Penetration of thought	Greatness of soul	Remission	......
Correctness of opinion	Endurance	Patience	......
(Awareness of subtle actions and of the hidden evils of the soul)	Gentleness	Liberality	......
	Fortitude	Good calculation	......
	Suppression of anger	Contentment	......
	Correct Evaluation of Self	Abstinence	......
	Amiability	Cheerfulness	......
	Nobility	Joy	......
	Manliness	Tenderness of character	......
		Self-discipline	
		Good appearance	
		Tranquility	......
		Honest dealing	......
		Righteous indignation	......
		Wit	......

Chapter III / RELIGIOUS-LEGAL VIRTUES

The preceding chapter has shown that the four principal virtues—namely, practical wisdom, courage, temperance, and justice—occupy a central position in Ghazali's treatment of philosophic virtues. He calls them the goods of the soul nearest to ultimate happiness. But he also shows that those goods can only be perfected when accompanied by the goods of the body—health, strength, beauty, and long life; and these bodily goods, in turn, cannot be useful without the external goods—wealth, family, fame, and noble birth. Ghazali calls all these goods "bounties" (*niʿam*), "forms of happiness (*saʿādāt*), and "virtues" (*faḍā'il*).[1]

We saw that in his discussion of the philosophic virtues Ghazali uses *faḍīlah* as virtue of the soul. However, when he applies this term to bodily and external goods, he means kinds of excellence which are necessary and useful instruments in bringing about the virtues. Ghazali's understanding of bodily and external goods is based to a large extent on the philosophic tradition as represented in particular by Aristotle and Miskawayh.[2] Aristotle speaks of external goods, goods of the body, and goods of the soul. Those of the soul are commonly held to be good in the fullest sense.[3] Nonetheless, according to Aristotle virtue needs the external goods as well.

> . . . for it is impossible, or not easy, to do noble acts without the proper equipment. In many actions we use friends and riches and political power as instruments, and there are some things the lack of which takes the luster from happiness, as good birth, goodly children, beauty.[4]

1. *C*, pp. 109-110. R, IV. 2. 2247-48; al-Rāghib al-Iṣfahānī, *Dharīʿah*, p. 35. Since al-Rāghib al-Iṣfahānī's account of these goods is identical with that of the *Criterion*, there will be no further reference to it. Ghazali discusses in detail some of the bodily virtues, e.g., beauty, and all of the external virtues, in *C*, pp. 110-114.
2. Miskawayh, *Tahdhīb*, pp. 79ff.
3. Aristotle *Nicomachean Ethics* 1. 8. 1098b12.
4. Aristotle *Nicomachean Ethics* 1. 8. 1099a31-34.

Virtuous actions, then, are not self-sufficient inasmuch as they presuppose external and bodily goods.

Ghazali's agreement with Aristotle goes beyond the mere enumeration of external and bodily goods which comprise the instruments for obtaining happiness. By calling these types of happiness bounties, Ghazali suggests that happiness is a gift which God bestows as a favor.[1] Aristotle also maintains that happiness is somehow a divine gift, even when it is achieved as a result of human actions. Ultimately, happiness does not depend completely on the human will for its realization. There remains some element of happiness which cannot be acquired but must be bestowed as a God-given blessing:

> Now if anything that men have is a gift of the gods, it is reasonable to suppose that happiness is divinely given—indeed, of all men's possessions it is most likely to be so, inasmuch as it is the best of them all. This subject however may perhaps more properly belong to another branch of study.[2]

Aristotle may be suggesting here a "theology" or "metaphysics" of happiness, even though he does not reopen this question in the *Metaphysics* or elsewhere.[3] Ghazali, in contrast, treats this question explicitly when he discusses a fourth category of goods which he calls "the virtues of divine assistance" (*al-faḍā'il al-tawfīqiyyah*).

Theological Virtues

While regarding bodily and external goods as useful and important instruments for the attainment of the virtue of the soul, Ghazali considers the virtues of divine assistance necessary and essential to the virtues of the soul. Indeed, no virtue at all can be acquired without divine assistance.[4] According to Ghazali, assistance (*tawfīq*) is a divine favor, which he defines as the concord of man's will and action with God's decree and determination.[5] (In his theological work the *Golden Mean* he mentions "assistance" as a theological concept but does not discuss it.)[6] This

1. *C*, p. 109.

2. Aristotle *Nicomachean Ethics* 1. 9. 1099b11-14.

3. Aristotle *Nicomachean Ethics* trans. H. Rackham, p. 44 (footnote).

4. *C*, p. 110; *R*, IV. 2. 2249, where he says that none of the virtues of the third and second categories are of any use without the virtues of the fourth category, which act as intermediaries between them and the interior virtues of the soul.

5. *R*, IV. 2. 2255; *C*, pp. 114-115.

6. Ghazali, *al-Iqtiṣād fī al-I'tiqād*, ed. by I. A. Cubukçu and Hüseyn Atay (Ankara: Nur Matbaasi, 1962), p. 221.

notion may have its origin in Islamic theology (*kalām*), for al-Juwaynī, Ghazali's teacher and an eminent Ash'arite theologian, devotes a special section of his book *al-Irshād* to a discussion of divine assistance, equating it with the capacity for obedience which God creates in man.[1]

Faḍīlah as divine assistance is fundamentally different from *faḍīlah* as virtue of the soul or as excellence. Ghazali's use of this term here is closely related to *faḍl*, which derives from the same verb root. The term *faḍl* signifies any gift where the giving is not obligatory, i.e., a free gift, a gratuity, an act of bounty, a favor, or a benefit.[2] In the Koran *faḍl* is several times attributed to God alone; for instance, "That is the free gift of God; He giveth it to whom He willeth."[3] Koranic verses even combine *faḍl* and *ni'mah*, such as, ". . . joyful in blessing (*ni'mah*) and bounty (*faḍl*) from God,"[4] and in all these cases the virtues of divine assistance are spoken of as gifts or favors from God (*faḍl min Allah*).

Thus, by applying the term virtue to divine assistance, Ghazali attributes it to God. In so doing he emphasizes that no other virtues can be achieved without divine assistance. He even maintains that without divine assistance man's own effort in seeking virtue is in vain and may even lead to what is wrong and evil.[5] This statement suggests that the virtues of divine assistance are fundamentally different from the philosophic virtues: philosophic virtues can be understood completely in terms of human choice, whereas the basis of the virtues of divine assistance must be sought in the bounties of God. Within this new framework, divine support of morality becomes crucial for the realization of ultimate happiness. In the final section of Book 1 of Quarter III of the *Revival*, which is the key to the discussion of vices and virtues, Ghazali says that some people are created for paradise and others for hellfire, and that each person will be divinely directed toward that for which he is created.[6] In the final analysis, therefore, everything, including all the virtues, is a divine bounty.

1. Imām al-Ḥaramayn al-Juwaynī, *al-Irshād* (Cairo: Maktabat al-Khānjī, 1950), p. 254.

2. Lane, *Arabic-English Lexicon*, I. 6. 2421.

3. Koran 5:59. also verses such as, "the bounty is in God's hands." Koran 3:73; 3:57; 57:29.

4. Koran 3:171; see also 3:174; 49:8.

5. *C*, p. 115 where Ghazali quotes a line of poetry to the effect that if man is not assisted by God, then his own independent effort will destroy him.

6. *R*, III. 1. 1429. The same point is repeated over and over again in several Books of the *Revival*; cf. *R*, IV. 2. 2225; *R*, IV. 5. 2518.

In order to understand this position, it is necessary to discuss the virtues of divine assistance in greater detail. Since they are related to God and are discussed in a theological context by Ghazali as well as Muslim theologians, the virtues of divine assistance are in fact theological virtues. Ghazali maintains that there are four of these virtues, namely God's guidance (*hidāyat Allāh*), His direction (*rushd*), His divine leading (*tasdīd*), and His support (*ta'yīd*).[1] Ghazali intentionally makes these virtues correspond in number to the external and bodily goods, as well as to the four principal virtues of the soul.[2]

1. Divine guidance (*hidāyah*), according to Ghazali, is a virtue which is the precondition for the attainment of any other virtue because it is the source of all the goods. He supports this statement with the Koranic verse, "He gave unto everything its nature, and further, gave it guidance."[3] In the *Supreme Purpose* Ghazali states that the "Guide" (*al-Hādī*) is one of the attributes of God and that it means "He who guides par excellence." Ghazali quotes the Koranic verse cited above and says that this attribute can be applied only metaphorically to prophets and learned men. For these appear to guide others on the right path; but in reality it is God who guides men. Anyone else is an instrument of His absolute guidance.[4]

The question of divine guidance was important, of course, for Muslim theologians. Abū al-Ḥasan al-Ash'arī, founder of the Ash'arite theological school, as well as Abū Bakr al-Bāqillānī and al-Juwaynī, two leaders of the school who came after him, all dealt with this question, arguing that God alone is the source of guidance.[5] Ghazali's general position on divine guidance agrees with the established doctrine of the Ash'arite school of theology to which he adhered. What distinguishes his particular view is that he goes beyond the general position which

1. *C*, p. 110; *R*, IV. 2. 2249.

2. *C*, p. 110.

3. Koran 20:50; cf. *C*, p. 115. Most of the verses quoted in relation to these virtues were subjected to extensive analysis by the Muslim theologians, especially those who belonged to the Ash'arite school.

4. *Maqṣad*, p. 95.

5. Abū al-Ḥasan 'Alī Ibn Ismā'īl al-Ash'arī, *al-Ibānah 'an Uṣūl al-Diyānah* (Haydarabad: Majlis Dā'irat al-Ma'ārif, n.d.), pp. 78-80; *Kitāb al-Luma' fī al-Radd 'alā Ahl al-Zaygh wa al-Bida'*, ed. by Richard J. McCarthy (Beirut: al-Maktabah al-Sharqiyyah, 1952), p. 156; Abū Bakr al-Bāqillānī, *Kitāb al-Tamhīd*, ed. by Richard J. McCarthy (Beirut: al-Maktabah al-Sharqiyyah, 1957), pp. 334-36; al-Juwaynī *Irshād*, pp. 210-13.

regards guidance as belonging to God only and introduces what he calls the three phases or stages (*manāzil*) of guidance. The first stage is concerned with knowing how to distinguish between good and evil. He claims that this is implied in the Koranic verse, "And guide him to the parting of the two mountain ways."[1] This type of guidance, he says, is given by God to all men, "some of it through reason (*bi al-'aql*) and some by revelation to prophets."[2] Reason and revelation, in his view, are available to all men either directly or indirectly; only love of worldly things and bad habits prevent men from availing themselves of this general guidance (*al-hidāyah al-'āmmah*).[3] In the second stage of guidance, God constantly helps man in each state in proportion to his progress in knowledge and his improvement in performing good deeds. This suggests that man has already received general guidance, as understood in the Koranic verse, "But to those who follow guidance, He increases their guidance, and bestows on them their piety (*taqwāhum*)."[4] The third and final stage of guidance is identified with the light (*nūr*) which illuminates the condition of prophet and saint (*walāyah*). Through this light man attains what cannot be attained by means of reason. This, for Ghazali, is absolute guidance, and he bases himself on the interpretation of the Koranic verse, "Say: God's guidance is *the* guidance."[5] Ghazali describes the third stage of guidance in relation to his own experience in seeking certainty. After having lost confidence in all necessary truths of the intellect, he says he regained trust in them once more, not on the basis of rational demonstration, "but by a light which

1. Koran 90: 10; cf. *C*, p. 115; R, IV. 2. 2256.

2. *R*, IV. 2. 2256; *C*, p. 115, lines 11-12, where I read *ba'ḍahu* (some of it, i.e., guidance) instead of *ba'ḍahum* (some of them, i.e., men). This reading is from Esad Efendi MSS, 1759, fol. 92b. It agrees with the *Revival*, with al-Rāghib al-Iṣfahānī, *Dharī'ah*, p. 44, and, finally, with Ghazali's well-known view that reason alone is not a sufficient source of knowledge, cf. *Munqidh*, pp. 61-63.

3. *R*, IV. 2. 2256-57; cf. *C*, p. 115. What Ghazali calls general guidance seems to resemble the Mu'tazilite notion of guidance in general. The resemblance, however, is incomplete, because general guidance is one stage in Ghazali's treatment of guidance. Whereas for him God guides men to what is right and what is wrong (which is an Ash'arite doctrine), the Mu'tazilites refuse to admit that God guides men astray. Abū al-Ḥasan 'Ali Ibn Ismā'īl al-Ash'arī, *Maqālāt al-Islāmiyyīn* ("Die Dogmatischen Lehren der Anhanger des Islam"), ed. by Helmut Ritter, Bibliotheca Islamica, 1, 2d ed. (Wiesbaden: Franz Steiner Verlag, 1963), pp. 259-62.

4. Koran 47:17; cf. *C*, p. 115; *R*, IV. 2. 2257.

5. Koran 6:71; cf. *C*, p. 116; *R*, IV. 2. 2257.

God most high cast into my breast. That light is the key to the greater part of knowledge."[1]

In concluding his account of these stages of guidance, Ghazali reminds his reader that all three derive from God. This seems to rule out any apparent contradiction between the first two stages of guidance and the third with respect to man's freedom of choice.[2] In addition to raising the question of freedom of the will, these stages of guidance reflect Ghazali's tendency to synthesize different aspects of his moral theory, which, in this instance, are represented by the terms "reason," and "sainthood." Finally, divine guidance is related only to knowing the right thing, not to doing it. A consideration of action is postponed until his inquiry into the rest of the virtues of divine assistance.

2. Direction (*rushd*),[3] for Ghazali, means divine providence (*al-'ināyah al-ilāhiyyah*). In the *Supreme Purpose,* Ghazali lists direction as one of the attributes of God: "the one who directs" (*al-Rashīd*), meaning He who gives direction to all men in proportion to their guidance.[4] Direction consists in the divine care and protection which man receives when he aims at the good end. Such a virtue strengthens man for that which is good and weakens his inclination to what is bad. An example of direction is seen by Ghazali in the Koranic verse, "And we verily gave Abraham of old his direction, and were aware of him."[5] A man may be guided to the point where he knows what is good, but not seek it because he lacks direction. In this sense direction supersedes guidance.

3. Leading (*tasdīd*) is the third of the virtues of divine assistance. It is present when man's will and actions aim at the right end. It facilitates his action so that he may achieve his end in the shortest time.

1. *Munqidh*, pp. 13-14, where Ghazali quotes a koranic verse (which he quotes elsewhere in relation to the third stage of guidance), "Whenever God wills to guide a man, He enlarges his breast for surrender [to Him] (*islām*)." Koran 6:125; cf. *C*, p. 116; *R*, IV. 2. 2257.

2. *R*, IV. 2. 2257. This agrees with the fact that Ghazali introduces the same three stages with a tradition of Muḥammad according to which no one enters paradise, even the Prophet himself, except by God's guidance. (Cf. *R*, IV. 2. 2256.)

3. *C*, p. 116. Direction is used here in the active sense of moving the subject towards the goal.

4. *Maqṣad*, p. 97; cf. al-Juwaynī, *Irshād*, p. 155.

5. Koran 5:115; *C*, p. 116; *R*, IV. 2. 2257. Divine providence is also discussed by Muslim philosophers. Cf. al-Fārābī, *Fuṣūl*, p. 160; Avicenna, *Shifā'*: *Metaphysics*, II, 415.

It suggests moving man toward his end while direction only inspires him to move toward an end himself.[1]

4. Support (*ta'yīd*) is the last and the sum of all of these virtues. It sustains man in his actions internally by giving him insight, and externally by strengthening him and providing suitable conditions to attain what is desired with the means at his disposal. This virtue, according to Ghazali, is implied in the Koranic verse, "How I supported thee with the holy spirit."[2]

The virtues of divine assistance are not to be found within the strict limits of the philosophic tradition.[3] Rather, Ghazali is inspired here by the Islamic theological tradition, and his special contribution consists in his effort to define, classify, and relate these virtues to those of the soul. In dealing with these virtues, he emphasizes primarily that man cannot attain virtue without God's assistance. For him, God is the ultimate source of good and evil because He is the cause of everything. This view corresponds to Ghazali's famous critique of causation, where he denies that there is power in the cause to produce a specific effect. There is only succession of events and God alone is the sufficient cause of all things. Such a theory implies that in reality God is the only Doer (*fā'il*).[4] In spite of this, however, Ghazali speaks of voluntary actions and man's responsibility for them.[5] His method of resolving this apparent difficulty is that of the theologians, in particular that of the "adherents of the truth" (*ahl al-ḥaqq*), i.e., the Ash'arites:

When fire burns, it burns because of pure determinism. God's action is pure freedom

1. *C*, p. 116; *R*, IV. 2. 2257.

2. Koran 23:24; cf. *C*, p. 116; *R*, IV. 2. 2257.

3. It was mentioned above that, although Aristotle points out the divine character of happiness, he does not elaborate on this idea in detail. Cf. Simon van den Bergh, "Ghazali on 'Gratitude towards God' and its Greek Source," *Studia Islamica*, VII (1957), 77-98. Van den Bergh tries to find a Greek origin for each virtue in the goods of the soul, as well as the bodily and external goods mentioned above. However, when he comes to the "virtues" of divine assistance (which comprise the fourth category of goods), he admits that "The fourth category, of course, lies wholly beyond the scope of Stoicism" (p. 98). Cf. al-Fārābī, *Fuṣūl*, p. 160, where he regards the view accepted by Ghazali about divine providence, direction, and leading as utterly wrong.

4. *Maqṣad*, p. 91; *R*, IV. 5. 2495, 2511-12, 2518.

5. *R*, III. 2. 1442; *R*, IV. 5. 2518-23. For example, Ghazali defines practical wisdom as a state of the soul in which it distinguishes right from wrong in connection with all voluntary actions (*al-af'āl al-ikhtiyāriyyah*).

of choice. Man's position lies midway between these two; it is determined choice (*jabr ʿalā al-ikhtiyār*).[1]

Ghazali identifies his resolution by the term "acquisition" (*kasb*), a notion which the Ashʿarite school of theology propagated and made famous. He claims that the doctrine of acquisition opposes neither choice nor determinism, but combines the two.[2] Man "acquires" (*yaktasib*) his actions, that is, they become his by virtue of man being the place or channel (*maḥall*) of God's power (*qudrah*). Reward and punishment are determined on the basis of God's will and not man's efforts. The Muʿtazilites had argued that God's justice requires Him to reward those who do good and punish those who do evil. In contrast, Ghazali understands by God's justice His absolute freedom to do what He pleases with His creatures.[3] A man may spend his entire life performing "virtuous" deeds without attaining happiness unless he receives divine aid. Once a person realizes that God is the creator of all things and, hence, recognizes the virtues of divine assistance, he can look for deeds which are instrumental in producing the virtues of the soul.

The virtues of divine assistance as characterized above are different from the philosophic virtues and indeed are even opposed to them. Their basis is a theological concept of divine determinism, whereas the basis of philosophic virtues is human will and habituation. Both kinds of virtues, however, are regarded as "means" and not "ends" in themselves. Those of divine assistance are the means by which God helps man attain happiness, while the philosophic virtues are the means by which man attains happiness by his independent effort, and it is obvious that there is a fundamental difference between them. The basic issue here is the assertion that without God's aid man cannot attain happiness and thus there is no assurance that the philosophic virtues will lead to the happiness which is their end. They may even be self-defeating, according to Ghazali, because they can be signs of man's insubordination to God's will.

We have seen that Ghazali made certain changes and modifications in the philosophic virtues in order to make them acceptable, and now

1. *R*, IV. 5. 2511, where he also says that "man is forced to choose (*majbūr ʿalā al-ikhtiyār*)."

2. *R*, IV. 5. 2511, 2516; cf. al-Ashʿarī, *Ibānah*, p. 63; *Lumaʿ*, pp. 37-60; al-Bāqillānī, *Tamhīd*, pp. 31-41; al-Juwaynī, *Irshād*, pp. 187-215.

3. *R*, I. 1. 195; Ghazali, *al-Risālah al-Qudsiyyah* ("The Jerusalem Tract") ed. and trans. by A.L. Tibawi in "Al-Ghazali's Tract on Dogmatic Theology," *Islamic Quarterly*, IX (1965), 89; *R*, III. 1. 1429; cf. al-Juwaynī, *Irshād*, p. 208.

his introduction of the virtues of divine assistance implies a radical critique of the self-sufficiency of the philosophic virtues which undermines their efficacy. For Ghazali, everything in the world, including man and his actions, is created, determined and ordered by God's will. In such a world, it is impossible for man to have free choice and consequently, on his own, to acquire the philosophic virtues. In order for man to do anything, he is in constant need of divine aid. The philosophic virtues can have efficacy in this world only when they are conditioned by the theological virtues. Thus Ghazali not only denies the philosophic virtues their fundamental characteristic of being originated in man's free will, but also ranks them below some character qualities which serve better the cause of seeking divine assistance.

In this new context we face a situation in which philosophic virtues are destroyed as means to the attainment of happiness. Their acquisition does not assure man of anything. The only reliable things in this situation are the virtues of divine assistance, and it has been explained above that the virtues of divine assistance are "virtues" in a special sense for in reality they are gifts and favors of God over which man has no direct control. Indirectly, however, there are certain things which man can do in order to call forth God's blessing. These are, obviously, actions which are directed toward God, even when they are done in relation to other people or things, and now we must inquire what are these things which can be used as means of appealing for God's assistance? Surely, they cannot be the philosophic virtues because Ghazali does not believe that unaided reason is able to know the exact nature of such things. Furthermore, anything which comes about as a result of an assumed free will of man is only an illusion. Thus the only way for man to know the real things which call forth God's assistance is through God's revelation in the form of commandments. Therefore, only by fulfilling these commandments can man assure for himself the possibility of acquiring virtue and consequently of attaining happiness.

Because living according to the divine commandments increases the likelihood of receiving God's gifts, these commandments become the means of teaching virtue in the religious community. Here the divine commandments take precedence over everything (including philosophic virtues which must in any case be modified here) because they embody specific precepts which can never be known by unaided human reason. In this context "virtue" becomes primarily religious virtue. Ghazali even goes so far as to equate virtue here with the act of obedience to

God (*ṭā'ah*),[1] and therefore investigation of the Islamic virtues is fundamentally a description of the proper way of carrying out the divine commandments.

Only a member of a religious community favored with divine revelation, therefore, can acquire that virtue which leads to happiness, because human reason alone cannot apprehend the states and activities which are likely to elicit divine guidance. This is true even when the philosophic virtues and the divine commandments appear to be identical; for acknowledging these virtues and actions simply because they have been commanded is a precondition to receiving divine aid.

In Ghazali's view, divine commandments and the judgments derived from them are divided into two parts: those which are concerned primarily with beliefs and actions directed towards God, and those which consist of the actions which man directs towards his fellow men. The former he calls acts of worship (*'ibādāt*), and the latter customs (*'ādāt*)

Acts of Worship

In discussing acts of worship in the first Quarter of the *Revival*, Ghazali maintains that moral refinement is compatible with scrupulous observance of ritual laws. The function of the acts of worship is to help man preserve his relation with God and enable him to appeal to God for the divine assistance necessary for the attainment of happiness in the hereafter. Ghazali charges the Muslim philosophers with not observing and even with rejecting some of the acts of worship.[2] A Muslim philosopher, such as Avicenna, points to the importance and usefulness of the acts of worship in sustaining the multitude's remembrance of God and the resurrection in the hereafter, which are essential for the continuance of political life.[3] In contrast, Ghazali finds in the acts of worship very little of political and social values, and his apparent aim in dealing with them is to stress their importance for the individual and the part they play in helping him master his passions, schooling him in virtue, and above all, enabling him to seek divine assistance in order that he may attain happiness.

1. *R*, III. 5. 946.
2. *Tahāfut*, p. 4.
3. Avicenna, *Shifā'*: *Metaphysics*, II, 445; cf. al-Fārābī, *Millah*, p. 47, where he relates religious practices to philosophy.

In the "Book of Knowledge," the first book of the first Quarter of the *Revival*, Ghazali points to the Islamic view that the acquisition of knowledge is a religious duty. Every Muslim is enjoined to obtain, not only knowledge of spiritual practice, but also knowledge of the Koran and of the Sunnah, that is, the words and deeds of the prophet Muḥammad.[1] Moreover, the Muslim should acquire a detailed familiarity with ritual law and all its subsidiary sciences insofar as he requires them for the proper observance of the acts of worship, for example, an understanding of the direction of the Ka'bah and the times of prayers.[2] The special branch of knowledge which deals with the external aspects of the divine commandments in general is known as Islamic jusriprudence (*fiqh*). Ghazali admits that this science contributes in some way to man's salvation in the hereafter, but he points out that, because they concentrate on the external aspects of worship alone and reject interpretation of their hidden meanings, jurists fail to understand the full range of the divine commandments.[3] An explanation of the acts of worship must disclose the importance of their external aspects and, at the same time, point to their hidden significance.

The specific things which the divine commandments require man to know are the articles of faith (*qawā'id al-'aqā'id*), and he must believe in these articles which are the basis of the acts of worship. Examples of these articles are that there is one God who created everything, who governs all things, and who does not resemble any of the created things; that He sends prophets to guide men with revealed scriptures; that Muḥammad is the last of these prophets and the Koran is the last of the scriptures; that the teachings of the Koran and the traditions of Muḥammad must be faithfully followed; that after his death man will be resurrected in the hereafter and he will be judged by God who will reward or punish him for his deeds during his life.[4] It is within the framework of these beliefs that the acts of worship acquire their significance.

1. The Islamic religious formula "There is no deity but God; Muḥammad is the apostle of God" is the foundation for these beliefs. The utterance of this formula marks man's acceptance of the religion of Islam and

1. *R*, I. 1. 25-28.
2. *R*, II. 7. 1116-24.
3. *R*, I. 1. 28-29, 31, 34.
4. *R*, I. 2. 154-220. This book is called "The articles of Faith" (*Qawā'id al-'Aqā'id*). Part of it contains Ghazali's book *The Jerusalem Tract* (*Al-Risālah al-Qudsiyyah*), which was written earlier. Cf. *Qudsiyyah*, pp. 79-94.

consequently implies his willingness to regard such beliefs as the framework within which he practices the acts of worship. This formula is known as the first of the five pillars of Islam.[1]

Ghazali devotes Books 3 through 7 of Quarter I of the *Revival* solely to the discussion of the rest of the pillars of Islam, that is, prayer (*ṣalāh*), introducing it with the act of ritual purity (*ṭahārah*), alms-tax (*zakāh*), fasting (*ṣawm*), and pilgrimage (*ḥajj*). He deals with the external aspects of these acts of worship and he says that he is interested only in those external elements which are essential to the acts of worship. He suggests that detailed discussion of less essential elements can be found in the works of the Muslim jurists.[2] In explaining the external characteristics of the acts of worship, however, Ghazali continually points to the internal aspect underlying what is apparent. He discusses these acts of worship according to a range of degrees of excellence, and the number of intermediate levels may differ for each act of worship.

2. Ritual purity (*ṭahārah*) is arranged in four levels. The first and lowest of them is purity of the external parts of the body; the second level is cleaning the members of the body from sins; the third is purifying the heart from vices; and finally comes purifying the "inmost of the heart" (*as-sirr*) from anything other than God.[3] The explicit subject of the third book of "The Quarter on the Acts of Worship" is limited to the first level only. In his account of the several practices of ritual purity Ghazali concentrates on washing the whole body (*ghusl*) and ablution (*wuḍū'*), which are preconditions for the act of ritual prayer (*ṣalāh*), and explains how they are performed, the number of prayers, and their different times. Islamic religious teachings stipulate that a Muslim must give his sincere, undivided attention to prayer so that he does not perform it mechanically, and Ghazali considers such "intangible" consideration the most crucial element in praying. For prayer to be complete and perfect there are certain character traits that must accompany its performance, namely, "the presence of the

1. *R*, I. 2. 158; cf. *R*, I. 2. 204; *R*, I. 5. 378, where Ghazali mentions the famous tradition of the Prophet Muḥammad, "Islam is built on five pillars: testifying that there is no god but God and that Muḥammad is the Apostle of God; performing prayer; giving alms-tax; fasting the month of Ramaḍān; and performing the pilgrimage to the House of God by those who have the means to it."

2. *R*, I. 3. 228-242.

3. *R*, I. 3. 222-23, 227.

heart" (*ḥuḍūr al-qalb*), understanding (of its actions and words) (*fahm*), glorification (*ta'ẓīm*), reverence (*haybah*), hope (*rajā'*), modesty (*ḥayā'*), and submission (*khushū'*), which is the most essential of all these to prayer.[1]

3. The duty of paying alms-tax (*zakāh*) is analyzed in a similar way. It is an act of worship with regard to man's property. Ghazali explains, in a summary way, the amount to be given, to whom it can be given, and the conditions that must be fulfilled by the giver so that he can meet this duty. To point out the hidden qualities which lie behind the external practices of this duty, Ghazali arranges men into three groups, according to their attitude toward giving wealth. The highest rank comprises those who are truly dedicated to worshiping God, and give away all their possessions. They are therefore not obligated to pay the alms-tax since they no longer possess the required minimum amount from which the percentage of alms-tax is given. Such men rid themselves of the trivial task of accounting and bookkeeping, dedicating themselves to the spiritual refinement of their souls. The intermediary rank consists of those who keep their wealth and at the same time give to those who are in need beyond the specific percentage prescribed by the duty of alms-tax. The third and lowest of the three ranks applies to those who only give what the religious law prescribes without exceeding or falling short of the limit. This is the rank of the multitude which is dominated by an apparent love of wealth.[2]

4. Fasting (*ṣawm*). Ghazali gives an account of the specific obligations associated with it, namely, refraining from satisfying the desires for food and sex, from dawn till sunset every day during the lunar month of Ramaḍān. Fulfilling the minimal requirements of fasting marks the "fasting of the multitude" (*ṣawm al-'umūm*), which is the lowest of three ranks of fasting. The second rank consists in keeping all members and organs of the body from committing any sin. This is the rank of the few (*khuṣūṣ*) which is practiced by pious men (*ṣāliḥūn*). The third and highest rank of fasting is that of the elect few (*khuṣūṣ al-khuṣūṣ*); it requires training the soul to refrain from thinking of anything except God. Such fasting is broken by thoughts directed away from God or the hereafter.[3]

1. *R*, I. 4. 289-90, 307-310.
2. *R*, I. 5. 387-88.
3. *R*, I. 6. 428-32.

5. Pilgrimage (*ḥajj*) is usually enumerated as the last of the five pillars of Islam. It is the only one which takes account of the means necessary to perform it, such as health of the body, safety on the way to Mecca, and sufficient money to sustain oneself on the journey and one's family during his absence. Ghazali then mentions that the time of pilgrimage is the beginning of the tenth lunar month of the Hijrah year through the ninth day of the twelfth month. There are five principal conditions without which the performance of the pilgrimage is invalid, namely, the state of ritual consecration in and around Mecca (*iḥrām*), circumambulation of the Ka'bah (*ṭawāf*), the ceremony of running seven times between Ṣafā and Marwah (*sa'y*), standing on mount 'Arafah (*al-wuqūf bi 'Arafah*), and shaving (*ḥalq*).[1] Ghazali explains these conditions and other related practices essential to the performance of this act of worship.

Ghazali differs from the Muslim philosophers who see in the pilgrimage social and political significance. Miskawayh, for example, states that the Legislator made it incumbent upon people to perform pilgrimage so that,

> the inhabitants of the distant cities can come together, as do the inhabitants of the same city, and can achieve the same state of fellowship, love, and community of good and of happiness as those who are brought together every year, or every week, or every day. With this innate fellowship they meet to seek the goods common [to them], to renew their devotion to the law.[2]

In contrast, Ghazali interprets the internal significance of this ritual with reference to individual salvation only. He maintains that the essence of pilgrimage is in reality the way to God. It is the monasticism (*rahbāniyyah*) of the Muslim, which replaces the discontinued ancient monastic orders.[3] His interpretation of the above basic conditions of pilgrimage focuses even more emphatically on the internal aspects of these rituals. For example, he interprets circumambulation of the Ka'bah as permeating the heart by invoking the Lord of the Ka'bah, whereas running seven times between Ṣafā and Marwah is regarded as the sign of devotion in the service of God and hope for His mercy.[4]

1. *R*, I. 7. 448-49. *Iḥrām* is also the state during which the pilgrim wears two seamless woolen or linen sheets, usually white, neither combs nor shaves, and observes sexual continence.

2. Miskawayh, *Tahdhīb*, p. 141. Cf. Avicenna *Shifā'*: *Metaphysics*, II, 444.

3. *R*, I. 7. 484.

4. *R*, I. 7. 489-90.

In his treatment of the major Islamic acts of worship, Ghazali repeats the traditional Islamic descriptions. At the same time, he adopts certain procedures that call attention to the internal benefits hidden in the rituals, interpreting them in terms of their significance for individual spiritual salvation. The traditional understanding always recognized, even if it did not give priority to, the social and political significance of these acts of worship. For instance, the ritual of holy strife (*jihād*) was important enough to Muslims that they considered it the sixth pillar of Islam. Ghazali, however, does not regard it essential and does not devote to it even a single section of any of the books of the *Revival* which deal with acts of worship. Instead, he prefers to discuss things such as "The Rules for Reciting the Koran," "Invocation and Supplication," and "The Arrangement of Specific Times of the Day and Night to be Devoted to Private Worship and Meditation," which are the themes of the last three Books of the "Quarter of Worship" of the *Revival*. In these books he concentrates on practices which are primarily concerned with individual spiritual refinement, indeed spiritual refinement of the "few."

In concluding his account of the acts of worship, Ghazali emphasizes that invoking God's name (*dhikr Allāh*) is the most virtuous and useful act of worship. All other practices lead to this and they are necessary as means to it.[1] There is no difficulty in reconciling this view of invocation with the tenets of Islam; for in all acts of worship invoking God's name and glorifying Him is an essential element. Ghazali's special way of interpreting invocation and how to go about it, however, seems to open the way for certain states of the soul which are beyond those acquired through the traditional understanding of the acts of worship. In explaining these rituals, both in terms of their external as well as their internal significance, Ghazali shows that they are crucial and necessary intruments in acquiring and preserving a number of character traits, e.g., modesty, submission, patience, understanding, and piety.

Acts of worship are "virtues" in that they are means to the attainment of happiness. Indeed, they are the most important means to such an end because, through them, man appeals directly to God for divine assistance without which it is impossible to achieve anything. It is obvious from Ghazali's discussion of the acts of worship that, in all of them, man makes different uses of his body to worship God and express devotion to Him. In this sense they can be considered "external" or outward practices.

1. *R*, I. 9. 593.

However, when Ghazali speaks about the "external aspect" of the acts of worship, he means something more than that. He means that characteristic of them which is the subject matter of jurisprudence. According to Ghazali, the jurist concerns himself with judging the external appearance of an individual's performance of the acts of worship, and thus the individual is immune to political or social punishment in the religious community. But this does not help him to escape afflictions in the hereafter unless there is sincerity and devotion in performing such acts of worship.[1] To appeal for God's aid, one has to do better than act out the performance of worshiping God. For Ghazali, worshiping God is the most serious task that man can perform to achieve his salvation and thus he begins with a brief explanation of its external characteristics, considered as the minimum expected effort, and then he points to the internal significance of these acts.

Customs

Ghazali devotes all of the second Quarter of the *Revival* to the discussion of customs or manners (*'ādāt*), which are religiously prescribed and approved "habits," and originate in God's commandments (in the form of legal injunctions) as well as in moral imperatives. Like the acts of worship, therefore, customs owe their validity to a divine command and are a condition for receiving the divine assistance, which is necessary for the attainment of happiness. Unlike the acts of worship, which are primarily directed toward God in the form of rituals, these customs are primarily concerned with behavior toward others. In this sense, customs are external practices among men, but they are practices which are performed with the aim of obeying God and seeking His aid. Ghazali enumerates as customs Islamic religious manners in regard to food, marriage, business transactions, permissible and forbidden things, companionship, and travel. In dealing with all such customs, Ghazali gives explanations of the Islamic legal requirements which make such practice Islamic. For example, he explains the requirements for performing marriage, preserving family ties, and obtaining divorce. In business transactions he explains the Islamic requirements for buying and selling, entering contracts, and so on. He considers such legal injunctions a necessary and important guide so that a man may deal with other men in a manner which satisfies God's commandments.

1. *R*, I. 1. 31-33.

Since man must appeal to God for assistance in attaining happiness, he must learn these legal injunctions in order to know what he should do and should avoid. However, as he did when writing about the acts of worship, Ghazali points out here that he does not intend to give a detailed treatment of legal questions. This must be sought in textbooks of Islamic jurisprudence, including his own manuals on the subject, and such details are primarily related to business transactions with which one can dispense if one limits his property to the minimum legal level.[1] Ghazali's attitude toward these legal injunctions can be understood in terms of his view of jurisprudence, which he says is a "worldly science" since it deals with the application of divine commandments in their literal meaning. We have seen that in discussing the acts of worship Ghazali considered that jurists deal only with external practice and that it is necessary to look for internal significance if one aims at the other-worldly happiness. Likewise, in regard to customs, the jurist is limited by legal injunctions. In this, he helps to preserve the "political" life of the religious community, but this task has only indirect relevance to the happiness of the hereafter, for in the community man has to train himself to perform these customs sincerely and not merely for fear of the political authority.

In Ghazali's view religious law is essential to the well-being and the common good of the multitude, whereas the "way of religion" (*ṭarīq al-dīn*), the way of mystical devotion, is suited only to a "few individuals" (*āḥād*). It is in the interest of those few that most men turn away from the path of devotion and prefer worldly goods which are regulated by the law. For if all men become "devoted souls," the order of the world will be disturbed, living will become difficult, and consequently those who seek the way of devotion will not be able to achieve their goal. Thus, by ordering the lives of all men, the religious law gives an opportunity to the "few" to seek the means of ultimate spiritual salvation.[2] This, however, does not mean that the "few" can dispense with the religious-legal injunctions, but rather that while abiding by these injunctions, they look beyond their external significance for internal aspects conducive to the ultimate happiness of the hereafter.[3] The

1. *R*, II. 4. 817. Ghazali's own manuals on jurisprudence include: *al-Basīṭ*, *al-Wasīṭ*, and *al-Wajīz*; cf. Badawī, *Mu'allafāt*, pp. 17-20.

2. *R*, II. 4. 845-46.

3. It may be said that the whole corpus of Islamic religious teachings constitutes a handbook of Islamic ethics, inasmuch as the generally accepted Muslim view is that

religious law is the *minimum* effort expected from the member of the Islamic community.

Ghazali's view of the role and position of the religious law explains his approach in dealing with the Islamic customs. He moves away from the religious-legal aspect of the given custom to discuss the moral imperatives implied in it or taught by it. In other words, he moves beyond the strict legal injunctions to explain the specific religious-legal virtues. This attitude can be explained by an examination of the concluding book of the "Quarter of Customs," namely, "The Book of the Manners of Life and Prophetic Character" (*Kitāb Ādāb al-Ma'īshah wa Akhlāq al-Nubuwwah*). In the introduction of this Book Ghazali states:

> I had resolved to end the "Quarter of Customs" of this book [i.e., the *Revival*] with a comprehensive Book dealing with the manners of living, in order that deducing them from all of these Books would not be difficult for the student. Then I realized that each Book of the "Quarter of Customs" had already dealt with a particular class of manners. Since I find the task of repetition painful and tedious . . . I have decided to restrict myself in this Book to the character of the Messenger of God [i.e., Muḥammad] as related by tradition.[1]

This statement conceals another important reason for restricting the subject of this Book. By avoiding any mention of the legal injunctions dealt with in parts of the "Quarter of Customs," Ghazali is able to limit himself to moral considerations as distinguished from legal questions. He also seeks to emphasize the importance of these moral considerations by showing how the prophet Muḥammad practiced them. In doing this he considers them Islamic religious- legal virtues.

According to Islamic teaching, Muḥammad was the highest of God's creatures both in nobility and power, and for this reason, Ghazali says, the knowledge of prophetic traditions which describe Muḥammad's character restores and strengthens the faith as well as the character traits of Muslims.[2] Ghazali approaches Islamic religious-legal virtues according to a method known to Islamic traditional moralists such as Ibn Abī al-Dunyā and al-Ḥarbī.[3] However, whereas both of these

the correct performance of religious duties and understanding of religious duties are the basic elements of moral life; see R. Walzer and H.A.R. Gibb, "Akhlāḳ, "*EI*[2], I, 326.

1. *R*, II. 10. 1284.

2. *R*, II. 10. 1284.

3. Both are Ḥanbalite traditionists. The former is Abū Bakr 'Ali b. Muḥammad b. 'Ubayd Ibn Abī al-Dunyā, d. 281 A.H./894. In his *Makārim al-Akhlāq* "The Noble Qualities of Character" he deals with ten Islamic virtues. Cf. *GAL*, I, 160; *GAL*(*S*),

regard the chain of transmitters (*isnād*) as an important part of these traditions which teach a certain virtue or group of virtues and repeat traditions simply because of their different chains of transmitters, Ghazali states that in using prophetic traditions to learn about the virtues of Muḥammad, he "will weave together the reports, section by section, without their chains of transmitters."[1] This enables him to discuss certain issues raised by these traditions, whereas traditional moralists usually limit themselves to quoting the report which teaches or supports the virtue in question. Aside from this, however, Ghazali agrees with the view of traditional Islamic moralists, especially Ibn Abī al-Dunyā, that prophetic traditions provide a sufficient basis and authority for proper conduct.[2] He also agrees with him in omitting material that is not within the best authenticated Islamic traditions when dealing with the noble character of Muḥammad. Thus there is no allusion to philosophers.

Ghazali asserts that Muḥammad was endowed with an ideal moral character so as to teach Muslims how to achieve virtue. Quoting the prophetic tradition, "I was sent to complete the noble qualities of character," he comments, "thereafter the Messenger of God explained to mankind that God loves the fine qualities of character and detests the bad qualities of character."[3] Thus, virtue is based here on a divine sanction embodied in the Prophet's practice and is acquired primarily for the sake of obedience to God's command. Ghazali quotes prophetic traditions to strengthen this notion.[4] He maintains that all of the Prophet's good qualities are due to God's action:

> God taught him all fine qualities of character, praiseworthy paths, reports about the first and last affairs, and matters through which one achieves salvation and reward in future life, and happiness and reward in the world to come.[5]

I, 247-48. See James A. Bellamy, "The Makārim al-Akhlāq by Ibn Abī-'l-Dunyā," *Muslim World*, LIII (1963), 106-119. The latter is Ibrāhīm b. Isḥāq b. Bashīr b. 'Alī al-Ḥarbī, d. 285 A.H./899. In his *Ikrām al-Ḍayf* ("Hospitality to Guests") (Cairo: Maṭba'at al-Manār, 1349 A.H.) he deals with a single virtue simply by bringing together the relevant prophetic traditions.

1. *R*, II. 10. 1284.

2. *R*, II. 10. 1286; *R*, III. 2. 1443; cf. Ibn Abī al-Dunyā, *Makārim*, fols. 2a-2b.

3. *R*, II. 10. 1286.

4. *R*, II. 10. 1287. For example, "By Him in whose hand is my life, no one shall enter paradise except him who is of good character." It must be noted that, when discussing Islamic virtues in Book 10 of Quarter II of the *Revival*, Ghazali uses the term *makārim al-akhlāq*, a term used in the same sense by Ibn Abī al-Dunyā.

5. *R*, II. 10. 1299.

Unlike Ibn Abī al-Dunyā, who bases his enumeration of the Islamic virtues on a tradition of Muḥammad's wife, 'A'ishah, which limits them to ten,[1] Ghazali does not restrict his list of these virtues to one single tradition, nor does he limit them in number. His list consists of a selected sample:

> Among these qualities there are: having good social relations, doing noble actions, being submissive, bestowing favor, feeding others, extending greetings, visiting the sick Muslim whether he be pious or profligate, escorting the bier of a Muslim, behaving honorably toward your neighbor whether he be a Muslim or a disbeliever, honoring the aged Muslim, accepting the invitation to food and the inviting of others, bestowing pardon, making peace between people, liberality, magnificence, kindness, being the first to extend greeting, repressing anger, and pardoning people.[2]

When introducing these virtues, Ghazali does not explain whether they are means between two extremes; nor does he specify whether the vices that oppose them are extremes of defect or excess. Yet the word *'ādah*, which is used by Ghazali to mean custom, means habit as well. Since he equates virtue with good habit in his discussion of philosophic virtues, his usage of the same term here suggests that customs constitute a class of Islamic religious-legal virtues comparable to the philosophic virtues. Furthermore, in his account of the philosophic virtues, Ghazali concludes that all these virtues are explained in detail and supported by prophetic traditions which are to be found in the "Book (*Kitāb*) of the Character Traits of the Prophet (peace be upon him), and in other Books."[3] The only book which seems to fulfill this promise is Book 10 of the "Quarter of Customs" in the *Revival* which we are about to discuss.

In a more detailed account of Islamic religious virtues, the first group of these virtues which Ghazali attributes to Muḥammad consists of gentleness, courage, justice, and temperance,[4] and Ghazali maintains that only the prophet Muḥammad has perfectly achieved these four

1. Ibn Abī al-Dunyā, *Makārim*, fols. 4b-5a, where he says that his book deals specifically with each of the ten noble qualities of character enumerated by Muḥammad's wife, 'Ā'ishah, who said: "There are ten noble qualities of character: speaking the truth, firm courage in obeying God, giving to him who asks, repaying good deeds, strengthening family ties, keeping faith, behaving honorably towards neighbors, behaving honorably towards friends, hospitality to guests, and modesty which is the chief of them all." Ghazali quotes the same tradition but does not make it the basis of his table of noble character traits (*R*, II. 5. 1031).

2. *R*, II. 10. 1287.

3. *C*, pp. 101-102; cf. Asad Efendi MSS, 1759, fols. 81b-82a.

4. *R*, II. 10. 1288-89: "He [Muḥammad] was the most gentle, courageous, just, and temperate of men."

principal philosophic virtues.[1] Practical wisdom has been dropped from the list of these four principal virtues and replaced by gentleness, which, in his discussion of the philosophic virtues, Ghazali classifies under courage. Furthermore, in his detailed discussion of the above four virtues, Ghazali overlooks justice and only mentions courage briefly. The rest of the account is mostly devoted to gentleness, temperance, and their subordinate virtues. Thus Ghazali's approach here is closer to the Islamic traditional moralists than the Muslim philosophers. Likewise, Ghazali's purpose in giving an account of the character of the Prophet is to refine the individual through Islamic traditional customs, while in contrast, Avicenna pays more attention to the prophetic teaching which concerns the political well-being of the community. Avicenna viewed the substance of the prophet's moral teaching as fundamentally identical with the ethics taught by the philosophers:

> It is necessary that the Legislator should also prescribe laws regarding morals and customs that advocate justice, which is the mean . . . As for courage, it is for the city's survival . . . By wisdom as a virtue, which is the third of a triad comprising in addition temperance and courage, is not meant theoretical wisdom . . . but rather, practical wisdom pertaining to worldly actions and behavior.[2]

Although one can locate a number of the accepted philosophic virtues in Ghazali's account of Islamic customs, he refuses to follow the order, state the definitions, and give the grounds of the philosophic virtues. This approach is part of his effort to adopt the philosophic virtues into this new religious context of moral life. Thus he favors virtues that have a closer tie to religious devotion. Humility, for example, becomes so important that Ghazali devotes a special section to its discussion.[3] The only way to understand the significance of these virtues and their relation to each other is to consider the special sections devoted to the discussion of particular virtues within Book 10 of Quarter II of the *Revival*,[4] and to keep in mind the detailed treatment of some of these virtues in the rest of the Books of the "Quarter of Customs."

It must be remembered that all Islamic religious virtues dealt with in the "Quarter of Customs" are external practices. Knowing this, one can

1. *R*, III. 2. 1443.
2. Avicenna, *Shifā'*: *Metaphysics*, II, 454-55.
3. *R*, II. 10. 1333.
4. For example, "An account of his pardoning" (*R*, II. 10. 1326); "An account of his liberality and generosity" (*R*, II. 10. 1329); "An account of his courage" (*R*, II. 10. 1331); "An account of his humility" (*R*, II. 10. 1333).

see that in his treatment of virtues such as temperance, courage, liberality, magnificence, gentleness, and modesty, Ghazali deviates slightly from his discussion of them as philosophic virtues. They are accepted here on the authority of the Prophet, and the legal requirements attached to practicing some of them are spelled out in greater detail. Justice, in its social context, is less prominent. No one can truly seek the happiness of the world to come unless he trains himself in observing the religious-legal injunctions with respect to wealth. Observing these injunctions which govern all practices of transactions is justice. But justice is merely a means of escaping punishment; by going beyond social justice to acquire the virtue of benevolence (*iḥsān*) one can receive a reward. To be just, that is, to fulfil the legal requirement, is to be of the rank of pious men (*ṣāliḥūn*), whereas to be benevolent is to be of the rank of those who are brought near to God (*muqarrabūn*.)[1]

In connection with liberality and magnificence, Ghazali mentions the virtue of "hospitality to guests." In part, this virtue is subsumed under liberality and magnificence, but it is also a virtue in its own right. Being hospitable to guests does not necessarily mean giving to those in need, or giving for the public good, for this is a special aspect of generosity. Rather Ghazali agrees with Muslim traditional moralists in regarding hospitality as one of the pre-Islamic virtues which were approved by the Prophet. 'Ā'ishah is reported to have said, "Islam came when there were sixty-odd good qualities among the Arabs, all of which Islam intensified; among these are hospitality, good-neighborliness and faithfulness to one's engagements."[2]

Ghazali orders the virtues of human association as follows. First, there are the virtues which he calls involuntary types of companionship in travel, in office, in school, or in the king's court. Second, there is voluntary companionship, which, like companionship in general, reflects man's good nature. It has both material and spiritual benefits for the individual, and to be successful, it must be based on good character, righteousness, observance of the law, and absence of greed for wordly goods.[3] But, above all, true companionship can only be founded on love. Analyzing

1. *R*, II. 3. 760, 793-807.

2. Ibn Abī al-Dunyā, *Makārim*, fol. 4b; cf. *R*, II. 1. 664, 671-77. Ghazali relates that Muḥammad freed the daughter of Ḥātim al-Ṭā'ī, a famous pre-Islamic man known for his generosity and hospitality, because of her father's noble character qualities even though he died before Muḥammad's mission (*R*, II. 10. 1287).

3. *R*, II. 5. 954.

the different objects and degrees of love, Ghazali divides companionship into different categories. The most private type is blood-kinship. The more general type is Islamic brotherhood. Friendship and fellowship are two subspecies under the category of brotherhood:

> When friendship becomes stronger it becomes brotherhood, when this increases, it becomes, in turn, "true love," and finally it becomes bosom-friendship (*khullah*), which is a relationship between man and God.[1]

In his account of the virtue of strengthening blood-kinship (*ṣilat al-raḥim*), Ghazali agrees so completely with the traditional moralist Ibn Abī al-Dunyā that he limits himself to quoting traditions which teach how to behave honorably toward parents, offspring, and immediate relatives. Muḥammad helped his kindred without preferring them to those who were more virtuous than they.[2]

Brotherhood among the believers in their obedience to God is an important relationship underlying most of the kinds of companionship. It is within this relationship that we find many of the Islamic virtues which have a social significance. Ghazali points to the special obligations that must be fulfilled so that the "covenant" of brotherhood becomes virtuous. These obligations, which must be exercised in a way which supports brotherhood, include everything that belongs to the parties participating in the covenant—heart, speech, life, and property. Thus, the duty of Islamic brotherhood means full participation in all kinds of activities with fellow Muslims. A Muslim should wish his coreligionists well and not harm them. He should be humble with them, forgive them, protect their honor, and visit their sick.[3] To illustrate some of these virtues of Islamic brotherhood, Ghazali relates how the Prophet visited the sick Muslims in the farthest section of the city, always attended their funerals, and was the first to extend greetings to whomever he met. Likewise, he was modest, forgiving, and merciful.[4] His humility fascinated everyone. His companions did not rise for him when he passed by, because they knew that he disliked that. When a man, frightened by his reverential fear of Muḥammad, was brought to him, Muḥammad said, "Be at rest. I am not a king. I am only the son of a woman of [the tribe of] Quraysh who eats dried meat."[5]

1. *R*, II. 5. 993.
2. *R*, II. 5. 1032-34; II. 10. 1295-96; cf. Ibn Abī al-Dunyā, *Makārim*, fol. 23a.
3. *R*, II. 5. 995-1027.
4. *R*, II. 10. 1293, 1301-1304.
5. *R*, II. 10. 1295-96.

Although neighborliness is an involuntary type of association, Ghazali, following the traditional Islamic practice, gives it an important role among the voluntary relations in the community. He quotes the prophetic tradition, "He who believes in God and the last day, let him honor his neighbor."[1] In order to show its relation to the most private type of association, namely, blood-kinship, and the more general one, i.e., Islamic brotherhood, Ghazali quotes the prophetic tradition:

> There are three kinds of neighbors, one with three claims upon you, one with two claims, and one with one. The one with three claims is the Muslim neighbor who is related to you, for Islam, kinship, and neighborliness each has its due; the one with two claims on you is your Muslim neighbor, and the one with one claim is your neighbor who is a polytheist (*al-mushrik*).[2]

The important thing about these virtues of association is that all of them aim ultimately at the highest kind of relationship, namely, bosom-friendship (*khullah*) which, according to Ghazali, can exist only between the devoted person and God. Now this bosom-friendship does not necessarily require association with other men, at least not all the time; in fact it can only be truly practiced away from other people who may disturb it, and for this reason Ghazali devotes one of the books of the "Quarter of Customs" to the "Manners of Isolation" (*Adāb al-'Uzlah*) in which he discusses private devotion and meditation.[3] Thus, while giving an account of the practice of these virtues as customs of the religious community, Ghazali directs attention to what lies beyond them and points to what he regards as the higher stages of salvation to be sought by those who can do more than observe the external froms of these virtues. He expresses the same attitude in his book on the "Manners of Travel" (*Adāb al-Safar*). There, while explaining the conditions of traveling, he periodically reminds his reader of a more important kind of traveling, namely, traveling the way of God and seeking nearness to Him.[4]

Therefore, in his treatment of "customs," Ghazali brings to the fore areas of human activity which are not of primary importance to Islamic teachings, although these teachings touch upon them. Ghazali suggests

1. *R*, II. 5. 1028; cf. Ibn Abī al-Dunyā, *Makārim*, fol. 35b.

2. *R*, II. 5. 1028; cf. Ibn Abī al-Dunyā, *Makarim*, fol. 37a, where he reports the concluding part of this prophetic tradition as follows, " . . . your neighbor who is not of your religion."

3. *R*, II. 6. 1044-82.

4. *R*, II. 7. 1093, 1108, 1116-24.

that Islamic religious virtues point to good qualities concerned with man's relation to God and to the hereafter, quoting the prophetic tradition directed to Mu'ādh b. Jabal, one of the close companions of Muḥammad:

> O, Mu'ādh, I command you to fear God, to report truthfully, to fulfill the promise, to act loyally, to avoid perfidious actions, to care for the neighbor, to have mercy on the orphan, to be soft-spoken, to be liberal in extending greeting, to perform fine acts, to limit expectation, to cleave to the faith, to study the Koran, to love the other life, to be anxious in regard to the reckoning, and to act humbly.[1]

In comparing this list of Islamic virtues with the one given above, one sees that fear of God, adhering to the faith, study of the Koran, love of the other life, and being anxious in regard to reckoning, are signs of devotion which Ghazali tries to interpret as indicative of the path to be chosen by the few.

We have noticed that Ghazali concludes his account of the acts of worship by emphasizing invocation, meditation, and supplication, and he proceeds in the same way when dealing with customs, as can be seen in Book 8 of Quarter II of the *Revival*, i.e., "The Manners of Singing and Ecstasy" (*Ādāb al-Samā' wa al-Wajd*). Because of the controversial character of singing, Ghazali takes pains to show that Islamic religious law does not prohibit listening to songs except in five cases: when the singer is a female, when the musical instruments used are of the kind associated with drinking parties, when the words of the song are obscene, when the listener is a person who is overcome by the desire for sex, and when the singer or the listener is a person who is vulgar. The last case means that such a person may become so overwhelmed by singing that he wastes his time instead of performing his duties.[2] The discussion about who can engage in singing rests finally on a distinction between the many and the few, and Ghazali's analysis parallels his understanding of the possibility of spiritual salvation for those who can penetrate behind religious customs and see their hidden meanings. Since Ghazali considers the music as important as the words of the song, and since the most noble words one can utter are those invoking God's name, the ecstasy of love resulting from rhymed invocation adds significance to the mere utterance of words. Ghazali equates such ecstasy with the full tranquility of the soul which is a sign of its health.[3]

1. *R*, II. 10. 1288.
2. *R*, II. 8. 1130, 1146.
3. *R*, II. 8. 1138.

Conclusion

Ghazali's discussion of the religious-legal virtues is introduced by an investigation of the theological virtues. By regarding divine assistance as necessary for the attainment of happiness, Ghazali calls the efficacy of philosophic virtues into question. Since the only way for man to elicit divine assistance consists in appealing to God for His aid, and because in Ghazali's view unaided reason cannot know the way of seeking God's assistance, it is necessary for man to have recourse to the commandments revealed by God. Thus, the Islamic religious-legal virtues are indispensable for the attainment of human happiness. In this new context of living in obedience to divine commandments, the philosophic virtues can regain their relevance by assuming the basic characteristics of the religious-legal virtues: they are sanctioned by God and are means of seeking His assistance. The philosophic virtues are easily incorporated into customs because of their common ground; both deal with man's relation with other men. Despite this resemblance, however, Ghazali's approach in dealing with customs agrees more closely with that of the traditional Islamic moralists who deduce their views from the practices of the prophet Muḥammad.

We saw that Ghazali deals with both groups of religious-legal virtues —the acts of worship directed towards God and customs directed towards fellow men—in their external aspects and at the same time points to their internal significance. Likewise, he plays down the political aspects of these virtues in order to accentuate their importance for individual spiritual salvation.

Thus, according to Ghazali, the religious community must live up to the acts of worship and customs and apply them properly so that its members may receive what he calls general guidance, necessary for the attainment of the happiness of paradise in the hereafter. If a few members of the religious community are capable of interpreting these acts of worship and customs and of living in accordance with their inner meanings while at the same time observing the practices required by their external meaning, they may receive the absolute guidance which leads to ultimate happiness in the hereafter. The notion that those in a religious community who understand inner meanings may attain two kinds of happiness is based ultimately on Ghazali's well-known distinction between the multitude (*al-ʿāmmah* or *al-ʿawāmm*) and the few (*al-khāṣṣah* or *al-khawāṣṣ*).[1] According to Ghazali the multitude can only understand the external aspects (*ẓāhir*) of divine commandments, whereas the few can understand both the external and internal (*bāṭin*) aspects. By repeatedly linking the external commandments to the activities of the body, he suggests that the external aspects rank below the internal. With the same purpose, he openly praises the internal aspects of the commandments and reiterates that, in giving an account of the external acts of worship or customs, his primary intention is to reveal their mysteries (*asrār*) and hidden significance.[2] In spite of this attitude, the external aspects of the divine commandments remain essential because they are meant for every member of the community: they comprise the only means at the disposal of the many for attaining happiness, while for the few the external meanings provide the important surface without which true understanding of the internal meanings cannot be attained.[3] Moreover, the few cannot dispense with observing the external practices without subsequently losing sight of the true internal sense of the commandments.[4] This last stipulation means that Ghazali rejects those doctrines taught by some Islamic philosophic and mystical schools, according to which some or all Islamic religious practices could be disregarded by the few on the grounds that they are of secondary importance or good for the masses only.[5]

Ghazali's position can only be understood in the light of the theological virtues which are crucial for his ethical theory. Unlike the philosophers, who claim that the acquisition of certain virtues itself makes men's nature capable of seeking hapiness, Ghazali maintains that living according to the commandments in their external sense *may* elicit the gift of divine guidance, and thus that living according to the commandments in their external sense is the necessary, but not the sufficient condition for the attainment of happiness. For Ghazali, then, it is divine

1. This point is stated in the general introduction of the *Revival* (*R*, p. 5) as well as in the introduction to the second half of it (*R*, III. 1. 1349). In Book 2 of Quarter I of the *Revival*, Ghazali points out the difference between what is external and what is internal. *R*, I. 2. 173-80.

2. *R*, p. 4. The titles of "Books" dealing with acts of worship in Quarter I of the *Revival* reflect the same view of Ghazali. For example, he calls the book on prayer, "The Mysteries of Prayer" (*Asrār al-Ṣalāh*); the one on fasting, "the Mysteries of Fasting."

3. *R*, I. 3. 223.

4. *C*, pp. 204ff.

5. Ghazali charges the philosophers with this practice in his *Munqidh*, p. 113.

guidance, and not the religious-legal virtues themselves, which makes happiness possible. For this reason, the actions of anyone who dispenses with the external commandments in his search for their inner meaning will have as their basis independent human effort, and as a result, such a man will be in the same position as those who did not receive the divine commandments at all and cannot be the recipients of divine aid necessary for happiness. Ghazali further supports his position by asserting that, had God meant the external aspects of the divine commandments to be dispensed with by some men, He would have revealed this; but judging from the way Muḥammad and his companions understood and carried out the commandments, Ghazali concludes that this is not the case.

In their external aspects the religious-legal virtues, whether they are acts of worship or customs, provide the religious community in general with the opportunity for attaining happiness through obedience to God's divine commandments. However, in order to attain *ultimate* happiness, the members of the religious community must discover the internal meanings of these divine commandments and live according to them. This difficult task can only be mastered by a few members of the community. Anyone who is capable of undertaking such a task should spare no effort, for in this lies the highest, supreme, and ultimate happiness. Thus, the religious-legal virtues which supersede the philosophic virtues as the precondition for the attainment of happiness are not sufficient to assure that some men will reach *ultimate* happiness. Indirectly, however, they provide the opportunity to go beyond their external aspect and capture the significance of their internal aspect so that some men may attain the ultimate happiness. And thus Ghazali points to still another kind of virtue which must be higher than the religious-legal virtues.

Chapter IV / MYSTICAL VIRTUES

Ghazali and Mysticism

THE virtues appropriate to the few who seek ultimate happiness in the hereafter, that is, the vision of God, are established by Ghazali on the basis of a careful and elaborate interpretation of the hidden meanings of the divine commandments. This interpretation can be mastered by the truly learned men (*'ulamā'*) only. These are not jurists, theologians, or philosophers, but only the mystics (*ṣūfiyyah*); and Ghazali identifies himself with the mystics:

> I learned with certainty that it is above all the mystics who walk in the path of God; their life is the best life, their method the soundest method, their character the purest character (*wa akhlāquhum azkā al-akhlāq*).[1]

Relating how he came to accept mysticism, Ghazali points out that he found that this discipline includes both knowledge and practice. It was relatively easy for Ghazali to acquire the mystics' knowledge. In a statement about his sources, he begins with al-Makkī's work, the *Food of Hearts* (*Qūt al-Qulūb*), which he seems to consider his textbook of mysticism. Then he mentions "the works of al-Muḥāsibī," followed by "the various scattered sayings (*mutafarriqāt*)" of al-Junayd, al-Shiblī, and al-Bisṭāmī, and finally "the discourses" of unnamed mystics.[2] Ghazali starts with al-Makkī and al-Muḥāsibī, two mystics known for their effort to reconcile mysticism with Islamic religious teachings. Al-Bisṭāmī, who was known for his mystical heresies, is mentioned last. The reference to the "discourses" of unnamed mystics may refer to other mystics with

1. *Munqidh*, p. 101, where Ghazali's admiration of the mystical character traits culminates in his assumption that what is worthwhile in philosophic ethics is borrowed from the teachings of the mystics (cf. *Munqidh*, p. 81).

2. *Munqidh*, pp. 95-96: "I began to acquaint myself with their belief by reading their books, such as the *Food of Hearts* (*Qūt al-Qulūb*) by Abū Ṭālib al-Makkī (may God have mercy upon him), the works of al-Ḥārith al-Muḥāsibī, the various scattered sayings (*mutafarriqāt*) of al-Junayd, al-Shiblī, and Abū Yazīd al-Bisṭāmī (may God sanctify their spirits), and other discourses of their leading men."

the reputation of al-Bisṭāmī.[1] Ghazali, therefore, identifies himself more specifically with a tradition of mysticism which stood for synthesizing mystical and Islamic religious ideas. Al-Makkī's book, in particular "is of primary importance, as being the first and a very successful attempt to construct an overall design for orthodox Sufism."[2] Ghazali quotes extensively from the *Food of Hearts* in the *Revival*, especially in Quarter IV, which deals with the mystical virtues. Whole sections are simply reproduced, and even the sayings of earlier mystics and learned men, prophetic traditions, and the traditions of the Companions, are set forth as presented by al-Makkī.[3] This book, then, appears to be one of the sources through which Ghazali acquainted himself with the "scattered sayings" of early mystics.[4]

Ghazali's originality can be seen in his selection, arrangement, and synthesis of the material he extracted from al-Makkī. Ghazali achieves a degree of clarity in his presentation of the basic features of mysticism by introducing a rational, theoretical framework to explain certain otherwise inexplicable aspects of mysticism. He had learned the language of the philosophers and theologians before he acquired a personal experience of the mystical life and was ready to perfect the work begun by al-Makkī and mystics like him.[5] The speech (*kalām*) of the mystics, Ghazali points out, is incomplete and sometimes even defective because it is the habit of each one of them to give an account of his own spiritual state alone, without any regard for the states of others; consequently, their explicit statements diverge markedly. Because of this, Ghazali feels

1. On al-Bisṭāmī see ʻAbd al-Raḥmān Badawī, *Shaṭaḥāt al-Ṣūfiyyah I. Abū Yazīd al-Bisṭāmī* (Cairo: Maktabat al-Nahḍah al-Miṣriyyah, 1949), pp. 21-29; cf. R.C. Zaehner, *Hindu and Muslim Mysticism* (New York: Schocken Books, 1969), pp. 86-134.

2. A. J. Arberry, *Sufism: An Account of the Mystics of Islam* (London: George Allen & Unwin Ltd., 1950), p. 68.

3. Especially Books 1-7 of Quarter IV of the *Revival*. cf. al-Makkī *Qūt al-Qulūb* (2 vols.; Cairo: Muṣṭafā al-Bābī al-Ḥalabī ,1961), I, 364ff., II, 1-164; Arberry, *Sufism*, p. 68, where he says that *Qūt al-Qulūb* "was carefully studied by al-Ghazalī and exercised considerable influence on his mode of thought and writing"; L. Massignon, "al-Makkī," *EI* II, 174, where he points out that whole pages of the same book have been copied by Ghazali in the *Revival*. The commentator on the *Revival*, al-Zabīdī, shows that Ghazali was influenced in his mystical views in a substantial way by al-Makkī; see his *Itḥāf*, I, 30; VIII, 499; the same view was expressed by an earlier authority on Ghazali, al-Subkī, *Ṭabaqāt*, IV, 126.

4. Ali Hasan Abdel-Kader, *The Life, Personality and Writings of al-Junayd* (London: Luzac & Company Ltd., 1962), p. 55.

5. Arberry, *Sufism*, p. 68.

that rational knowledge is capable of giving a better and more objective account of spiritual experience.[1]

Comparing the mystical and rational ways of achieving happiness, Ghazali remarks that the validity of the mystical way cannot be disputed. It brings those who practice it to their goal, which is the sublime state enjoyed by saints and prophets. But this kind of discipline is not without serious dangers. The mind may be adversely affected, the health of the body destroyed, and melancholy may ensue:

> If the soul has not been exercised in the sciences that deal with fact and demonstration, it will acquire mental phantasms and suppose that truths are descending upon it. Many a Sufi has continued for ten years in one such fancy before escaping from it, whereas if he had a sound scientific education he would have been delivered from it at once.[2]

Thus, mysticism is accepted by Ghazali as a superior way to true happiness, but it must always be rooted in and remain under the control of trained reason. For this reason he uses mysticism to explain and modify the philosophic and religious-legal paths to happiness and at the same time clarifies the mystical approach through the use of Islamic teachings and the philosophic tradition. He points out continuously that the mystic must always observe religious law and practice, making this the sign of the first resting place of those who are travelling the road to God (*'alāmāt al-manzil al-awwal min manāzil al-sā'irīn*).[3] In Ghazali's view, the so-called earlier theorists of Sufism, such as al-Makkī, al-Sarrāj, and al-Qushayrī, did not fully succeed in their effort to reconcile mysticism with the tenets of Islam and at the same time clarify the mystical spiritual experiences. His own rational, theoretical explanation of these experiences is meant to give a clear account of them and, in addition, to synthesize or harmonize them with both Islamic and philosophic teachings in a homogeneous whole with a single ultimate end.[4]

1. *R*, IV. 3. 2316.

2. *C*, p. 46; cf. *R*, III. 1. 1379; Arberry, *Revelation and Reason in Islam*, (London: George Allen & Unwin, 1965), p. 110.

3. *C*, p. 204.

4. Ghazali's rational approach to mysticism in general was perceived and commented upon by some later Muslim thinkers as well as by his contemporaries. Ibn Taymiyyah, for example, states that "Ghazali was inclined toward philosophy, presented it in a mystical form, and expressed it in Islamic terminology" (Ibn Taymiyyah, *Naqḍ*, p. 56; *Radd*, p. 195). Abū Bakr Ibn al-'Arabī, a friend and one-time student of Ghazali, maintains that Ghazali had penetrated deeply into philosophy, and when he wanted to leave it, he could not. (Quoted by Ibn Taymiyyah in his *Muwāfaqat* I, 2.) On the basis of this statement, 'Abd al-Raḥmān Badawī concludes that Ghazali's

Characteristics of Mystical Virtues

It has already been mentioned in the Introduction to this study that the core of Ghazali's mystical doctrine can be considered not only an ethical theory but also a theory of virtue. Ghazali distinguishes between the "knowledge of revelation" and the "knowledge of devotional practice." The former, in his view, cannot and must not be expressed or laid down in writing. Since only the latter can be expressed, and because Ghazali equates that with ethics in general and virtue in particular, the study of Ghazali's mysticism means essentially the study of the mystical virtues. The few, with whom Ghazali is concerned, on the highest level of moral refinement, are the mystics whose end is not knowledge or paradise, but nearness to God. The special "qualities" which these few can acquire for their special kind of ultimate happiness, therefore, lie beyond the specific limits of philosophic and religious-legal virtues. These qualities of the few which we call "mystical virtues" are concerned in the first place with the spiritual well-being of the individual in his special relation to God.

Ghazali discusses these mystical virtues in Quarter IV of the *Revival*. He also deals with them in a summary way in the fourth part of the *Book of the Forty, Concerning the Principles of Religion* (*Kitāb al-Arbaʿīn fī Uṣūl al-Dīn*), which is an abridgement of the *Revival*. A longer summary in Persian known as the *Alchemy of Happiness* (*Kīmiyā-yi Saʿādat*) deals with the same mystical virtues. However, the number and the order of these virtues differ from one book to the other. The arrangement of

opposition to philosophy meant the rejection of Aristotelianism in favor of Neoplatonism; see his article "al-Ghazālī wa Maṣādiruh al-Yūnāniyyah," *Abū Ḥāmid al-Ghazālī fī al-Dhikrā al-Miʾawiyyah al-Tāsiʿah li Mīlādih*, ed. Zakī Najīb Maḥmūd (Cairo: al-Majlis al-Aʿlā li-Riʿāyat al-Funūn, 1961), pp. 221-37; the same article appeared in his book: *Dawr al-ʿArab fī Takwīn al-Fikr al-Awrubbī* (Beirut: Dār al-Ādāb, 1965), pp. 150-73. Simon van den Bergh, on the other hand, tries to trace Stoic and Neoplatonic sources for at least two mystical qualities discussed by Ghazali, namely, gratitude and love; see his articles, "Ghazali on 'Gratitude towards God' and its Greek sources," *Studia Islamica*, VII (1957), 77-98; and "The 'Love of God' in Ghazali's Vivification of Theology," *Journal of Semitic Studies*, I (1956), 305-321. Although inquiring into the possible Neoplatonic or Stoic philosophic origin of Ghazali's mysticism may be important and useful in clarifying certain issues, the first question which the student of Ghazali must face is not whether he borrowed this or that particular idea, but how he understands the views he holds and what use he makes of them. To answer this question, it is necessary to reconstruct and obtain a comprehensive view of Ghazali's thought and understand the way he synthesizes the different traditions whose sources are already present in the writings of Muslim philosophers, theologians, and mystics.

mystical virtues in these books is given in Table 2[1] (p. 159). Ghazali's various arrangements of mystical virtues can also be compared with those of other mystical writers who preceded him, such as al-Kharrāz, al-Sarrāj, al-Makkī, al-Kalābādhī, al-Qushayrī, and al-Anṣārī al-Harawī, which are given in the table of the Sufi's lists of mystical virtues (Table 3, p. 160).[2]

We pointed out in Chapter II above that Ghazali uses the expressions *khuluq ḥaṣan* and *khuluq maḥmūd* to mean the same things as *faḍīlah*, i.e., virtue. When dealing with the religious-legal virtues, however, he uses the first two terms more often than the third. This can be explained by the fact that, for the Islamic traditional moralists, virtue is known as *khuluq maḥmūd*, *khuluq ḥasan*, or *khuluq karīm*, while *faḍīlah* is the term commonly used by Muslim philosophers for virtue.[3] In dealing specifically with mystical virtues, Ghazali calls them "commendable character traits" (*akhlāq maḥmūdah*). In the introduction to the *Revival*, he says "As for 'The Quarter on Things Leading to Salvation (*Rub' al-Munjiyāt*)' I shall mention in it every commendable character trait (*khuluq maḥmūd*)";[4] and in the *Book of the Forty*, he uses the same expression as the title of the fourth part, which deals with the mystical virtues.[5] He also calls these mystical virtues the "qualities of salvation" (*al-ṣifāt al-munjiyāt*).[6]

1. The order of mystical virtues in the *Alchemy of Happiness* is given according to the Tehran edition (Ghazali, *Kīmiyā-yi Sa'ādat* [2 vols., 2d ed., Tehran: Kitāb-furūshī va Chāpkāne-yi Markazī, 1333/1954], II, 507-977); but according to Badawī the manuscript of the *Alchemy of Happiness* in Dār al-Kutub al-Miṣriyyah MSS, 13 Mysticism, has the same order of these virtues as the *Revival*; see Badawī's *Mu'allafāt*, p. 176.

2. Abū Sa'īd Aḥmad Ibn 'Īsā al-Kharrāz, *Kitāb al-Ṣidq*, ed. by 'Abd al-Ḥalīm Maḥmūd (Cairo: Dār al-Kutub al-Ḥadīthah, n.d.), pp. 24-87; Abū Naṣr al-Sarrāj, *Kitāb al-Luma'*, ed. by 'Abd al-Ḥalīm Maḥmūd and Ṭāha 'Abd al-Bāqī Surūr (Cairo: Dār al-Kutub al-Ḥadīthah, 1960), pp. 65-97; al-Makkī *Qūt*, I, 364ff., II, 1-164. Abū Bakr Muḥammad al-Kalābādhī, *al-Ta'arruf li-Madhhab Ahl al-Taṣawwuf*, ed. by 'Abd al-Ḥalīm Maḥmūd and Ṭāha 'Abd al-Bāqī Surūr (Cairo: 'Isā al-Bābī al-Ḥalabī, 1966), pp. 86-134; Abū al-Qāsim 'Abd al-Karīm al-Qushayrī, *al-Risālah*, ed. by 'Abd al-Ḥalīm Maḥmūd and Maḥmūd bin al-Sharīf (2 vols.; Cairo: Dār al-Kutub al-Ḥadīthah, 1966), I, 252-408, II, 421-632; 'Abd Allāh al-Anṣārī al-Harawī, *Manāzil al-Sā'irīn*, ed. by S. de Laugier de Beaurecueil (Cairo: Imprimerie de l'Institut Français d'Archéologie Orientale, 1962), pp. 9-113.

3. Bishr Fāris, *Mabāḥith 'Arabiyyah* (Cairo Maṭba'at al-Ma'ārif, 1939), pp. 21-31, where he discusses the term *khuluq karīm* and gives an account of the traditions about *makārim al-akhlāq*.

4. *R*, p. 4; cf. *R*, I. 1. 36.

5. *Arba'īn*, p. 175.

6. *R*, IV. 9. 2811.

Furthermore, he calls these virtues "stations" or "stages" (*maqāmāt*), terms which are more at home in the mystical tradition.[1] Thus, to identify virtue, Ghazali moves from *faḍīlah*, which is more commonly used by the philosophers, to *khuluq ḥaṣan* or *khuluq maḥmūd*, which are preferred by the Islamic traditional moralists, to *ṣifah* and *maqām*, which are better known to the mystics. The term *khuluq ḥaṣan*, however, seems to be the central expression which connects all the other terms, since it is used throughout Ghazali's treatment of philosophic, religious-legal, and mystical virtues.

Ghazali's identification of the virtues, character traits, and qualities of salvation is more than mere terminological usage. The mystical qualities, like the philosophic virtues, comprise the means to attain happiness. The philosophers understood passions as the stuff of virtue. Yet, most of the mystical qualities (in particular fear, hope, and love) are basically passions. Love, the last of these, is the highest mystical virtue man can acquire during his life.

According to Aristotle, the passions are: "desire, anger, fear, confidence, envy, joy, friendship, hatred, longing, jealousy, pity, and generally those states of consciousness which are accompanied by pleasure or pain."[2] He argues that:

> Neither the virtues nor the vices are passions, because we are not called good or bad on the ground of our passions, but are so called on the ground of our virtues and our vices, and because we are neither praised nor blamed for our passions (for the man who feels fear or anger is not praised, nor the man who feels anger blamed, but the man who feels it in a certain way), but for our virtues and our vices we are praised or blamed.[3]

Only when a passion is felt in a certain way can it become a virtue. Virtue is a state of character. It is concerned with passions and actions, in which both excess and deficiency are blamed, while the intermediate is praised and is a form of success; and being praised and being successful are both characteristic of virtue, which is a state of character concerned with choice, lying in a mean relative to us.[4]

Ghazali follows this Aristotelian approach when dealing with the philosophic virtues, as we saw in Chapter II above.[5] But when dealing

1. *R*, IV. 2. 2179.
2. Aristotle *Nicomachean Ethics* 2. 5. 1105b20-22.
3. Aristotle *Nicomachean Ethics* 2. 5. 1105b29-1106a2.
4. Aristotle *Nicomachean Ethics* 2. 5. 1105b25-35.
5. *R*, III. 2. 1441.

with mystical virtues, he diverges sharply from it. Making use of the more elaborate and detailed treatment of the passions in Aristotle's *Rhetoric*,[1] Ghazali takes the same passions which are used as the basis for the philosophic virtues, and looks at them in the light of his views of nearness to God. This is the genesis of Ghazali's "new" virtues which we have called mystical. For example, because the philosophers regard death as the object of the greatest human fear, they conclude that fear is a defect for which the corresponding virtue is courage. Ghazali, on the other hand, looks at the same passion in the light of man's relation to God, who ought to be feared both in this life and the next, and concludes that the right state of character is "fear of God." Thus the passions are raised to higher levels beyond the usual low rank assigned to them in the treatment of "philosophic virtues." In the same way, Ghazali frequently takes a disposition generally understood in terms of man's relation with his fellow men, abstracts it from the political context, and reformulates it in terms of his concept of nearness to God. For example, he takes "trust" as exercised by man toward his fellow men, and modifies it in terms of man's special relation to God, thus establishing the mystical virtue of "trust in God."

In addition, Ghazali establishes these mystical virtues through methods similar to those by which the philosophic virtues are established. The only change he introduces concerns the object and the end of virtue. The ultimate end, according to him, necessitates purifying the soul and freeing it from the body as far as possible, so that it may devote itself entirely to the highest passion, namely, love of God. Since this highest passion is private, the end of the mystical virtues transcends political activity: they free man, not only from the body, but from the city as well.

After establishing the mystical qualities as virtues, Ghazali emphasizes what he calls their basic characteristics. In his view, each one of these virtues comprises three elements which follow one another consecutively. The first is knowledge, which produces the second, a positive disposition (*ḥāl*), which in turn causes the third, action.[2] This distinction reflects

1. Aristotle *Rhetoric* 2. 1. 1378a-11. 1389a. It is likely that Ghazali had access to the discussion of the passions in the writings of Avicenna. See, e.g., Avicenna's *Fī al-Akhlāq wa al-Infi'ālāt al-Nafsāniyyah* in *Memorial Avicenna* IV *Miscellanea*, contribution de M. L. Massignon, Mme Denise Remondon et M. G. Vatom (Cairo: Publications de l'Institut Français d'Archeologie Orientale, 1954), pp. 23-26.

2. Ghazali mentions these common characteristics in several places in Quarter IV of the *Revival*; cf. *R*, IV. 2. 2179, 2305. I have translated *ḥāl* here as a "positive disposition" rather than "a state" because in this context Ghazali means by *ḥāl* a per-

Ghazali's independence from earlier Sufi accounts of these virtues inasmuch as he uses nonmystical doctrines to explain mystical notions. This kind of analysis of the essential components of the mystical virtues obviously belongs to the philosophic tradition. However, whereas he enumerated four basic elements in connection with the philosophic virtues—namely, faculty, knowledge, positive disposition, and action—he eliminates the category, faculty, in relation to the mystical virtues. He does not give his reasons for doing so. One can only assume that, while a psychic faculty is of importance in a system which depends primarily on unaided reason, it is of secondary importance in relation to a discipline which relies on divine assistance. Moreover, in his discussion of philosophic virtue, Ghazali maintains that virtue applies only to the positive disposition from among the four above-mentioned elements, whereas here he considers three of these as necessary components of mystical virtues. It seems that Ghazali's emphasis on all the three basic elements, here, is a theoretical orientation which he introduces into his discussion in order to clarify these mystical virtues, which are usually extremely vague in the mystical manuals. Nonetheless, in the course of his detailed discussion of some of these virtues, Ghazali himself singles out the positive disposition as that which is most properly called virtue; knowledge is something which leads to it, and action is its product.[1]

Ghazali's independence from earlier Sufi accounts is also revealed in his manipulation of mystical terminology. Although he chooses certain technical terms current in mystical literature, he tends to define them in his own way. Station (*maqām*) was usually distinguished by earlier mystics from state (*ḥāl*). According to al-Qushayrī, a station signifies a spiritual plateau in the novice's progress to God, which is the result of the mystic's personal effort and endeavor, whereas a state is a spiritual mood depending, not upon the mystic, but upon God: " 'States' are gifts; while 'stations' are earnings."[2] In general, Sufi authors insist upon the effort of the soul as it approaches the station, just as they emphasize the received character of the state. Furthermore, stations are

manent character trait in the soul and not "a passing state." *Ḥāl*, here, is similar to the term *hay'ah*, which Ghazali uses in his discussion of the philosophic virtues. *Hay'ah* is also a positive disposition which results from knowledge and, in turn, produces action; cf. *R*, III. 2. 1441.

1. *R*, IV. 2. 2180, where Ghazali applies the term "patience" to the "positive disposition."

2. al-Qushayrī, *Risālah*, I, 193.

permanent, while states are transitory.[1] Al-Sarrāj, the author of a well-known early Sufi manual, regards stations as moral habits and states as psychological conditions of mind.[2] According to Ghazali, in contrast, the difference between states and stations is one of degree and not of kind. When a character trait of the soul becomes permanent and persists, it is a station; if, on the other hand, it occurs sporadically, it is a state.[3] This definition is reiterated in the *Dictation* (*al-Imlā'*), a book Ghazali wrote to defend the *Revival* and explain the mystical terms used in it.[4] This view of states and stations shows that only stations can be regarded as virtues, since stability is an essential characteristic of virtue. It is for this reason that Ghazali calls mystical virtues stations.[5]

Because of the fact that various stations and states are closely related to each other, and each Sufi has his own doctrine of spiritual refinement, mystical writers differ with regard to the definition and arrangement of these stations and states.[6] Ghazali, likewise, presents his own arrangement of these stations, but he does not enumerate a specific number of them as do some of the Sufi writers who preceded him. (Al-Makkī, for instance, maintains that they are nine).[7] Nevertheless, Ghazali preserves the notion of order or hierarchy in mystical virtues, that is, which virtue must be acquired first, which one should follow, and, finally, which is the highest virtue which one can acquire. He agrees with most of the earlier Sufis in regarding "repentance" (*tawbah*) as the first station for the novice. At the other pole, he follows al-Makkī in regarding love (*maḥabbah*) as the highest station possible for man in this life. In his view, repentance, patience, gratitude, hope, fear, poverty, asceticism, divine unity, and trust, in this order, all lead to love; whereas yearning, intimacy, and satisfaction are the fruits (*thimār*) or the by-products of love.[8]

1. L. Gardet, "Ḥāl, "*EI*², II, 83.
2. al-Sarrāj, *Luma'*, pp. 65-66; cf. al-Hujwīrī, *The Kashf al-Maḥjūb*, trans. by Reynold A. Nicholson (Leyden: E.J. Brill, 1911), p.. 180-81.
3. *R*, IV. 3. 2316.
4. Ghazali, *al-Imlā' 'alā Ishkālāt al-Iḥyā'* in *Mulḥaq Iḥyā' 'Ulūm al-Dīn* (Cairo: al-Maktabah al-Tijāriyyah al-Kubrā, n.d.), p. 16.
5. For example, he calls them the "stations of those who travel the way to God" (*maqāmāt al-sālikīn*) (*R*, IV. 3. 2316), and the "stations of religion" (*maqāmāt al-dīn*) (*R*, IV. 3. 2360). By religion (*dīn*), Ghazali says, "we mean the relation of devotional practice (*mu'āmalah*) between man and his Lord" (*R*, IV. 9. 2810).
6. Shihāb al-Dīn al-Suhrawardī, *'Awārif al-Ma'ārif* in *Mulḥaq Iḥyā' 'Ulūm al-Dīn*, p. 225.
7. al-Makkī, *Qūt*, I, 364.
8. *R*, IV. 6. 2580.

These virtues, which are also known as stations, are the principal mystical virtues because they are presented as the major plateaus to be reached by the few in their pursuit of ultimate happiness. In this, Ghazali agrees with al-Makkī.

In addition to these mystical virtues, Ghazali enumerates six more qualities of the soul which he does not specifically call stations. These are not presented by al-Makkī as stations, although he deals with some of them as separate and independent mystical attributes.[1] Nevertheless, they are mystical virtues in the sense that they are attributes and qualities of salvation which must be acquired by the mystic. According to Ghazali, these six mystical virtues can be classified in three groups. They are ordered as follows: resolve, sincerity, truthfulness; vigilance, self-examination; and finally, meditation.

Ghazali deals with these six virtues at the end of the *Revival*, after completing his discussion of love and its by-products. There is no transition in his presentation between love and resolve, the first of these virtues. Indeed, he does not mention any of the six mystical virtues when describing the order of the virtues that lead to love of God.[2] In the *Alchemy of Happiness*, however, Ghazali (who orders these six virtues in the same way as in the *Revival*) places all of them after "asceticism" and before "divine unity,"[3] but in the *Book of the Forty*, Ghazali places the first three of these virtues between gratitude and trust, and does not mention the other three virtues at all.[4] That Ghazali moves these six virtues back and forth together and that in every case he presents them as a group in the same order, suggests that they form a cohesive group somehow outside the principal mystical virtues. Ghazali describes the mystical virtues in question as a means of bringing about, supporting, and perfecting the principal mystical virtues. In this respect they pertain equally to all principal mystical virtues. Thus, a man may be truthful in his repentance and, when he acquires love, he may become truthful in his love. Finally, although this group of mystical virtues shares with the principal mystical virtues the characteristic of being directed toward

1. al-Makkī, *Qūt*, II, 311, where he discusses "sincerity."

2. *R*, IV. 6. 2580. The six mystical virtues in question are discussed in Books, 7, 8, and 9 of the fourth Quarter of the *Revival*. The arrangement is the same in *RB*. and *RM*.

3. *Kīmiyā-yi*, I. 855-911. However, Badawī quotes a Cairo manuscript of the same work (Dār al-Kutub al-Miṣriyyah MSS, 13 Mysticism) as having the same order Ghazali assigns to these six mystical virtues in the *Revival*; see his *Mu'allafāt*, p. 176.

4. *Arba'īn*, pp. 206-217.

God, they seem to be primarily concerned with the internal relationships of the faculties within the soul.

Therefore, the basic characteristic of these six mystical virtues is to prepare the way and provide the psychological basis for the major mystical virtues. To distinguish between these two groups, we call the major ones principal mystical virtues and the others supporting mystical virtues. The function of these supporting mystical virtues in preparing the soul for the fulfillment of a perfect acquisition of each principal virtue suggests the desirability of dealing with them first.

Supporting Mystical Virtues

We mentioned above that these mystical virtues are particularly concerned with the internal relationships of the faculties of the soul. They make it submissive and obedient to the will of God, and enable the mystic to struggle against the whims of the soul and seek its purification so that it can ascend through the spiritual "stations." These six supporting mystical virtues can be divided into three groups following Ghazali's own division in the *Revival.* The first includes resolve (*niyyah*), sincerity (*ikhlāṣ*), and truthfulness (*ṣidq*), all of which are the subject of Book 7 of Quarter IV of the *Revival.* The second group is composed of vigilance (*murāqabah*) and self-examination (*muḥāsabah*), dealt with in Book 8 of Quarter IV of the *Revival.* The third is meditation (*tafakkur*) which is the sole subject of Book 9 of Quarter IV of the same work.

Resolve

This is the first of the three virtues in the first group; it is inseparable from the other two since according to Ghazali resolve is useless without sincerity, and sincerity is nothing unless truthfulness is connected to it and perfects it.[1] For him, resolve is the basis of action in that action needs a special resolve to become good; resolve, however, is good in itself even if no action results from it. Although Ghazali says that resolve, will (*irādah*), and intention (*qaṣd*) are all words which are used to mean one and the same thing, his assertion that it is good with or without action suggests that he means by resolve "good intention." In this he is clearly thinking of resolve in terms of *niyyah* as understood in Islamic law, especially in connection with performing religious ritual duties.

1. *R*, IV. 7. 2694; cf. *Arba'īn*, p. 206, where he says that "sincerity" has three elements which lead to one another, namely, resolve, sincerity, and truthfulness.

For example, the first principal obligation with regard to the act of prayer is *niyyah* in the sense of deciding in one's mind what kind of prayer this is and that it is for the sake of God. It is because of this usage that Ghazali says that resolve is a virtue confirmed by the Koran and prophetic tradition.[1]

As a mystical virtue, resolve is composed of the three elements characteristic of mystical virtues, namely, knowledge, positive disposition, and action, but Ghazali modifies the terminology slightly here to emphasize its resemblance to the states of the soul. Thus, will replaces the positive disposition, and power the action, whereas knowledge is the same. When man knows with certainty that something is valuable and must be done, then the will for doing it emerges and, in turn, incites the powers which move the members of the body to action. Since Ghazali equates resolve with will, this means that he identifies resolve as a mystical virtue with the positive disposition.[2] The relation between resolve as a positive disposition and the action which results from it is of special interest to Ghazali. In his view, voluntary action may be done because of either one or two motives. When there are two motives for an action, the second motive may be a comotive, an associate, or an aid. After describing the relationships possible between resolve and action in terms of the motive or motives of an action, Ghazali interprets the prophetic tradition, "the resolve of the believer is better than his action" as supporting his view that resolve without action is superior to action without resolve.[3] He intends thereby to establish the view that the activities of the soul or the heart (*a'māl al-qalb*) are more important than the actions of the members of the body. Moreover, among the states of the soul, resolve is regarded as the most excellent because it means the inclination of the soul to what is good.[4]

For resolve to be a mystical virtue, the mystic must have the necessary knowledge which leads to it; he will not acquire the resolve for

1. *R*, IV. 7. 2694.

2. *R*, IV. 7. 2700.

3. *R*, IV. 7. 2702; however, al-Ḥāfiẓ al-'Irāqī in his *Mughnī*, p. 2702, says that the prophetic tradition quoted by Ghazali is "weak" (*ḍa'īf*).

4. *R*, IV. 7. 2704. According to Ghazali, resolve plays different roles in relation to the different kinds of actions. If the action in question is that of disobedience and evil, having a resolve for it does not make it good. However, resolve is necessary with respect to actions of obedience, without which they cannot be good. Finally, resolve elevates permissible action to the level of those that bring man near to God; cf. *R*, IV. 7. 2708-2710.

doing something merely by uttering the words expressing his intention to act. Ghazali insists that the mystic must give undivided attention to all the actions he contemplates doing and must act only after truly resolving to undertake a particular thing. Some men resolve to do good deeds out of fear and others out of hope. But once a man has attained spiritual refinement, he will intend by all his actions the pleasure of God alone.[1]

Sincerity

When an action is motivated by one intention alone, the state of the soul is called sincerity, that is, single-mindedness in purpose, whether the purpose is good or bad. But in Islamic religious terminology the word "sincerity" (*ikhlāṣ*) is used only when the intention is nearness to God, unadulterated by any wordly or selfish motive. Ghazali points out that the merit and excellence of sincerity is confirmed by the Koran and prophetic tradition. Particularly important in his view are the verses which deal with Satan's power in leading men astray because, according to the Koran, all men are considered potential victims of the devil's intrigues, with the sole exception of those who are sincere.[2]

As a mystical virtue, sincerity means that man's actions are only motivated by a desire to approach God. In other words, sincerity requires that there be one basic resolve for man's actions. When this is mixed with other intentions, such as when a person fasts for the sake of health as well as for reverence, the situation becomes complicated. To attain sincerity means to transcend the pleasures of this world and to dedicate one's life to the world to come. When an action is not purely for the sake of God, but mixed with some worldly desires, it cannot be characterized by sincerity.[3] Therefore, while remorse means good intention, sincerity means specifically intending nearness to God as the basic and sole resolve which stands behind all of man's actions.

Truthfulness

Truthfulness is the last of the three virtues of the first group of supporting mystical virtues. Ghazali enumerates six aspects of truthfulness

1. *R*, IV. 7. 2716.
2. *R*, IV. 7. 2721; cf. Koran 38:82-83: "Satan said: 'Then by Thy power, I will beguile them all, save Thy sincere servants among them.' "
3. *R*, IV. 7. 2724-31.

in general, namely, truthfulness in speech, in intention, in resolution, in executing a resolution, in action, and in accomplishing all the spiritual "stations," i.e., the principal mystical virtues. Although we are primarily concerned with the last aspect of truthfulness, a very brief statement about each of the first five may be helpful: (1) Truthfulness in speech consists in making a statement which is not only true but is also unequivocal, so that the person who hears it cannot interpret it in a different way, and this is the first kind of perfect truthfulness in speech, with certain exceptions being permitted in those situations when telling the truth may cause harm.[1] The second kind requires that man observe truthfulness in the words he uses when he is conversing (*munājāh*) with God. He should not use any word unless he knows that it truly expresses his spiritual state. This truthfulness reaches ultimate perfection when the person becomes free from all worldly things and occupies himself completely with God.[2] (2) Truthfulness in intention is related to sincerity in that it applies to the case when man has only one aim for whatever he does and in that this aim is nearness to God. (3) Truthfulness related to a resolution (*'azm*) means the intention to accomplish a lofty purpose which is contingent upon circumstances which do not presently exist, e.g., to resolve that "should an occasion present itself, I will gladly lay down my life in the service of God." The truthful man is he whose resolution for all good things is always accomplished with full power and no hesitation. (4) Truthfulness in the execution of a resolution requires that when the time to act arrives one carries out what he has resolved to do. (5) Truthful action lies in the perfect correspondence of the inward state of the person with his outward action without the slightest indication of hypocrisy.[3] (6) The highest truthfulness is that which accompanies the full and complete realization of the various mystical stations such as fear, hope, asceticism satisfaction, trust, and love.[4] Since each of these stations has a beginning and a higher limit, truthfulness in each of them means to reach their utmost limits. Thus when a man reaches perfection with regard to repentance, he acquires truthfulness in repentance. In this sense one

1. *R*, IV. 7. 2738; Ghazali mentions three occasions in which one is allowed to compromise with untruth; they are: war tactics, restoring good relations between two people, and keeping good relations between husband and wife.

2. *R*, IV. 7. 2739.

3. *R*, IV. 7. 2740-42.

4. *R*, IV. 7. 2744.

can speak of "truthful fear," "truthful hope," and so on. It is rare, however,to find a mystic who has attained truthfulness with regard to all the principal mystical virtues. But when such a person is found, he is the "truthful one" (*ṣiddīq*) who has attained the highest virtuous station possible for a human being on this earth.[1]

Vigilance and Self-Examination

The fourth and fifth supporting mystical virtues form the second group. They are related to each other because both apply to the states of the soul in its inner struggle against its baser faculties. Attainment of vigilance and self-examination as mystical virtues requires knowledge of God and of the day of judgment. When man knows that he has to account for everything he does in this life, he will watch over his desires and examine his motives so as to guard against what may bring God's wrath upon him in the hereafter.[2]

In order to understand Ghazali's analysis of these two mystical virtues, it is necessary to know what he means by "self" (*nafs*) in this context. In his discussion of the soul in Book 1 of Quarter III of the *Revival* which is an introduction to the second half of the whole work, Ghazali says that "self" has two meanings. One is the meaning which applies to the faculties of anger and appetite; this he says is the usage common among the Sufis who mean by "self" the source of evil qualities in man, and therefore man must strive against it. The second meaning is synonymous with "soul."[3] According to Ghazali the virtues of vigilance and self-examination are two of six steps which man has to go through in his struggle to subdue his "self" as understood in its Sufi meaning: (1) The first step, known as preconditioning (*mushāraṭah*), is to assign special duties to the self for the purpose of purifying it. This step helps man to know what to expect from his self. (2) Vigilance (*murāqabah*) is the second step in which man watches over the execution of what he has assigned to his self. (Literally, *murāqabah* means to watch another; here, however, it means being alive to the conviction that God sees man even if man does not see Him.) The knowledge that God knows everything that lurks in man's heart as well as everything that he does, brings about the positive disposition of vigilance which, in turn, produces actual watching over one's self. There are two degrees of vigilance: the

1. *R*, IV. 7. 2745.
2. *R*, IV. 8. 2749.
3. *R*, III. 1. 1351.

higher consists in being fully occupied with observing God's majesty alone. This degree of vigilance is restricted to the activities of the soul, to the exclusion of the actions of the body. For Ghazali, this is the degree of those who are near to God (*muqarrabūn*) and who are altogether oblivious to everything other than God. They do not perform even permissible bodily actions and hence they are in no need to watch over such actions. The lower degree of vigilance is that of men of piety who are fully conscious that God knows everything about them, both their inward and outward activities, and they do not execute any act except after making sure that it is religiously approved. It is because of this that men of piety are in constant vigilance over their outward actions. Thus, the basic requirement for both degrees of vigilance is to make certain that one's activities, whether inward or outward, are carried out for the sake of God and in accordance to His satisfaction.[1] (3) The third step that man must take in his struggle to subdue his "self" is self-examination (*muḥāsabah*). Thus, the second of the two virtues in question here follows the first immediately. After executing the action, man must examine in detail how far it has been fulfilled in accordance with the conditions originally imposed on the self and, in particular, to what extent errors entered into the action.[2]

In the restricted sense, self-examination does not go beyond giving a detailed account of all aspects of the finished action; however, the realization of shortcomings automatically calls forth the last three steps essential to subdue the self. Thus, if one finds that his self has committed mistakes, he should not be lax in chastising it; otherwise it will transgress more easily the next time. (4) Punishment (*mu'āqabah*), therefore, should immediately follow the realization that a transgression has been committed. It should be appropriate to the transgression; e.g., if a man has eaten food from a dubious source, he should punish himself by hunger. (5) The fifth step is known as striving for virtuous purification (*mujāhadah*). If one finds that his self did not commit any vice and is only deficient in fully executing virtuous actions, then he must force it to do more difficult and severe actions of this same variety. In the event that he finds this too difficult, he can overcome his weakness by accompanying pious men or, if none are to be found, by reading reports about

1. *R*, IV. 8. 2754-64.

2. *R*, IV. 8. 2767-70. Ghazali's discussion of self-examination is influenced by al-Muḥāsibī, see Josef van Ess, *Die Gedankenwelt des Ḥārit al-Muḥāsibī* (Bonn: Das Orientalische Seminar der Universität Bonn, 1961), pp. 139-43.

their experiences.[1] (6) The final step for subduing the lower faculties of the soul is continuous reproach (*mu'ātabah*). According to Ghazali, the "self," i.e., anger and appetite, is the most invidious enemy against which man must constantly guard. Thus, in addition to the five above-mentioned steps of controlling and examining the activities of the self, man must rebuke it so that it remains subjugated to the rational part of the soul. The way to rebuke the self (*tawbīkh al-nafs wa mu'ātabatihā*) is to stress its ignorance, inferiority, and insignificance. Ghazali quotes at length an account of the manner in which unnamed earlier learned men (*al-qawm*)used to reproach and rebuke their selves.[2]

It is significant that in his treatment of vigilance and self-examination, Ghazali follows the philosophic analysis of the soul, particularly the distinction between the rational faculty on the one hand, and the concupiscent and irascible faculties on the other. He identifies the "self" with the two lower faculties and examines and explains the mystical way of purifying the soul on this basis. This approach clarifies the mystical teachings with respect to self-examination and other related psychic experiences which otherwise are ambiguous and vague.

Meditation

Ghazali considers meditation a major element underlying all the virtues related to the special states of the soul and, consequently, to all the mystical virtues. Meditation, according to Ghazali, is the source of all three of the characteristics which the mystical virtues have in common: it produces knowledge, which in turn, produces the positive disposition of the soul that brings about action.[3] Ghazali uses the two terms *tafakkur* and *fikr* to mean meditation; however, in order to preserve his distinction in terminology, we shall render the latter term as "reflection." According to Ghazali, reflection consists of bringing together two ideas in order to produce from them a third one, e.g., in

1. *R*, IV. 8. 2770-84. This explains why Ghazali mentions a large number of stories about the way earlier prophets and mystics purified their soul.

2. *R*, IV. 8. 2789ff. In its form, style, and sometimes even content, this account corresponds to the *Book of Rebuking the Self* (*Kitāb Mu'ādhalat al-Nafs*), which belongs to the Hermetic literature (cf. Badawī, "Al-Ghazālī wa Maṣādiruh," pp. 225-29). It is said that the Sufi Dhū al-Nūn al-Miṣrī (d. 861) was familiar with Hermetic wisdom (Arberry, *Sufism*, p. 50). If this is so, then Ghazali may have had some access to such Hermetic writings through this mystic whom he mentions in many places in the *Revival* as well as in other works.

3. *R*, IV. 9. 2808.

order to know that (3) the hereafter is more worthy of choice, one has to know that (1) eternal things are better objects of choice, and (2) that the hereafter is eternal.[1] This syllogistic reasoning, in Ghazali's view, depends both on man's having some knowledge to start with as well as being acquainted with the process by which a conclusion is produced. When a conclusion is reached, it can, in turn, be joined to another proposition for the sake of producing yet another conclusion; and this syllogistic process goes on until it is terminated by death.

Ghazali emphasizes the importance of reflection by quoting the prophetic tradition "An hour's meditation is more excellent than a year's worship."[2] Since everything can be an object of meditation, to enumerate such objects would be an impossible task. The only possible approach is to investigate in general the ways of reflecting about objects, especially as they relate to the mystical "stations." With respect to the spiritual practice directed toward God, reflection may be either about man, his character qualities, and states, or about God, His attributes, and His works.[3]

In Ghazali's view, the most important kind of meditation that man must engage in with respect to himself is to reflect upon his character traits and actions in order to distinguish what is good from what is bad. The good and the bad are in turn divided into external and internal qualities, and thus four themes result from this division: acts of obedience, acts of disobedience, qualities that lead to salvation, and qualities that lead to destruction. The first two are related to the religious-legal duties. The qualities that lead to salvation must be carefully considered in order to find out what is essential in bringing man nearer to God, whereas reflection on the qualities that lead to destruction helps man to avoid what impedes nearness to God. This outline of meditations on character qualities and actions reflects the general theme of the *Revival.*[4] It shows how the *Revival* can help man to effective reflection on himself. But Ghazali maintains that this reflection, though superior to other acts of worship, is not the true aim of the few who seek God alone and occupy their souls with Him to the point of being unconscious of themselves and of their mystical states. These few meditate only on God's majesty and greatness.

1. *R*, IV. 9. 2806-2807.
2. *R*, IV. 9. 2803.
3. *R*, IV. 9. 2810.
4. *R*, IV. 9. 2810-14. In his enumeration of these qualities Ghazali indicates the Quarter and Book of the *Revival* where they can be found.

Now, reflection on God's majesty and greatness can be achieved in two ways. The highest is to meditate on the essence of God, His attributes, and the meaning of His glorious names. But since the human intellect is so limited that it cannot grasp the reality of God directly, Ghazali asserts that men have been forbidden to follow this higher method.[1] Instead, they are advised to reflect on God's mysterious and wonderful works as manifested in His creations because all these show His glory, majesty, knowledge, and power. Ghazali divides created things into two categories. The first includes those which cannot be known at all and consequently man cannot reflect on them. The second category includes things which can be known. Some of these, however, cannot be seen with the eye, such as angels, genii, and Satan. Others, such as the sky, the earth, and what is between them, can be seen with the eye. To reflect on these works of God for the sake of knowing Him, one should begin by reflecting on his own being, and then proceed to the wonders of the universe.[2] As a mystical virtue, meditation is the means through which the soul performs its "natural" role of reflecting on the highest truth. Since this can only be expected of a soul which has subjugated its lower faculties, meditation is a virtue which ranks higher than self-examination, and indeed is the highest of the supporting mystical virtues.

The discussion of these virtues shows that we are dealing here with a special kind of psychological ethics, one which aims at nearness to God. Ghazali associates these virtues particularly with the states of the soul as he endeavors to establish a psychological basis for the principal mystical virtues. In so doing, he clearly adheres to the analysis of the soul as understood in the philosophic tradition. His study of the first three supporting virtues, namely, resolve, sincerity, and truthfulness, is primarily a study of intentions. The fourth and fifth, i.e., vigilance and self-examination, are related to the analysis of appetite and anger and, consequently, to the method of subordinating them to the rational faculty. The sixth virtue, meditation, is connected with the rational faculty and shows the role of this faculty in helping the one who seeks God by reflecting on His creation. The attainment of these supporting mystical virtues, therefore, brings about a complete and integrated state of the soul in all its faculties. This state can be the basis which

1. *R*, IV. 9. 2820.
2. *R*, IV. 9. 2822-44.

prepares the few to acquire the principal mystical virtues and, ultimately, achieve nearness to God.

Principal Mystical Virtues

These are the mystical qualities which Ghazali calls "stations" in order to underline the importance of their hierarchy. Each of these virtues is looked at as a consequence of the one which precedes it and as a step which leads to the one after it. The first principal mystical virtue in Ghazali's hierarchy is "repentance" and the highest is "love." Between these two he arranges the rest of the mystical virtues in such a way as to help the mystic in the end to acquire "love." Most of the earlier mystics paid great attention to the arrangements of mystical stations, and emphasized that the mystic cannot acquire a station unless he has mastered the one which precedes it. But these earlier mystics differed in their arrangements of such stations. In his treatment Ghazali takes issue with the earlier mystics, including al-Makkī, not only in his arrangement of these stations, but also in the way he defines and justifies them. Unlike the earlier mystical authors who do not usually go beyond registering their own experiences or the experiences of other famous mystics about these stations, Ghazali explains the essential elements of each station and emphasizes the role this station plays in the mystical refinement of the few. He takes into consideration those special characteristics we mentioned in the introduction to this chapter and thereby provides a coherent framework for these mystical virtues and clarifies their precise nature which was often left vague in the writings of earlier mystics. The significance of these general remarks will become clear if we examine the way Ghazali analyzes each of the principal mystical virtues.

Repentance

Repentance (*tawbah*), which is the starting point of the path of those who seek God, i.e., the mystics, is the first principal virtue that must be acquired by the few.[1] Repentance here means a kind of conversion, a conscious resolve on the part of the novice to abandon worldly life and devote himself completely to the service of God. It is thus that Ghazali

1. *R*, IV. 1. 2078. Repentance is the subject of the first book of the fourth quarter of the *Revival*. It is the first of the "Things Leading to Salvation" in the *Revival* as well as in the *Book of the Forty* and the *Alchemy of Happiness*.

himself, after achieving a great reputation as a jurist and a theologian, turned away from formal religious learning and declared himself to be a Sufi.[1]

According to the Islamic religious teachings, the repentance which is required of Muslims is the abandoning of any action which violates the religious law and resolving not to commit a similar act in the future. Furthermore, the Muslim must atone for his sins in the special way prescribed by the religious tradition. The meaning of repentance as a mystical virtue, however, extends beyond this. Ghazali applies it to actions other than those which are merely violations of the religious law. In this sense, repentance means abondoning everything which stands between man and his ultimate goal of nearness to God. The mystic must repent for doing anything or thinking of anything other than what leads to this goal.

Instead of appealing to an eminent Sufi for definition of repentance, as was the procedure of earlier mystical writers, Ghazali formulates his own definition of this virtue by considering how it is composed of the three elements he established as characteristic of all mystical virtues, namely, knowledge, positive disposition, and action.

> The knowledge is the recognition of the great harmfulness of sins, and of the fact that they are the veil between man and all he loves. If his knowledge of this is certain and sure, and his heart is convinced, there springs from his knowledge a heartfelt pain for the loss of what he loves . . . The name we give this pain caused by an action which resulted in the loss of the beloved, is remorse (*nadam*). If this pain constrains the heart and holds it in thrall, then it produces . . . resolve to act.[2]

Knowledge, remorse, and resolve are three distinct elements which make up a single complex notion. The term "repentance" properly refers to the whole notion, although often it is used to mean remorse only, that is, the positive disposition. Repentance looks to the past in terms of renouncing a sin, and to the present and future in terms of resolving to accomplishing reparation.

Ghazali maintains that all men should acquire the virtue of repentance in the broad sense, and that both reason and religious teachings confirm this obligation. Tradition must guide those whose rational capacity is not yet fully developed; however, men of intellect will perceive by themselves that true happiness consists in nearness to God and that repentance is essential to achieve this nearness. Ghazali maintains further that

1. *Munqidh*, pp. 98-102; cf. Arberry, *Sufism*, p. 75.
2. *R*, IV. 1. 2080.

repentance is an obligation for man as man, because it is of the essence of the human soul that it is made up of higher and lower faculties. The perfection of the soul occurs when the rational faculty subordinates the concupiscent and irascible faculties to its control, and it is not the simple destruction of these lower faculties. Repentance is a perpetual obligation and has its basis in the eternal tension between good and evil (i.e., domination of the soul by its higher or lower faculties) which characterizes the human condition. Ghazali here goes beyond traditional Islamic teachings which require repentance when a specific sin has been committed. Unlike the Christian understanding of repentance based on original sin inherited from Adam, Ghazali explains his doctrine in terms of a psychological analysis of human nature which is derived from the philosophic tradition.[1]

Because repentance means basically to refrain from committing sins, Ghazali regards knowledge of what a sin is to be crucial for the realization of this virtue. In general, sin includes anything which distorts the relation between man and God. There are various kinds of sins and various ways of avoiding and atoning for them. The variety of sins gave rise to the famous theological debates about grave and venial sins (*al-kabīrah wa al-ṣaghīrah*), which were current among the early Islamic schools of dialectical theology (*kalām*). Dissatisfied with the earlier views, Ghazali argues that since the ultimate aim of the religious law, which is to lead men to God, can only occur as a result of knowing Him and His prophets, and since such knowledge can only be attained in this life, therefore both preservation of life and knowledge of God are essential for attaining nearness to Him. Whatever obstructs knowledge of God is infidelity and should be considered the gravest sin, followed by any act which shortens man's life or deprives man of what he needs to preserve his life, such as theft, etc.[2]

After realizing what sins are, man must repent immediately. He should recall all his past sins, reflect upon them one by one, minute by minute, and discard each and every one. If a man has, for example, neglected any religious duty, he should discharge it. For sins against God, one should grieve and seek pardon from Him. If there are sins against one's fellow man, one should atone for them all. If one has injured another he should comfort him and make up for his suffering. If one

1. *R*, IV. 1. 2081.
2. *R*, IV. 1. 2103-2110.

has deprived anyone of his possessions, one should restore what he took and ask for forgiveness. According to Ghazali, atonement for sins can be made through the heart, speech, or the body. Atonement by the heart is the core of repentance. It is done by seeking forgiveness from God. By speech one atones by acknowledging transgression and by reciting formulae of forgiveness. The body atones by performing good deeds and certain types of devotional practices.[1] Ghazali discusses in detail religious practices of repentance and how to accustom oneself to performing them. He points out that repentance for transgressions of the body and for the nonperformance of religious practice is decidedly less difficult than the task of the mystic, which is repentance for errant thoughts and the anxiety of his heart. In this sense repentance is present throughout the process of conversion from worldly to otherworldly desires; it must also accompany the mystic throughout his life or he risks falling short of his ultimate goal.

This doctrine is most striking in its consequences for the way of life of the few. Even if a man is free of sins committed by his body, he will still have anxiety for his sins; even if he is free from this anxiety, he will still be subject to deficiencies and neglect in the remembrance of God; even if he is free of these shortcomings, there will still be inadequacies in his knowledge of God, His attributes, and His works.[2] Thus, as a mystical virtue, repentance is something without which the mystic cannot even begin traveling the path to the nearness to God, and to attain the most noble kind of repentance, the mystic needs both knowledge and patience. In addition to showing the mystic the necessity of repentance, knowledge is the best means of guarding against obstinacy in postponing repentance. Patience, on the other hand, helps the mystic to resist bodily and worldly desires which continuously interfere with every effort of preserving repentance, and because patience is a prerequisite for the highest form of repentance, Ghazali discusses it as the second mystical virtue.[3]

1. *R*, IV. 1. 2152.

2. *R*, IV. 1. 2148-51.

3. *R*, IV. 1. 2171; cf. *Kīmyā-yi*, II, 77. This is in agreement with al-Makkī, *Qūt*, I, 217. In the *Book of the Forty*, however, Ghazali classifies "fear" as the second virtue (it follows after repentance) and "patience" as the fourth virtue (it follows "asceticism"); see *Arbaʿīn*, p. 182.

Patience

While patience (*ṣabr*), like the other mystical virtues, is composed of the three elements, knowledge, positive disposition, and action, Ghazali maintains that the expression patience applies particularly to the positive disposition; knowledge in this case is an introduction to the positive disposition, and action a result of it. To define patience, he again gives the analysis of the soul derived from the philosophic tradition and replaces the philosophic terms with others which are common in the Islamic tradition. Man possesses two powers: one, the motive of religion (*bā'ith al-dīn*), is reason (*'aql*); the other, an irrational motive, is known as passion (*hawā*) and includes both appetite and anger.[1] Patience is the persistence of reason in its effort to control the passions. When all passions are subdued and reason reigns supreme, man achieves the highest rank of patience. Thus understood, patience is strictly a human habit, and does not apply to angels or animals.[2]

There are many kinds of patience and they can be classified on the basis of the objects they treat. Endurance of bodily hardships and pains is a lower kind of patience. The most perfect and commendable kind of patience consists in steadfastly resisting the demands of the passions. Patience can thus be found in conjunction with other virtues, and consequently may be given different names according to the circumstances in which it is manifested. Ghazali asserts further that man needs patience at every step of his life. This is so because life presents only two types of situations: those which are congenial to man's natural inclinations, and those which are not. Examples of the former are health, safety, wealth, and honor, and man needs patience so as not to indulge them excessively. The situations which oppose man's inclinations are divided into three categories: (1) Those in which man must choose between obedience and disobedience. To perform the former and refrain from the latter, man needs a great deal of patience; (2) Those whose occurrence is not subject to man's will in which he can choose to react correctly. For example, to resist the desire for revenge, once a

1. *R*, IV. 2. 2180. Ghazali uses these two terms, i.e., the motive of religion and reason, interchangeably;see also *R*, IV. 2. 2181, 2189. In the *Supreme Purpose*, Ghazali says patience is "the persistence of the motive of reason (*'aql*) or religion (*dīn*) against the motive of appetite and anger' (*Maqṣad*, p. 97). This attitude confirms the view of Ibn Taymiyyah that Ghazali expresses philosophic ideas in Islamic terms; see his *Naqḍ*, p. 56.

2. *R*, IV. 2. 2181, 2188.

man has been harmed by speech or deed, requires patience; (3) Occurrences which are not subject to man's control in any way, such as the death of a beloved person or loss of wealth or health. Ghazali considers patience displayed in these situations to be the highest. In such circumstances the patient man does not indulge in a violent outburst of passion; rather, he expresses satisfaction with God's decree.[1]

As a mystical virtue, patience is particulary important for the mystic who seeks complete subordination of the passions and isolates himself from social life. In his isolation, the mystic needs patience to endure the hardships of loneliness and to train himself in carrying out practices which bring him nearer to God. Even if the mystic perfectly masters all essential spiritual practices, he still needs patience to guard against the whims of his thoughts which cannot be completely controlled until the soul is overwhelmingly engaged with God alone.[2]

Patience and gratitude are the two mystical virtues that are in addition attributes of God.[3] Patience is the only virtue which Ghazali treats both in the context of philosophic as well as mystical virtues, but his treatment of it as a philosophic virtue is brief and follows the Muslim philosophers such as Avicenna and Miskawayh, for Aristotle does not regard patience as even a quasi-virtue. Ghazali's rather detailed discussion of patience as a principal mystical virtue reflects his interest in the mystics' analysis of it as a spiritual station, especially as it is presented by al-Makkī.[4]

Ghazali links patience with gratitude by dealing with them in the same book in the *Revival* and presenting them as the two fundamental responses of man to what befalls him. In affliction he must be patient; in prosperity he must be grateful. Thus gratitude, as a mystical virtue, follows patience in a logical way.[5]

Gratitude

As a virtue, gratitude (*shukr*) describes man's best response to favorable events. Ghazali asserts that all previous discussions of gratitude fail to

1. *R*, IV. 2. 2191-98.
2. *R*, IV. 2. 2199-2201.
3. *R*, IV. 2. 2176; *Maqṣad*, p. 97.
4. al-Makkī, *Qūt*, I, 396-413.
5. In all the three books that deal with mystical virtues, i.e., the *Revival*, the *Book of the Forty*, and the *Alchemy of Happiness*, Ghazali deals with "gratitude" after "patience." This agrees with al-Makki's *Qūt*, I, 411-413.

define it completely, and in order to improve them he seeks in gratitude the three elements characteristic of the mystical virtues. Gratitude consists, according to him, of (1) knowledge of the gift, (2) the positive disposition of joy caused by the gift, and (3) an action which will please the one who bestows the gift.[1] Knowledge will take account of (a) the gift itself, (b) the man who receives it and how it is a benefit to him, and (c) the benefactor who chose to bestow the gift. All of this must be known about gifts in general. As to the gifts of God, the knowledge that God is truly the one and only benefactor completes the understanding of His uniqueness, for only then can man understand that everything which exists in the world receives its being from Him, that everything is His gift, and that consequently, gratitude is appropriately due to him above all else. This knowledge is sufficient to bring about the positive disposition of joy in relation to the benefactor. This joy can be considered true gratitude only if it is concerned neither with the gift nor with the giving, but only with the benefactor. (a) Joy in terms of the gift contains no gratitude whatsoever, because it is not related to the benefactor. (b) Joy in relation to giving involves a kind of gratitude because giving embodies the notion of a benefactor, but the benefactor is at most a secondary consideration for this kind of joy. This category includes men who are grateful to God for the sake of His reward. (c) Only in the third case does man acquire true joy by rejoicing in God as the only benefactor (*mun'im*). The action resulting from the positive disposition of joy expresses itself through the heart, the tongue, and the limbs: through the heart by searching for the good, through the tongue by extolling God's glory, and through the limbs by making use of God's bounty for acts in obedience to His will.[2]

After establishing the definition of gratitude in general and gratitude toward God in particular, Ghazali is faced with the problem of how man, the creature, can thank the Creator who creates everything including the gratitude of the creature. His general solution of this problem was discussed in Chapter III. God is the creator of everything and man is the vehicle and place (*maḥall*) of God's act; man's actions, then, become his own through his "acquisition" of them, which means that they are created by God but man is responsible for them. Thus, if a man is grateful, he is the receptacle of gratitude and not the creator of it. According to the ordinary understanding, the giver of a gift expects

1. *R*, IV. 2. 2212.
2. *R*, IV. 2. 2213-16.

something in return for it. But this is impossible in relation to God, for two reasons. First, He is too sublime to be in need of man's praise or his service. Secondly, the gratitude which man offers is itself a creation and gift of God. Ghazali admits that gratitude for a benefit which will require the benefactor to bestow another is problematical and one of the most obscure puzzles of mystical knowledge. He suggests that true knowledge of gratitude is only possible for him who perceives God's unique reality and knows that He is both the one who causes gratitude and the one to whom gratitude is extended. Understanding this, Ghazali says, means showing the highest gratitude to God.[1]

Genuine gratitude demands that one understand the purpose for which all gifts are given and makes proper use of them as he strives to reach the Benefactor. In order to be truly grateful, therefore, man must know what God approves and disapproves. Ghazali mentions two general ways of knowing God's designs. One is through the religious teachings contained in the Koran and prophetic traditions. The other is through rational inquiry which discerns God's purpose in everything created. At times this purpose is evident and at times it is hidden.[2] Such an eschatological view of all worldly things is clearly introduced for the purpose of showing that, to be grateful toward God, man must use everything according to its natural end which is to lead men to God.

To clarify the nature of gratitude, Ghazali turns to examine the bounties (*ni'am*) which are its proximate causes. He maintains that true good, pleasure, or happiness must be identified with the happiness of the hereafter; otherwise these words are being used either erroneously or metaphorically. They may, however, be applied in a less strict sense to anything that contributes, more or less directly, to ultimate happiness. On the basis of this understanding, Ghazali gives an elaborate classification of the bounties of this life. He includes every virtue, spiritual and material, to show that the bounties of God are so immense that they cannot be estimated.[3]

1. *R*, IV. 2. 2218-24.

2. *R*, IV. 2. 2225-35. Evident, for example, is God's purpose in the creation of the sun in order to separate night and day. Hidden, according to Ghazali, is God's purpose in creation or allowing the creation of money. Ghazali shows at length what the benefits of using money are. It is evident that he is in part influenced in his discussion by the philosophic tradition, particularly by Aristotle's discussion of money in relation to justice in the sixth book of the *Nicomachean Ethics*.

3. *R*, IV. 2. 2244-58.

Since gratitude means man's response to all acts of God, Ghazali raises the question of how to be grateful in the case of affliction (*balā'*). Affliction, he says, is either absolute or relative. Absolute afflictions are such things as being deprived of nearness to God in the hereafter and being a sinner or an evil man in this life. Relative afflictions include such things as poverty and sickness. Gratitude has to do with benefits and there can be no gratitude for absolute afflictions. However, man must be grateful for relative afflictions. Worldly goods are good for oneself or for others only because they serve the purpose God has in everything He creates.[1] Thus, as a mystical virtue, gratitude is directed toward God alone. The mystic thanks Him for everything that comes from Him, and uses his wordlly situation in a way which pleases God and leads to nearness to Him.

Hope and Fear

After gratitude, Ghazali discusses hope and fear as the next two mystical virtues. He relates them to each other in the same way as patience and gratitude. They are the subject of Book 3 of Quarter IV of the *Revival*. This same arrangement of hope and fear after gratitude is presented in the *Alchemy of Happiness*, and it is also in agreement with al-Makkī's arrangement of mystical stations.[2] However, in the *Book of the Forty*, Ghazali deals with hope within his discussion of "fear," which he classifies immediately after "repentance" as the second principal virtue.[3] Furthermore, he explicitly mentions in this book that fear should follow after repentance; whereas in both the *Revival* and the *Alchemy of Happiness*, Ghazali does not state explicitly that hope and fear should follow gratitude, nor does he mention what virtue should follow them.[4] In his introduction to the discussion of these two virtues, Ghazali says: "Hope and fear are two wings by means of which those who are brought near (*al-muqarrabūn*) fly to every commendable station (*kull maqām maḥmūd*)."[5] This means that, in addition to being stations themselves, hope and fear help the few to acquire other stations. Thus, by being silent about the relationship of these two virtues with what precedes them and what

1. *R*, IV. 2. 2289-92.
2. al-Makkī, *Qūt*, I. 432, 457, where he considers hope as the fourth spiritual station and fear the fifth.
3. *Arba'īn*, p. 182.
4. *Arba'īn*, pp. 181-82; cf. *R*, IV. 3. 2316, 2342, 2369.
5. *R*, IV. 3. 2316.

follows them, Ghazali seems to point to this special relation they have to all of the mystical virtues and not to some of them only.

Moreover, hope and fear differ from the mystical virtues we have discussed thus far, in that they are "passions" in their basic characteristics. These passions are well known in the philosophic tradition; and Ghazali's general definitions of both virtues, as we shall see, reflect the influence of this philosophic tradition.[1] Therefore, while dealing with hope and fear according to Ghazali's arrangement in the *Revival*, we shall keep in mind their special relation to all other mystical virtues and that they are basically passions.

Hope

Ghazali defines "hope" (*rajā'*) as the sentiment of the heart when it anticipates something desirable.[2] When the sentiment results from a reasonable appraisal of the probability of receiving that thing, it is correct to call it hope. However, anticipation directed towards an improbable occurrence is more properly called self-deceit or stupidity. If receiving something desirable is not impossible in itself, but the manner in which this may be brought cannot be ascertained, anticipation of that thing is called wishful thinking, because the term hope does not apply to what is determined. Therefore, hope properly refers to the expectation of something desirable when the means to attain that thing which are within human control have been discerned, and only that element beyond human action has been left to God.[3]

Applying this general meaning of hope to the particular case of the mystic who seeks nearness to God, Ghazali states that whoever obeys God and properly performs those devotional actions within his power should expect God to complete his efforts by bestowing on him His bounties. It is in this sense that Ghazali considers hope as a mystical virtue. He regards it as composite of the three elements characteristic of all mystical virtues, namely, knowledge, positive disposition, and action. As a positive disposition, hope results from the knowledge that God will fulfill the hopes of those who seek His nearness, and, in turn, it results in the action of further engagement in devotional practices.[4]

1. Aristotle *Rhetoric* 2. 5. 1382aff.; Avicenna, *Fī al-Akhlāq wa al-Infi'ālāt*, p. 24.
2. *R*, IV. 3. 2317; cf. Avicenna, *Fī al-Akhlāq wa al-Infi'ālāt*, p. 24.
3. *R*, IV. 3. 2317.
4. *R*, IV. 3. 2319.

Hope, therefore, is a praiseworthy sentiment because it impels men to action; despair, on the other hand, is objectionable because it enervates them. In this sense, despair and not fear, opposes hope, for fear impels men to action just as hope does. According to Ghazali, two kinds of men are in extreme need of hope. Firstly, those who, despairing of God's mercy, have ceased worshiping Him. Secondly, those who, dominated by excessive fear of God, devote all their time to worship and thereby neglect their duty towards their own well-being and that of their families. These two kinds of men incline away from moderation (*i'tidāl*) and therefore they are in need of hope which will restore moderation.[1]

Hope and fear are the only two mystical virtues to which Ghazali applies the doctrine of the mean. It is with regard to hope in particular that he reminds his reader that "what is sought after in all character traits is the mean."[2] The reason seems to be that hope and fear are passions. Since Ghazali starts with passions in this case, and analyzes them with a view to man's relation to God, he has to emphasize their mean state to guard against the problems involved in their extremes of excess. A too hopeful man may neglect spiritual practices necessary for mystical refinement and consequently fail in his purpose. If the extreme of defect dominates, Ghazali mentions two methods which can successfully bring the mean of hope. One method is reading Koranic verses and prophetic traditions which describe God's mercy and providence. The other method is reflection. By reflecting upon all of God's bounties and His care for men in this world, man will realize that such a majestic Creator will be even more generous with His servants on the day of judgment.[3]

After discussing hope as a mystical virtue which helps man to engage wholeheartedly in devotional practices, Ghazali begins his discussion of fear as the virtue which follows after it. He does not state why fear should follow after hope. In fact, he specifically says that actions on account of hope are of higher rank than those on account of fear, and on this basis, one might conclude that the order of these two virtues should be reversed.[4] However, Ghazali seems to think of them as two qualities which are closely related to each other and consequently should

1. *R*, IV. 3. 2323.
2. *R*, IV. 3. 2323.
3. *R*, IV. 3. 2324.
4. *R*, IV. 3. 2330; cf. al-Makkī, *Qūt*, I, 456, where he says "although hope is a way that leads to God, fear is nearer to it, and what is nearer, is higher."

be treated together. Nevertheless, the fact that Ghazali devotes more than three quarters of Book 3 of Quarter IV of the *Revival*, in which he discusses these two mystical virtues, to the discussion of fear alone, together with the fact that in the *Book of the Forty* he mentions fear by itself as a principal character trait, shows that he attaches a special importance to fear.[1]

FEAR

Like hope, fear (*khawf*) is related to something in the future which affects the soul. It differs from hope, however, in that this expected thing is dreadful and harmful. The knowledge that this thing can happen to one produces a certain positive disposition which is called fear.[2] Thus, fear is the expression for the soul's suffering when it anticipates something dreadful. Ghazali's general definition of fear corresponds to that of the philosophers. It is the "passion of fear,"[3] and in making use of this expression in order to establish fear as a mystical virtue, Ghazali has the following observations. He says that he wants to explain that fear, in a certain context, is commendable but it is false to suppose that all fear is commendable, or that the more powerful and frequent it is, the more commendable. Only if it is understood as a mean between two extremes can fear be considered a good character trait. A person who is deficient in fear tends toward effeminate softness. Whenever he sees a fearful thing, he is afraid, but when nothing terrifying is visible, his soul returns to hardness. A person with excessive fear inclines to hopelessness and despair. Excessive fear stultifies action and may result in sickness, depression, and intellectual atrophy. In its mean state fear is the means by which men are led to persevere in knowledge and action, so that by means of both of these they may attain their ultimate happiness.[4]

As a mystical virtue, fear here signifies the relationship between man and God. For Ghazali, fear in this context is essentially "fear of God" and not fear simply. He is concerned with discussing this human passion

1. For example, Ghazali treats hope in *R*, IV. 3. 2316-38, while he treats fear in *R*, IV. 3. 2339-96.

2. *R*, IV. 3. 2339-40.

3. Avicenna, *Fī al-Akhlāq wa al-Infi'ālāt*, p. 26; Avicenna, *al-Shifā': al-Manṭiq*, Vol. VIII: *al-Khaṭābah*, ed. by Muḥammad Salīm Sālim (Cairo: Wizārat al-Ma'ārif al-'Umūmiyyah, 1954), p. 138; cf. Aristotle *Rhetoric* 2. 5. 1382 1a1-3.

4. *R*, IV. 3. 2336-39.

with respect to man's view of God, and not of society or anything else. To explain what fear is as a mystical virtue, Ghazali discusses the three elements which characterize all mystical virtues, i.e., knowledge, positive disposition, and action, in their relation to God. With regard to knowledge, fear of God may sometimes be due to knowledge that God as the Lord of everything could decide to destroy the world out of indifference and nothing could interfere. Sometimes fear may result from a knowledge of human acts of disobedience which will call forth God's punishment. Or, this knowledge could involve a combination of both of these. The strength of man's fear of God is in proportion to the knowledge of his own sins and of the majesty of God. The positive disposition of fear which results from such knowledge produces, in turn, certain actions. In the body, fear produces pallidness, fainting, shrieking, weeping, and may even lead to death. It restrains the members of the body from disobedience, binds them to deeds of obedience, and makes them repair what is defective. As to character, fear stifles the passions and slackens the pleasures so that disobedience becomes abhorrent. The intensity of that fear pervades the character and is responsible, according to Ghazali, for the various ranks of mystical refinement. (1) Fear may cause man to resist the influence of his lower desires; this is temperance and it is the lowest degree. (2) It may restrain man from what is forbidden by religious law; this is abstinence. (3) It may discourage him from what is possibly forbidden; this is piety. (4) And at its utmost strength, fear may evoke in man thoughts of God during all his activities, however insignificant; this is truthfulness which is the highest rank. It is the most commendable product of fear, provided that it does not lead to sickness of the body or atrophy of the mind.[1]

Since the objects to be feared are of two kinds—those which are feared in themselves (such as hellfire), and those which are feared because they bring about what is dreadful (such as sins)—there are at least two categories of men who achieve the station of fear. (1) There are those whose hearts are dominated by what is not essentially dreadful but dreadful because of its consequences. Ghazali gives several examples of these things and discusses two of them at considerable length. One of these is the fear of being marked as an evil man at the time of death. This he calls the evil end (*sū' al-khātimah*). The other is being marked as an evil man in preexistence. This he calls the "evil beginning" ([*sū'*]

1. *R*, IV. 3. 2340-44.

al-sābiqah).[1] (2) The second category includes those who fear things dreadful in themselves, such as the terror of resurrection, hellfire, or being veiled from God (*al-ḥijāb*); the last is the highest fear and is characteristic of the mystics while the former two characterize men of piety.

From these two categories of fear emerge two ranks of fear of God. (1) The first is the fear which the multitude has of God's punishment in the hereafter; this fear is inferior because it results from negligence and weakness of faith. (2) The second is fear of being veiled from God and being denied nearness to Him. Indeed, whoever ascends to the apex of knowledge and knows God, fears Him of necessity, and has no need of a regimen which induces fear, just as whoever knows the lion and sees himself falling into its claws has no need of a regimen to induce fear; rather, he fears of necessity, whether he wills it or not. Thus, whoever knows God, knows that He does what He wills, and fears Him accordingly.[2]

As is the case with other mystical virtues, Ghazali seeks to prove that fear of God is praiseworthy on the basis of Islamic religious teachings as well by citing Koranic verses, prophetic traditions, and sayings of earlier companions and learned men. Rational consideration, however, is a more important method because it explains not only that fear of God is good, but also why. According to Ghazali, rational consideration shows that the excellence of anything is in proportion to its ability to lead to nearness to God in the hereafter. This ultimate goal can be realized only when the love of worldly things is completely uprooted from the heart. This can be done only when man subdues his base desires. Subjugation of these desires is best achieved under fear.[3]

It has been mentioned above that Ghazali considers fear next in rank to hope. However, he says that one must acknowledge that fear is more essential than hope in the same way that bread is more essential than oxymel, that is, because disobedience and self-deceit are more dominant traits of mankind. Thus, in his discussion of fear as a mystical virtue, Ghazali shows how it is related to hope, and both are considered by him not only as mystical virtues, but also as means which help the mystic to acquire the other principal mystical virtues. Ghazali therefore does not relate either of them to any other virtue in particular, and in concluding his discussion of fear, he does not specifically state which

1. *R*, IV. 3. 2344-47.
2. *R*, IV. 3. 2361-62.
3. *R*, IV. 3. 2347-48.

mystical virtue should follow after it. Instead, he just begins dealing with "poverty" as the sixth principal mystical virtue.

Poverty

While al-Makkī considers asceticism (*zuhd*) the sixth mystical station which follows fear, and treats poverty (*faqr*) as part of it, Ghazali regards poverty and asceticism as separate mystical virtues which follow one another.[1] He classifies poverty after fear and before asceticism. But he discusses it together with asceticism in Book 4 of Quarter IV of the *Revival*, to indicate the close relationship between the two virtues: both deal with the same subject matter, that is, absence of worldly possessions.[2] To distinguish between poverty and asceticism, Ghazali states that the true mystic should turn away from worldly things and cut himself off completely from all aspects of this life. This can take place in two ways: either material goods never present themselves and this is poverty, or a man deliberately turns away from them and this is asceticism. In this sense, poverty is defined as "the lack of things needed.... If what is needed exists and can be had, then he who needs it is not called poor."[3]

In Ghazali's view, everyone other than God is poor. The few, in particular, must realize that since everything needs God for its existence and preservation, God alone is rich (*ghaniyy*), and Ghazali calls this condition of all men "absolute poverty." Yet he asserts that his intention is not to discuss absolute poverty but to deal instead with a more restricted kind of poverty, namely, lack of needed wealth (*māl*). A man is called poor when he cannot get the things necessary for his sustenance,[4] but poverty as a virtue does not mean the lack of wealth simply; rather, it is a lack of wealth qualified by man's attitude toward it, and a poor man can be displeased or contented with his condition. The highest and most commendable attitude toward poverty is what Ghazali calls the state of indifference to wealth. A person who is indifferent to possessing

1. *R*, IV. 4. 2389-99; cf. al-Makkī, *Qūt*, I, 528. However, Ghazali's view of poverty as a separate virtue agrees with other earlier mystics such as al-Qushayrī, who regards "poverty" as a separate "station"; see his *Risālah*, II, 536-49.

2. *R*, IV. 4. 2398. However, in the *Book of the Forty*, Ghazali deals with poverty within his discussion of asceticism; see *Arbaʿīn*, p. 187. Cf. al-Zabīdī, *Itḥāf*, IX, 262, where he points out the difference between Ghazali and al-Makkī with regard to "poverty." In his commentary on the *Revival*, al-Zabīdī, following al-Makkī, does not call poverty a "station"; he regards "asceticism" as the sixth station.

3. *R*, IV. 4. 2399.

4. *R*, IV. 4. 2399-2400.

or lacking wealth will not be pleased or pained by material things, and he is rich because he is free from the distractions of wealth whether he possesses it or not. But he is rich in a qualified sense, since it is only God who is truly rich. The state of indifference characterizes the man who seeks nearness to God, because he is not occupied with anything other than God. Hating and detesting worldly goods as well as seeking them means to be occupied with something other than God. Hating wealth, however, can give way to indifference and, subsequently, nearness to God, whereas seeking wealth turns one away from God.

Comparing poverty and riches, Ghazali considers poverty superior and more virtuous. Even if the rich man is liberal and gives away his wealth to those who are in need, he is still inferior to the poor man, because possessing wealth inevitably makes a man preoccupied with worldly affairs, and distracts him from nobler pursuits. Indeed, possessing wealth increases a man's love of this world, while poverty causes him to shun it and consider it a prison from which he must free himself.[1]

Although Ghazali emphasizes that all mystical virtues are composed of three elements, namely, knowledge, positive disposition, and action, he does not mention these in connection with poverty, nor does he call this virtue a "station." But this does not mean that poverty is not a mystical virtue, because he implies the existence of the three elements in what he calls the conditions of poverty. The virtue of poverty requires the knowledge that God is the source of everything that affects him and therefore a man must not detest being poor. This is the minimum requirement for anyone who seeks to aquire the positive disposition of poverty. Higher than this disposition is satisfaction with poverty; and the highest level is seeking to be poor and being pleased with poverty because one realizes the dangers of richness. As to action, one should never complain about his poverty, but should hide it. More importantly, the one who seeks the virtue of poverty must not neglect or diminish his devotional practices; he must give what is beyond his immediate needs to those who need it, and should try not to accumulate possessions for more than one day's needs. Failing that, he may accumulate them for forty days' needs, or one year's needs at most.[2]

The usual way for a poor man to satisfy his necessary needs is to work for them. Because the few are engaged in higher and more important duties, Ghazali allows them to satisfy their needs without working. This

1. *R*, IV. 4. 2423-24.
2. *R*, IV. 4. 2425-27.

can be done in one of two ways. (1) They may receive free gifts without asking for them. In accepting free gifts, the mystic must make sure that he is qualified to receive them and that he will be under no obligation in return. More importantly, however, he must consider this gift as a gift from God and not from the giver, who is only an intermediary for God's bounty. (2) Or they may satisfy their needs by begging. Ghazali emphasizes that, in principle, begging is only permitted in extreme cases of want. This is so because it implies dissatisfaction with God's decree, forces man to humble himself to someone other than God, and embarrasses those from whom he begs. However, the mystic who is poor may beg for his food when he is hungry and for medicine when sick; but he should not beg for less important or unnecessary needs.[1]

Thus poverty as a mystical virtue does not mean that a person happens to be poor and is therefore virtuous. Rather, it requires that the person know the right attitude toward worldly affairs and fulfill the above-mentioned conditions. Ghazali gives a detailed account of the character traits of poor learned men to emphasize the importance of this virtue. Nevertheless, in his view, poverty can only be a virtue for someone who has always lacked possessions. It is inferior to the excellence of the man who has had possessions and rejected them. This is asceticism, with which he deals next.

Asceticism

Ghazali has no reservations about calling asceticism (*zuhd*) one of the noble mystical virtues. He calls it a station and analyzes it according to the three constituents of the mystical virtues, i.e., knowledge, positive disposition, and action. Asceticism is so important for him that he gives it particular attention in the *Deliverer* to show how mystical virtues in general are experienced.[2]

Asceticism requires a knowledge of the relative excellence of things which produces the positive disposition of turning away from lower things to those which are superior. But this knowledge is a general one which produces a general asceticism that applies equally to many things. For the realization of asceticism as a mystical virtue one must know that the pleasure of nearness to God and of the world to come is incalculable, durable, and real, while the pleasures of this life are only transitory and

1. *R*, IV. 4. 2422-26.
2. *Munqidh*, p. 97.

illusory.[1] Ghazali maintains that the term asceticism applies particularly to the positive disposition, even though knowledge is also necessary. He differentiates various levels of asceticism on the basis of the positive disposition. To renounce everything other than the desire for nearness to God is absolute asceticism. Below this is renouncing worldly goods for the pleasure of the world to come. To renounce some worldly goods and desire some is not asceticism, although it has some merit in training one for it. To renounce forbidden and evil things is not asceticism at all because, as a mystical virtue, asceticism applies only to the renunciation of permissible things. Moreover, the thing renounced must be within the reach of the ascetic; otherwise his condition will be due to his inability to acquire certain things and not to asceticism. The action which results from the positive disposition of asceticism is refraining from enjoying the things renounced and engaging in worthier activities.[2]

Thus, asceticism, unlike poverty, can only be attained by someone who has worldly possessions. In addition to distinguishing asceticism from poverty, Ghazali distinguishes it from other virtues that may tend to be erroneously identified with it. For him asceticism is not merely renouncing wealth or giving it away for the sake of liberality or magnificence. Rather, it is renouncing this world as insignificant when compared to the value of the hereafter. Giving wealth for the sake of liberality, for example, can be expected from those who are concerned with this world alone, as well as from those who seek happiness in the hereafter, but asceticism can only be attained by those who direct all their attention to happiness in the hereafter.[3]

To illustrate the essence of asceticism, Ghazali selects a statement of Abū Sulaymān al-Dārānī: "We have heard much about asceticism. According to us, it is the renouncing of everything which distracts from God."[4] Thus, the meaning of renouncing this world for God is to come to God with a heart filled with remembrance and meditation. But remembering God and meditating on His majesty are only possible as long as man is alive and life can only be preserved if man has some minimal means for his survival. Therefore, if a man limits himself to those worldly things that preserve his life while intending to use his life for

1. *R*, IV. 4. 2444.
2. *R*, IV. 4. 2444-45.
3. *R*, IV. 4. 2448.
4. *R*, IV. 4. 2464; cf. al-Qushayrī, *Risālah*, I, 295.

devotional practices, then he is in fact a true ascetic completely occupied with God.[1] Ghazali enumerates food, dress, and dwelling as necessary for survival and in agreement with asceticism and gives a detailed account of how the minimum amount of each, aquired for the shortest time, is what agrees with true asceticism. The true ascetic accumulates nothing; according to Ghazali, he does not even save some of his lunch for his supper.[2] It is for this reason that he emphasizes that the highest rank of asceticism becomes perfect by the attainment of trust in God. Ghazali states explicitly that trust in God, as a mystical virtue, necessarily follows asceticism.[3]

Divine Unity and Trust

We shall discuss divine unity (*tawḥīd*) and trust (*tawakkul*) together since Ghazali maintains that the former is the basis of the latter, that is, divine unity is the knowledge which produces trust, the corresponding positive disposition. (Divine unity means the state of awareness of the oneness of God and not simply the abstract notion of the unity of God.) Thus, while classifying divine unity as a separate mystical quality, Ghazali deals with it as a part of the mystical virtue of trust. This agrees with his approach in the *Book of the Forty*, as well as with the doctrine of his favorite mystical writer, al-Makkī, but the fact that he allocates a special section to divine unity conforms to the viewpoint of other earlier mystical writers, such as al-Qushayrī and al-Harawī who, however, make it a separate station.[4]

In discussing divine unity as the knowledge which produces trust, Ghazali states that those who profess belief in it are of four ranks. (1) Those who profess the unity of God with their lips but have no faith in their hearts. (2) Those who believe on the basis of authority and tradition, that is, they pronounce with their lips the formula "there is no deity but God" with the same devotion as the multitude of the Islamic community. (3) Those who believe God to be the only cause of all that exists on the evidence of discursive thought and through the

1. *R*, IV. 4. 2465.

2. *R*, IV. 4. 2466-83.

3. *R*, IV. 4. 2488, where Ghazali says: "Since asceticism can only be complete by trust (*tawakkul*), then let us begin by explaining it."

4. *R*, IV. 5. 2494. Indeed Ghazali says that "trust" is a "station" which comes after "asceticism," thus dropping any mention of "divine unity" (*R*, IV. 5. 2543-56). *Arbaʿīn*, p. 218; al-Makkī, *Qūt*, II, 3-75; cf. al-Qushayrī, *Risālah*, II, 581-88; al-Harawī, *Manāzil*, pp. 110-13.

light of intuition. (4) Lastly, those who have risen to the realization that nothing exists except God. Their hearts are filled with God and they even become unconscious of their own identity. This is the state of those who are truthful and have attained the stage of annihilation in divine unity (*fanā' fī al-tawḥīd*), because they see only God and are oblivious to everything else including their own existence. Of these four grades of belief in divine unity, the last is the highest but, because it belongs to the knowledge of revelation, and because trust, as a mystical virtue, is not based on this level of knowledge alone, Ghazali does not discuss it in this context. In the first or the lowest rank there is only hypocrisy, and in the second, the believer has the same status as the multitude who have faith. Although the second level of belief in divine unity is the one discussed by the dialectical theologians, Ghazali maintains that it can never produce the mystical virtue of trust. It is the third rank which truly produces the positive disposition of trust. This is so because the believer realizes that God is the only doer and that man in his actions is but a "channel" of God's action. In this way, as a mystical virtue, trust is understood as trust in God alone.[1] Lest this knowledge lead simply to naive resignation, Ghazali emphasizes that belief in divine unity must include the belief that God is the creator of everything that exists and that the whole world is the best possible world, that nothing can be added to it or taken from it to make it more perfect.[2]

Knowledge of divine unity combined with belief in the perfection of the existing world produces the positive disposition of trust in God or reliance of the heart on God alone. Once a man is convinced that God is the only doer, and that He has complete knowledge and power over men together with absolute mercy and providence, then his heart will inevitably rely on Him and have complete trust in Him.[3]

In order to explain the action which results form this positive disposition, Ghazali describes three levels of trust in God by giving examples from daily life. (1) Trust in God may resemble the relation between a man and the lawyer who represents him in a dispute. This is the weakest level of trust because man is always checking on and preparing part of the work of his lawyer. (2) Next is trust in God which resembles the

1. *R*, IV. 5. 2494-2513. It is here that Ghazali again discusses the problem of the seeming contradiction between God's act and man's choice. Since this question has been already discussed in Chapter III, there is no need to repeat it here.

2. *R*, IV. 5. 2517.

3. *R*, IV. 5. 2518-20.

relation between a child and his mother, for the child knows only his mother and calls for her help alone. A man who trusts God in this way is unaware of possessing this virtue; he simply has complete trust in God. (3) Finally, the highest level of trust in God characterizes the man who recognizes God's mercy with a certainty beyond any shadow of doubt, regards himself as a mere corpse, and would not even move a limb without the will of God. This man does not appeal to God for anything because of his complete trust in Him, whereas a man in the second level may ask for what he needs, but only asks from God.[1]

Ghazali, now, raises the problem of how far personal thought and effort are consistent with trust in God and faith in divine unity, since the various levels of trust in God mentioned above ought to issue in corresponding actions. This question does not arise with regard to the last level, because man in this level feels that he is inert flesh in the hands of God. Personal thought can enter in at the second level but man's only action consists in prayer to God for help. Personal effort is much more extensive at the lowest level of trust in God where man exerts himself in a way analogous to a client's cooperation with his lawyer. Such activity is not inconsistent with his trust in the lawyer; for distrust would result in seeking the aid of someone else, and Ghazali emphasizes that trust does not require man to abandon all action. At the same time, those actions which originate in a sense of power or control over events are inconsistent with trust in God. Rather, a man must perform whatever actions he is capable of, but depend on the will of God for the outcome.[2]

The balance between human action and trust in God, according to Ghazali, can be clarified according to the ends they aim at. These are (1) securing what is useful for sustenance, (2) preserving what one already possesses, (3) guarding against possible future evils, and (4) opposing present evils.[3] In a detailed discussion of these classes of actions, Ghazali shows that sometimes trust in God consists only in the knowledge that the thing is from God, while at other times, trust includes a positive disposition and action. Thus, as a mystical virtue, trust in God does not reject all action indiscriminately; rather, it rejects only those which are essentially contrary to man's reliance on God in what he does. However, according to Ghazali, the greater man's trust

1. *R*, IV. 5. 2521-22.
2. *R*, IV. 5. 2523-26.
3. *R*, IV. 5. 2529-66.

in God, the less he will desire to accumulate provisions or worry about harmful evils because of his conviction that, ultimately, God will supply his basic needs and protect him from what may harm him.[1]

Therefore, while accepting a number of essential human activities as consistent with trust in God as the virtue of the few, Ghazali considers that the mystic who acquires this virtue in its highest form will be constantly aware of his state as a helpless thing in the hands of God. In this sense, trust in God is an important mystical virtue which makes the method followed by the few in acquiring mystical virtues consistent with the theological virtues discussed in the first section of Chapter III above. Thus, trust in God teaches the mystic to gear all his activities to what pleases God and to rely completely on His providence. Ghazali discusses trust in God as the last of the mystical virtues before love. Although he does not specifically state that this mystical virtue should be followed by love, he discusses love immediately after trust in God in all three works which deal with mystical virtues.[2]

Love

By dealing with love (*maḥabbah*) immediately after trust, Ghazali departs from the method of al-Makkī who places satisfaction (*riḍā*) after trust, and then follows it with love.[3] For Ghazali, satisfaction, together with yearning (*shawq*) and intimacy (*uns*), are the fruits of love, that is, its consequences. Indeed, Ghazali calls Book 6 of Quarter IV of the *Revival*, in which he discusses love, "The Book of Love, Yearning, Intimacy, and Satisfaction," and so reveals the relative order he assigns to these mystical virtues. In spite of this, however, he agrees with al-Makkī that "love of God is the final aim and the highest station"[4] and emphasizes that any station beyond love of God, such as yearning, intimacy, or satisfaction, is but its product, and the stations before it, such as repentance, patience, asceticism, and the others mentioned above, only lead to and prepare for it.[5]

1. *R*, IV. 5. 2544-46, 2567-71; cf. Ghazali, *Ayyuhā al-Walad* in *al-Jawāhir al-Ghazālī* (Cairo: Maṭba'at al-Sa'ādah, 1934), p. 69, where Ghazali defines trust in God as complete reliance on Him alone with regard to all things that may affect man.

2. *R*, IV. 5. 2577; *Arba'īn*, p. 225; *Kīmiyā-yi*, II, 922-42.

3. *R*, IV. 6. 2580; *Arba'īn*, p. 227; *Kīmiyā-yi*, II, 943; cf. al-Makkī, *Qūt*, II, 99. Cf. al-Zabīdī, *Itḥāf*, IX, 544, where he points out the difference between Ghazali and al-Makkī with regard to the order of love among the mystical virtues.

4. *R*, IV. 6. 2580; cf. al-Makkī, *Qūt*, II, 99.

5. *R*, IV. 6. 2580.

Therefore, love as a mystical virtue is understood as love of God. In Ghazali's view, it is the most important mystical virtue but it is also one of the controversial mystical virtues. Some Islamic religious thinkers had contested the possibility of its existence and doubted its compatibility with Islamic teachings. Before analyzing such an important virtue, therefore, Ghazali considers it necessary to establish its existence and compatibility with Islam. Although Aristotle affirms that there can be no love between man and God because the distance between them is too great, Ghazali's argument against those who deny the love of God is primarily directed against Muslim traditionalists and certain dialectical theologians.[1] These thinkers interpret the Koranic verses "He loveth them and they love Him," and "Those who believe have stronger love for God," to mean not love but some other duty such as obedience.[2] They argue that love of God is impossible, because love exists only between members of the same genus and God is too high above us to inspire human emotions. According to Ghazali, this interpretation of love in terms of obedience is misleading because obedience is a consequence of love and love precedes it. On the basis of these Koranic verses and a score of prophetic traditions, and what he believes to be a unanimous agreement (*ijmāʿ*) in the Islamic community that love of God is a religious duty, Ghazali assures us that love of God is not only compatible with Islamic religious teachings but required by them. For him, objections to love of God are usually caused by a misunderstanding of its definition. To obtain a perfect definition of love of God, one must know what love is in general, its conditions, and finally its applicability to God.

What man perceives in the world can be divided into three classes: (1) what is harmonious with his natural disposition and, thus, produces pleasure and then love in the beholder; (2) what conflicts with his natural disposition, produces pain, and is therefore hated; (3) what is neutral and thus neither loved nor hated. A man of sound nature will love and seek that which gives him pleasure, and hate and avoid the

1. Aristotle *Nicomachean Ethics* 8. 7. 1159a3-4. However, a Muslim philosopher such as Miskawayh acknowledges love of God by the gnostic (*al-ʿārif*) who acquires true knowledge of Him; see his *Tahdhīb*, p. 147. Ghazali mentions one Aḥmad Ibn Ghālib, known as Ghulām al-Khalīl, as an example of the dialectical theologians who reject love of God because it may imply anthropomorphism (*tashbīh*); see *R*, IV. 6. 2655-56.

2. *R*, IV. 6. 2581; Koran 5:59, 2:160.

painful. Therefore, "love is the inclination of nature (*mayl aṭ-ṭab'*) to that which gives pleasure."[1]

There are five classes of pleasurable objects of love: those perceived by the five senses. Such pleasures can be shared by all animals. Were there no other senses, then God could not be loved, because He cannot be perceived by the senses or represented by images. But there is another, sixth sense, which characterizes man and differentiates him from animals. This may be called "intellect," or "light," or "heart," or something else. It is an inner sight, stronger than external sight. Its perceptions are more powerful, and the beauty of what is perceived by it is greater. The delight of the heart in perceiving sublime divine objects is, therefore, superior to the pleasures derived from the five senses.[2]

Ghazali discusses five categories of love. (1) Every living being loves itself first. Self-love means that by nature every living being has a desire to persevere in its existence and avoid death. Since that which is loved by nature is what is agreeable to the lover, and nothing is more agreeable to him than his own self, man loves his own existence and fears death, not only out of fear of pain or of punishment in the hereafter, but because death will put an end to his existence. This love naturally extends to the perfection of an individual's existence and everything that helps to preserve that perfection. Thus, each man's first love is for himself; then for the soundness of his members; then his property, children, kinsfolk, and friends. These things are only loved, in this sense, because man's existence and perfection depend on them. Ghazali gives an example of how man's love of his children is related to his self-love. He says that man loves his children when he does not receive any benefit from them, because they continue to exist after he does. The continuity of the existence of offspring is a kind of continuity of the existence of one's self. Still, if a man were motivated only by this natural disposition (*wa kāna ṭab'uhu 'alā i'tidālih*) and had to choose between being killed himself or having his child killed, he would choose his own existence rather than that of his child because the life of his child only resembles his own.[3] (2) The second category of love is benefit. Man loves those who

1. *R*, IV. 6. 2584.
2. *R*, IV. 6. 2584-85.
3. *R*, IV. 6. 2585-86. It must be noted here that Ghazali gives this example to show the exact nature of self-love. He deliberately uses the expression "when man is motivated by his natural disposition alone" in order to warn against confusing this meaning of self-love with other grounds of love. Van den Bergh in his "The 'love of God,'" p. 311, regards this example as "immoral."

benefit him and can thus love a stranger to whom no blood ties bind him. This second object of love concerns only the means to one's own existence. It is in the nature of the love of the means that, once the aim is attained, the means lose their value. (3) Man may love something other than himself for its own sake, not for any benefit he may receive from it. This love by itself causes him happiness. It is a true and perfect love, inasmuch as its object is beyond a man's own existence. Beauty, for instance, is loved in this way: for the perception of beauty is a delight, loved for its own sake and not for the satisfaction of physical desires. Verdant plants and running water are loved in themselves apart from their usefulness for man's survival.[1] (4) Man loves beauty in general. The term "beauty" (*ḥusn*) can be applied to things not perceived by the senses as well as to well-proportioned shapes and agreeable colors. Beauty in anything means that there exists in it the perfection that befits it. Thus, when we speak of a beautiful character of a man, for example, we refer to the good qualities which are not perceived by the senses but by the inner sight. Thus, the one who loves the saint or the prophet, loves him because of the beauty of his character. (5) The fifth category of love is the mysterious, hidden relationship (*al-munāsabah al-khafiyyah*) which exists between two persons, not because of beauty or any advantage, but solely as a result of a certain spiritual affinity between them.[2]

Were one man to have all five qualities which evoke love, he would inspire more intense love than someone endowed with only one or two qualities. However, only in God are all five qualities in their perfect form united. Hence, it is only God who is an object of love in the ultimate sense. For, although individual men may be objects of love in one of the five ways, that any human evokes love in all five ways is mere illusion.[3] Ghazali then applies these five categories to love of God. (1) As to man's love of his own existence, he who knows himself and God knows absolutely that his existence, survival, and perfection depend on God alone. Nothing exists by itself; everything receives its existence through God who truly exists by Himself. If a man does not love God, it is because he does not understand himself and because of his love of himself. (2) Love of benefit must lead man to love of God once he knows that God is the ultimate cause of all benefit. In the last analysis,

1. *R.* IV. 6. 2586-87.
2. *R*, IV. 6. 2589-91.
3. *R*, IV. 6. 2591.

a man bestows favors only on himself, never on others. When he gives to others, he aims at a reward such as entering paradise. Therefore, no man has a right to be thanked and loved for favors since it is God who enables him to act and since in doing good deeds he really seeks to benefit himself. (3) True love for a benefactor without expecting any favors from him also requires the love of God, because God is the benefactor of the whole of creation and all things created. Ghazali cites several examples of God's special favors for men and asks, how could there be another benefactor in addition to God? (4) As to the love of beauty for its own sake, he who loves the prophet or a saint does not love him for his external beauty but for the inner beauty which his actions and character suggest. But, in reality, the good qualities which form such inner beauty belong, in their most perfect state, to God alone. Being created implies being imperfect. All perfection but God's is relative. (5) Spiritual affinity is based on something visible or hidden. Ghazali says that this affinity also exists between man and God, but it cannot be expressed because of its relation to the knowledge of revelation, and only when one experiences the higher mystical station can he have a "taste" (*dhawq*) of love of God based on this affinity. However, Ghazali maintains that this kind of love is metaphorically mentioned in a prophetic tradition in which Muḥammad relates that God says: "My servant continues to approach Me with supererogatory practices till I love him, and when I love him, I become the hearing through which he hears, the sight through which he sees, and the tongue by which he speaks."[1]

This discussion of the objects of love in general and the way they can be applied to the love of God has been pursued in some detail in order to show how Ghazali uses nonmystical sources to explain a mystical virtue. It is clear that he appeals to the philosophic tradition, especially that of Aristotle, for an exposition of love in general which he applies to his analysis of the love of God.[2] In order to see how this procedure contributes to the systemization and clarification of a mystical virtue, one need only compare Ghazali's account of love of God with that of al-Makkī and al-Qushayrī.[3] However, the philosophers do not regard love as a virtue but rather as a passion.[4] By considering love of God

1. *R*, IV. 6. 2601.
2. Aristotle *Nicomachean Ethics* 9. 4. 1166a1-8, 1169b2.
3. *R*, IV. 6. 2580-2655; al-Makkī, *Qūt*, II, 99-141; al-Qushayrī, *Risālah*, I, 610ff.
4. Aristotle *Rhetoric* 2. 4. 1380b-1381b; Avicenna, *Fī al-Akhlāq wa al-Infi'ālāt*, p. 24.

as a mystical virtue, Ghazali shows how such a passion can become not only another mystical virtue, but also the highest mystical virtue. For this purpose, he relates this passion of love to God through the highest form of knowledge, that is, knowledge of Him.

In his discussion of love of God, Ghazali does not mention explicitly the three components of the mystical virtues, i.e., knowledge, positive disposition, and action. However, his discussion of the necessary relation between knowledge and love of God, which is obviously a positive disposition as he defines it, and his accounts of the activities of those who are experiencing love show that these three elements are assumed in this mystical virtue. The element of knowledge deserves special attention because, although knowledge, according to Ghazali, is an element in all mystical virtues, it is most prominent in his discussion of love of God, and we are even given hints of an esoteric (*bāṭin*) knowledge which is not to be written down in books. On the other hand, Ghazali does not deal with an independent mystical virtue called "knowledge" as al-Qushayrī, for example, does.[1]

When he speaks of knowledge of God Ghazali means an intuitive theoretical knowledge which produces a joy and a pleasure that do not end with death.[2] He distinguishes two ways which lead to this highest knowledge. (1) The way of those who are strong in their apprehension and devotion. These know God first and then know other things through Him. (2) The way of the weak, who know God's works first and, through these, gradually ascend to some perception of the Creator. The first way, according to Ghazali, is the esoteric knowledge which cannot be expressed in writing. Although he calls the second the way of the weak he says it is actually very difficult in itself. It can only be achieved through meditation which requires freedom from desires of worldly things. Because of the infinity of the objects to be known, this process can never be complete, but it can produce love of God.

Ghazali emphasizes that love of God can only be attained in this life, although it assures man of ultimate happiness in the hereafter. Ultimate happiness admits of degrees in proportion to the strength of man's love of God. Vision of God (*ru'yat Allāh*) is the highest happiness that man can attain in the hereafter if his love of God reaches the utmost degree in this life. The purification of the heart from worldly things is

1. al-Qushayrī, *Risālah*, I, 601-609, where he deals with "knowledge" (*ma'rifah*) immediately before dealing with "love."

2. *R*, IV. 6. 2604-2606.

attained through careful training in the mystical life. When this is done, knowledge of all that is God's is the means of securing, preserving, and strengthening the love of God.[1]

Since men differ in their desire for worldly things and their capacity for knowledge, it is natural that they differ in their love of God. Love of God and desire for worldly things pull man in opposite directions, so that love of God increases when the desire for worldly things decreases and vice versa. In contrast, there is a certain correspondence between love of God and knowledge in general; the more man understands, the greater his love will be.[2] Therefore, one reason for imperfect love of God is weakness in man's knowledge of Him. If God is the most evident of all things, then the knowledge of Him ought to come first in time and be the easiest to obtain. Nevertheless, things do not happen in this way. The reason, according to Ghazali, is that knowledge of God comes late in man's development, after he has acquired certain moral and intellectual habits. Furthermore, our intellects are too weak to grasp the majesty and splendor of God which illuminate everything. It seems strange that God's evidence is the cause of His being hidden. Generally, however, things are understood by means of their opposites. If some things indicated God's existence while others denied it, it would be much easier for us to perceive the difference. If the sun never set and if we lived in perpetual light, we would never be able to know the existence of light, which we learn only through its negation, darkness.[3] Therefore, a mystic who sets out to seek the highest mystical virtue, i.e., love of God, must achieve knowledge of God after he has already purified his soul from love of anything other than Him.

To distinguish true love of God from apparent love, Ghazali enumerates a large number of signs through which true love can be known. For example, a man who truly loves God will desire to meet Him and, consequently, will not fear death but love it. Hating death is a sign of incomplete love of God. But there is one case in which the man who loves God may not desire to die for the time being, namely, when he is not quite prepared to meet his Beloved and wishes to prepare himself better by means of more devotional practices. He who loves God will also prefer God's will to what he himself desires and will find obedience to God pleasing. Indeed, he who loves God will love to be alone so as

1. *R*, IV. 6. 2612, 2616-22.
2. *R*, IV. 6. 2623.
3. *R*, IV. 6. 2625-27.

to meditate upon Him, and will find pleasure in isolation and pain and discomfort in associating with others. He will love all those who obey God and hate all His enemies.[1] The different signs of true love of God and the examples of how true lovers of God behave show that there are infinite degrees of love of God. But Ghazali is interested in demonstrating the essential characteristics of the true love of God which is based on knowledge of Him. This is the love of God which is the highest mystical virtue. When this love of God is achieved, it leads to the vision of God in the hereafter, which is the highest rank of ultimate happiness, higher than the happiness of paradise. It is in relation to these two levels of ultimate happiness that Ghazali says there are two kinds of love of God: love of Him because of His majesty alone and love of Him because He is the true Benefactor.[2]

As to the question whether God loves His servants, Ghazali's approach changes when he ends his treatment of man's love of God. He admits that there are Koranic verses as well as prophetic traditions which speak of God's love of man, for example, the Koranic verse quoted above: "He loveth them, and they love Him." While he opposes the theologians and traditionalists who seek to interpret man's love of God as obedience, he himself maintains that as to the question of God's love of His creatures, the word love cannot have the same meaning as when it is applied to man. This is so because all the words we use have a different sense when applied to God and can be applied to God only metaphorically. Love in man implies a need and a deficiency, which are impossible for God, who possesses all perfection, all beauty, and all majesty eternally and necessarily. Therefore, God loves only Himself. What is said about His love of His servants must be taken in a metaphorical or allegorical sense, that is, it means that God lifts the veil from their hearts so that they can know Him and are enabled to draw nearer to Him, and that He wills this from eternity. God's love for man means that He brings man to His nearness, repels his sins, purifies his soul, and lifts the veil so that he can see Him with his inner sight.[3]

This discussion of God's love of man is meant to make clear that it is man's love of God which is the subject of the highest mystical virtue and not God's love of man. There remain only the mystical virtues which result from love of God and are, consequently, controlled by it.

1. *R*, IV. 6. 2640-48.
2. *R*, IV. 6. 2649, 2654-55.
3. *R*, IV. 6. 2635-37,2639.

Of the specific virtues which follow from love of God, Ghazali mentions yearning, intimacy, and satisfaction, and discusses them in this order.

Virtues produced by love

Yearning

Yearning (*shawq*) can be defined as seeking and longing for something. By nature, man yearns toward the object of his love when it is not present or is partly perceived, for one does not long for what is present and fully grasped. As a mystical virtue, yearning, therefore, is only possible for those who acknowledge the existence of love of God.[1] Ghazali points out two ways of yearning for God. The first is the way the gnostics (*al-'ārifūn*) perceive divine unity and is not absolutely pure, but mixed with some fancies characteristic of this life. Perfect clarity can only occur through the direct vision of God which occurs in the hereafter. Thus, those who have achieved perfect knowledge of God still "yearn" for full clarity in the hereafter. The second type of yearning arises from the fact that the number of divine things is limitless. An individual person can discover only some of them, while an endless number remains unknown to him. The mystic knows that such things exist and that they are all known to God and hence he yearns to know these unknown things. Therefore, while the first kind of yearning can be satisfied in the hereafter, through encountering God and having a vision of Him, the second kind does not seem to be satisfied either in this world or in the world to come because it is impossible that man should know all that God knows.[2]

Intimacy

Ghazali regards intimacy (*uns*) as somewhat higher than yearning since yearning is characterized by restlessness. Intimacy is the cheerfulness and joy of the heart when it contemplates the beauty of the beloved. As a mystical virtue, intimacy is attained when the mystic is overwhelmed with the joy of nearness to God. The sign of being intimate with God is to be annoyed when associating with fellow men and delighted when contemplating God alone.[3]

1. *R*, IV. 6. 2628-30; cf. al-Makkī, *Qūt*, II, 120, where he mentions it in passing.
2. *R*, IV. 6. 2629-30.
3. *R*, IV. 6. 2656-58.

SATISFACTION

The most important of the three virtues produced by love of God is the mystical virtue of satisfaction (*riḍā*) with whatever God decrees. Ghazali considers love of God as a necessary precondition of satisfaction. He deals with satisfaction after love directly or indirectly in all three books in which he treats mystical virtues.[1] He thus differs from al-Makkī who regards satisfaction as the eighth mystical station which immediately precedes the ninth and the final station, namely, love.[2] Both thinkers consider love as the highest station, higher than satisfaction but al-Makkī, on the other hand, seems to distinguish between two kinds of satisfaction—the first is produced by trust and therefore precedes love; the second comes after love, but he does not discuss it in detail nor does he regard it as a station.[3] Ghazali regards only this second kind of satisfaction as a mystical virtue because one has to love God first before he can truly be satisfied with His works.

The attainment of love of God is, therefore, the necessary and sufficient condition for the emergence of satisfaction; once a man loves God, he must necessarily be satisfied with God's works. In order to demonstrate this, Ghazali discusses the case of man's acceptance of and satisfaction with pains and hardships that may befall him. He suggests that there are two ways of being satisfied with these matters. (1) One may enjoy the love of a certain object to such a degree that he does not feel pain or hardship coming from other sources and thus, still more, he does not feel the pains which come from the beloved object. (2) Alternatively, a man may accept immediate pain and even desire it despite his natural aversion to pain because he expects pleasure to replace this pain in the future. Such is the case of a sick man who accepts the pain of surgery for the relief which will follow.[4] If man can be satisfied with what opposes his desires and natural disposition, then he is even more likely to find satisfaction in those things to which he is naturally inclined, and if this is possible with regard to worldly affairs, it is even more likely in connection with love of God and the pleasures of the hereafter.

1. *R*, IV. 6. 2663; *Arba'īn*, p. 227, where he calls it the ninth principle of character traits; *Kimiyā-yi*, II, 974; cf. al-Zabīdī, *Itḥāf*, IX, 646.

2. Al-Makkī, *Qūt*, II, 76-91.

3. al-Makkī, *Qūt*, II, 151. Other mystics who classify "satisfaction" before love are: al-Qushayrī, al-Sarrāj, al-Kalābādhī, and al-Harawī; al-Kharrāz, however, classifies it immediately after "love," followed by "yearning" and "intimacy"; see Table 3, p. 160.

4. *R*, IV. 6. 2669-70.

In his discussion of satisfaction and of the other two virtues produced by love of God, namely yearning and intimacy, Ghazali does not mention specifically the three elements necessary for every mystical virtue, i.e., knowledge, positive disposition, and action. However, in his discussion of satisfaction in particular, Ghazali deals with the positive disposition of satisfaction as well as the action produced by it. Knowledge is left out because satisfaction is a by-product of love of God and this love is impossible without the knowledge of God. As a positive disposition, "satisfaction" means delight in submitting to God's will. Ghazali enumerates three levels of such delight. (1) The first is hope of reward in the hereafter. (2) Next is cheerful acceptance of whatever befalls man because it is due to the will of God. (3) The highest level is reached when man's desire for anything becomes the same as God's will and gives rise to the highest joy.

Ghazali raises some questions about the action which is produced by the positive disposition of satisfaction. (1) Since man seeks to be completely satisfied with God's decree, this may lead to abandoning all actions, even acts of obedience, or else to licentiousness since all actions ultimately originate in God. If God is the source of all good and evil, should a man who is pleased with God welcome sin and evil in himself and in others? According to Ghazali, though evil is ultimately traceable to God, man should be neither pleased with it nor with the one who commits it. Only ignorant and feeble-minded people regard acceptance of evil as the virtue of satisfaction. A sin is an act of God in the sense of ultimately originating in Him, and, from this viewpoint, man should express his satisfaction in "knowing" its origin. However, since man acquires his capacity to act from God, he is in a qualified sense responsible for sins which must, therefore, be rejected and despised. (2) The second question is related to supererogatory practices such as supplication (*du'ā'*). Since the man who loves God must be satisfied with whatever He decrees, does supplication conflict with this mystical virtue? Ghazali's answer is a clear no. Indeed, believers have been divinely commanded, through the Koran and prophetic traditions, to ask God for forgiveness as well as for aid to help them attain what is good and refrain from what is evil. Muḥammad himself constantly used to supplicate God in spite of the fact that he had achieved the highest degree of satisfaction.[1] Thus recommended and praiseworthy actions do not conflict with satisfaction. Ghazali finds it necessary in connection with the relation

1. *R*, IV. 6. 2677.

of action to "satisfaction," to comment on a well-known prophetic tradition in which Muḥammad forbade fleeing from a plague-stricken place. In Ghazali's view, fleeing from a plague does not in itself convey dissatisfaction with God's decree; the tradition merely indicates that some healthy persons must remain in the stricken place to look after the sick and the dead. Indeed, Ghazali says that in general it is a "decree" and order of God to flee from harmful things.[1]

In order to show the superior merit of satisfaction as a mystical virtue, Ghazali compares the attitudes of three men toward death. The first prefers death because he yearns for an encounter with God. The second chooses to continue living so that he may serve God. The third says that he does not choose, but rather will be satisfied with whatever God chooses for him. The cases, Ghazali says, were presented before a well-known gnostic (*'ārif*), who sided with the one who displayed "satisfaction."[2] Therefore, satisfaction is the highest mystical virtue produced by love of God which is truly the highest principal mystical virtue.

Conclusion

Ghazali's analysis of the mystical virtues occupies all of Quarter IV of the *Revival*, the largest quarter of the entire book. In his analysis, Ghazali emphatically asserts that the mystical virtues are *the* virtues par excellence, not because they describe man's relation to God, but because they are primarily the virtues of the few. Although he says that by the few he means the mystics, he points out in several places of Quarter IV of the *Revival* that the mystics have failed to reach a scientific understanding of these virtues. It is for this reason that he introduces the rational theoretical framework which he calls the tripartite characteristic of the mystical virtues. Ghazali also had recourse to other philosophic doctrines, such as the distinction between the rational psychic faculties on the one hand and the irascible and concupiscent on the other, which underlies many mystical virtues, especially those related to the states of the soul, namely, the supporting mystical virtues.

It is clear that Ghazali's "theoretical" approach to the mystical virtues is derived from the philosophic tradition. However, many of the specific features of his discussion, his ordering these virtues into a hierarchy, and regarding them as stations or spiritual states, all belong to

1. *R*, IV. 6. 2681.
2. *R*, IV. 6. 2682.

the mystical tradition with which Ghazali identifies himself. Ghazali's discussion of mystical virtues resembles in a certain way his discussion of the philosophic virtues. In the latter case, the generally accepted interpretation is that Ghazali rejects the philosophic tradition; however, as his treatment of philosophic virtues develops, it becomes clear that he accepts the essential features of all the philosophic virtues while modifying them in terms of the religious-legal tradition and mystical teachings. In contrast, it is generally accepted that Ghazali accepts the mystical tradition completely; however, his method of dealing with the mystical virtues reveals his dissatisfaction with the usual mystical understanding of these virtues. By having recourse to the teachings of the philosophers, Ghazali creates a new framework within which the mystical virtues can be explained more consistently and precisely.

In addition to his attempt to explain certain aspects of the mystical virtues in terms of philosophic concepts, Ghazali deals with these virtues as essentially based on the Islamic religious tradition. In his view, and in the view of his major Sufi source, al-Makkī, these mystical virtues are nothing but the interpretation of the hidden meanings of the divine commandments; the only difference between these and the religious-legal virtues extracted from the external meanings of the divine commandments is the fact that the former are for the few, whereas the latter are for the many.[1] We have mentioned in the beginning of this chapter that, in selecting material for his mystical virtues, Ghazali singles out those mystics known for their effort to reconcile mysticism with Islamic teachings. He, in turn, tries to synthesize the mystical and Islamic traditions by showing that mystical virtues admit of degrees of excellence. The lower degrees are usually assigned to pious religious men, whereas the higher degrees can only be acquired by the mystics; it is to these higher degrees that the term mystical virtue most properly applies. In the cases of open conflict between some mystical virtues and Islamic teachings, Ghazali seeks to reconcile them by interpreting the religious teachings through the perspective of the mystical virtues.

In his description of the mystical virtues, Ghazali begins with everyday social or moral qualities, religious teachings, and human passions, abstracts them from their original context, and reformulates them in terms of the way of life of the few in search of nearness to God. It is particularly important to note, for example, that the first principal

1. al-Makkī, *Qūt*, II, 150.

mystical virtue, repentance, is a well-known Islamic religious practice which Ghazali develops beyond its original religious limits to make it a virtue of the few. The highest mystical virtue, love of God, on the other hand, is a human passion discussed by the philosophers but never developed as a virtue. Ghazali begins with this passion in its accepted philosophic sense and directs it toward a new object, God, thus making it the ultimate virtue which can be acquired by man during this life.

TABLE 2
GHAZALI'S LIST OF MYSTICAL VIRTUES

	Revival IV	*Forty* IV	*Alchemy* IV
Tawbah	Repentance	Repentance	Repentance
Ṣabr	Patience	Fear	Patience
Shukr	Gratitude	Asceticism	Gratitude
Rajā'	Hope	Patience	Hope
Khawf	Fear	Gratitude	Fear
Faqr	Poverty	Sincerity	Poverty
Zuhd	Asceticism	Truthfulness	Asceticism
Tawḥīd	Divine Unity	Trust	Resolve
Tawakkul	Trust	Love	Sincerity
Maḥabbah	Love	Satisfaction	Truthfulness
Shawq	Yearning		Vigilance
Uns	Intimacy		Self-examination
Riḍā	Satisfaction		Meditation
Niyyah	Resolve		Divine Unity
Ikhlāṣ	Sincerity		Trust
Ṣidq	Truthfulness		Love
Murāqabah	Vigilance		Yearning
Muḥāsabah	Self-examination		Satisfaction
Tafakkur	Meditation		

TABLE 3

Sufis' Lists of Mystical Virtues[a]

al-Kharrāz *al-Ṣidq*	al-Sarrāj *al-Luma'*	al-Makkī *Qūt*	al-Kalābādhī *al-Ta'arruf*	al-Qushayrī *al-Risālah*	al-Harawī *Manāzil*
1 Repentance	1 Repentance	1 Repentance	1 Repentance	1 Repentance	2 Repentance
6 Asceticism	3 Asceticism	2 Patience	2 Asceticism	6 Asceticism	3 Self-examination
7 Trust	4 Poverty	3 Gratitude	3 Patience	8 Fear	5 Meditation
8 Fear	5 Patience	4 Hope	4 Poverty	9 Hope	12 Fear
10 Gratitude	6 Trust	5 Fear	6 Fear	15 Trust	16 Asceticism
11 Love	7 Satisfaction	6 Asceticism	8 Sincerity	16 Gratitude	19 Hope
12 Satisfaction	1 Vigilance	7 Trust	9 Gratitude	18 Patience	22 Vigilance
13 Yearning	3 Love	8 Satisfaction	10 Trust	19 Vigilance	24 Sincerity
14 Intimacy	4 Fear	9 Love	11 Satisfaction	20 Satisfaction	27 Trust
	5 Hope		14 Intimacy	24 Sincerity	31 Patience
	6 Yearning		17 Love	25 Truthfulness	32 Satisfaction
	7 Intimacy		27 Divine Unity	36 Poverty	33 Gratitude
				41 Divine Unity	35 Truthfulness
				44 Love	46 Intimacy
				45 Yearning	48 Poverty
					61 Love
					63 Yearning
					100 Divine Unity

[a] The Sufi manuals are given in a chronological order. Only mystical virtues which correspond to Ghazali's lists are given, and the numbers indicate the place of the given virtue in the order of virtues in the respective manual.

Chapter V / CONCLUSION

The three preceding chapters have shown how Ghazali discusses and analyzes virtues in the philosophic, religious, and mystical traditions. Within each tradition, he explains what virtue is, justifies each virtue theoretically as well as in terms of religious teachings, and modifies it in a way that enables him to synthesize it with other virtues belonging to the other traditions within a special reconstructed concept of virtue. To assess precisely the significance of Ghazali's treatment of each one of the three kinds of virtues in question, it is necessary to recall some of our earlier findings. This will show that the extensive and detailed account of Ghazali's treatment of the three traditions of virtue presented in this study is necessary for understanding the essential characteristics of a composite theory of virtue.

What emerged from the second chapter was Ghazali's general acceptance of the philosophic virtues. He justified his approval of them by their usefulness for the attainment of happiness in general, and for Islamic teachings in particular. This initial acceptance, however, was later qualified by his singling out particular aspects of these virtues, introducing specific changes in some of them, and adding other elements in others. The purpose of all these changes and modifications was to prepare these philosophic virtues for a role that differs radically from their usual function in philosophic ethical theory. The accepted philosophic virtues were incorporated by Ghazali into a wider ethical system which also includes non-philosophic elements. For example, courage as a philosophic virtue is transformed by him from its meaning as bravery on the battlefield, to become the excellent quality which subordinates man's base animal faculties to his rational faculty—a virtue related to the refinement of the individual soul. Likewise, Ghazali minimizes the virtue of liberality, in the philosophic as well as the religious traditions, so as to make room for poverty as a higher virtue in the mystical tradition. Similarly, Ghazali intends by his brief treatment of justice(and he maintains this attitude in connection with all virtues related to justice in the philosophic as well as the Islamic religious traditions) to indicate his understanding of ethics as by and large independent of politics—which view is intimately bound up with Ghazali's theory of individual human salvation.

Thus, Ghazali sees in the philosophic virtues a natural starting point (natural in the sense that man arrives at them by unaided reason) which can serve as a basis for the higher levels of virtue. That is why, in concluding his discussion of the four principal philosophic virtues, Ghazali states that any further inquiry into them must be sought in Islamic moral teachings. Unlike some other Muslim thinkers who welcome any device which can be used to reconcile philosophic ethics with Islamic moral teachings, Ghazali does not consider the partial modifications he introduces into philosophic virtues sufficient to justify synthesizing those virtues with their Islamic counterparts; a more comprehensive approach, transforming these virtues into an integral part of a new, wider framework, is necessary. Ghazali finds the key to this restructuring in the theological virtues, forms of divine assistance which are necessary means to the attainment of happiness. Because divine assistance is a gift from God which does not depend on man's free choice, it calls the efficacy of philosophic virtues into question. The only way for man to elicit divine assistance is to appeal to God for His aid. Unaided reason does not know how to seek God's assistance; for this, man must have recourse to divine commandments which become known through revelation. Thus, Islamic religious-legal virtues, which are the fulfillment of the divine commandments, are indispensable for the attainment of human happiness. The accepted philosophic virtues continue to play an important role in this new context of virtue, and because it is based on the analysis of the faculties of the soul, for instance, the philosophic exposition provides a firmer ground for the reconstructed concept of virtue.

The religious-legal virtues consist in the fulfillment of the divine commandments. They consist of worship directed toward God, and of those practices directed toward fellow men which are necessary for men to live in a particular religious community which makes possible devotional life. However, these virtues, which supersede the philosophic virtues as the precondition for the attainment of happiness, are insufficient to assure the attainment of ultimate happiness by the few. Rather, the religious-legal virtues, which are the practice of the divine commandments taken literally, make it possible for the few to attain the highest happiness by inviting them to explore an internal, nonliteral significance. For instance, from alms-tax (*zakāh*) as a religious-legal virtue one can reach asceticism, a virtue related to the internal significance of the commandments.

To harmonize the religious-legal virtues with the mystical virtues, Ghazali presents the latter as the internal (*bāṭin*) aspects of the divine commandments. While the literal (*ẓāhir*) meaning of these commandments must be observed by every member of the religious community, some devoted members may be able to penetrate to their inner significance and conduct their lives accordingly, thereby acquiring the mystical virtues. The incorporation of the mystical virtues, therefore, is based on Ghazali's well-known distinction between the external and internal meanings of the religious law on the one hand, and between the many and the few on the other. The many can only understand the external aspects of the religious law, whereas the few can understand both the external and the internal aspects. He suggests that the external aspects rank below the internal by repeatedly linking the external with the activities of the body, and with the same purpose, he openly praises the internal aspects and reiterates that, in giving an account of the external acts of worship or customs, his primary intention is to reveal their hidden significance. However, the few, in their effort to acquire mystical virtues, cannot in any way dispense with the religious-legal virtues. Any attempt in this direction will result in losing sight of the true internal sense of the commandments.

Ghazali's treatment of the mystical virtues is distinctive, not only because he endeavors to merge them into the Islamic religious tradition, but because he seeks as well to provide them with a rational, theoretical framework derived from the philosophic tradition. This is especially clear in what Ghazali calls the tripartite characteristic of the mystical virtues as well as in his account of the psychological basis for these virtues. This theoretical approach reflects Ghazali's way of freely moving from one tradition to another, filling in the gaps in the one with the complementary elements of the other, and modifying those aspects which cannot, in their original form, be incorporated into his new framework. The fact that Ghazali applies this method throughout his treatment of the three kinds of virtue mentioned above shows that the charge of inconsistency and the attempt to explain his discussion of certain traditions of virtue in terms of the development of his thought are ultimately untenable.

Ghazali's discussion of the mystical virtues points out their hierarchy and order. He asserts emphatically that, as a whole, the mystical virtues are the highest kinds of virtues—the virtues par excellence. Not only does he show that they are the means to ultimate happiness; he indicates as well how the three basic views of virtue, namely, the philosophic, the religious, and the mystical, are synthesized on the highest level of moral training. Indeed, Ghazali never merely copies or combines diverse ideas in a random way, but selects, transforms, and weaves certain aspects of them together with a view to a particular end, ultimate happiness.

We shall develop briefly the central notions which make Ghazali's composite theory of virtue possible. These are (1) his use of the theological virtues and (2) his special view of happiness.

We showed in Chapter III how the theological virtues call into question the efficacy of the philosophic virtues and of any virtue which is acquired through unaided reason, unless it is incorporated into a system governed by divine revelation. In this way, Ghazali presents Islamic religious-legal virtues as necessary and essential for the attainment of human happiness. It is only when life is ordered by the divine commandments and man knows how to appeal for divine guidance that virtue is possible.

While the theological virtues bridge the gap between the philosophic and religious concepts of virtue, Ghazali's doctrine of happiness integrates the mystical virtues with the religious-legal virtues on the one hand, and on the other, serves as the end which determines the form of the resulting composite theory of ethics and orders its component virtues. We have alluded to Ghazali's view of happiness in the course of our discussion of the various kinds of virtues, and now we discuss what Ghazali means by happiness in order to understand how his view influences the construction of his theory of virtue and how it gives this theory its special character.

True happiness, for Ghazali, is otherworldly happiness (*al-sa'ādah al-ukhrawiyyah*) but he also calls some worldly goods forms of happiness inasmuch as they are means to this otherworldly happiness. In this sense, anything that helps man realize the ultimate end can be called happiness in a qualified sense, and each of the four principal philosophic virtues can thus be called happiness.[1] Ghazali emphasizes that true happiness can be attained in the hereafter only and he means that man

1. *C*, pp. 109-110; *R*, IV. 2. 2247-48.

must die and be resurrected before he can attain the true end of his virtue.

In his two major ethical works, the *Criterion* and the *Revival*, Ghazali shares with the Muslim philosophers the view that man should not fear death; instead he should accept its reality, prepare himself for it, and be pleased with it.[1] In the *Revival* Ghazali deals with the subject in detail and he devotes Book 10 of Quarter IV of the *Revival*, the last and longest book in this work, to the discussion of "Death and What Comes After It" (*Fī Dhikr al-Mawt wa mā Ba'dah*).[2] He explains that what actually dies is man's body but not his intellect, which does not change at death (*al-'aql lā yataghayyar bi al-mawt*).[3] After death, man is resurrected and faces divine judgment for his deeds during this life. In the *Revival*, Ghazali states clearly that after death the soul returns to the body on the day of resurrection, and it may even return to it in the grave.[4] In this, he maintains the opposition to the philosophers' rejection of bodily resurrection which he expressed in the *Incoherence* and to which he continued to adhere in books he wrote after the *Revival*, such as the *Decisive Distinction Between Islam and Unbelief* (*Fayṣal al-Tafriqah Bayn al-Islām wa al-Zandaqah*) and the *Deliverer*.[5] Ibn Ṭufayl, however, points

1. *C*, pp. 198-204; *R*, IV. 10. 2846-2924. Cf. Abū Yūsuf Ya'qūb Ibn Isḥāq al-Kindī, *Risālah fī al-Ḥīlah li Daf' al-Aḥzān*, ed. by H. Ritter and R. Walzer in "Studi su al-Kindi II, uno scritto morale inedito di al-Kindi," *Memoire della Reale Academia Nazionale die Licei*, ser. VI, III, Fasc. 1 (1938), 44-46; al-Kindi's views on death are repeated by Miskawayh in his *Tahdhīb*, pp. 209-217. Ghazali apparently repeats al-Kindī's arguments against fear of death, especially in *C*, pp. 203-204. Indeed, in the *Criterion*, Ghazali's discussion of fear of death follows immediately after a section entitled "rejection of grief" in which he presents arguments similar to those of al-Kindī; see *C*, pp. 193-198; al-Kindī, *Ḥīlah*, pp. 33ff.; Miskawayh, *Tahdhīb*, pp. 217-21.

2. *R*, IV. 10. 2846-3034.

3. *R*, IV. 10. 2944, Ghazali explains here that the soul's departure from the body means that it ceases to manage the body. Soul, he says, is that essence in man which perceives sciences and feels pleasures and pains. These things do not depend on the body and, therefore, remain in the soul after death; see *R*, IV. 2926-27.

4. *R*, IV. 10. 2926. It should be noticed here that Ghazali briefly mentions bodily resurrection. In his brief statement, he judges the view that only the soul is resurrected as "bad suppositions" (*ẓunūn fāsidah*) while he calls the view which rejects resurrection altogether as the "opinion of the atheists" (*ra'y al-mulḥidīn*). Beyond this, bodily resurrection is not discussed at all in the concluding sections of either the *Book of the Forty* or the *Alchemy of Happiness*.

5. *Tahāfut*, p. 354-76; Ghazali's arguments here seem to be directed against Avicenna's view as expressed in the *Risālah Aḍḥawiyyah fī al-Ma'ād*, ed. by Sulaymān Dunyā (Cairo: Dār al-Fikr al-'Arabī, 1949), pp. 59, 112-25; Ghazali, *Fayṣal al-Tafriqah bayn al-Islām wa al-Zandaqah*, ed. by Sulaymān Dunyā (Cairo: 'Īsā al-Bābī al-Ḥalbī, 1961), pp. 191-92; *Munqidh*, p. 79.

out that Ghazali's esoteric view on the question of physical resurrection agrees with that of the philosophers, and he refers the reader to Ghazali's statement in the *Criterion* that the mystics reject the resurrection of the body.[1] Since Ghazali identifies himself with the mystics in the *Deliverer*, Ibn Ṭufayl concludes that this must have been Ghazali's belief as well.[2]

It is rather difficult to evaluate beyond any doubt Ibn Ṭufayl's assessment of Ghazali's belief. But even if it were true, it would not substantially alter the character of Ghazali's theory of virtue.[3] However, in the *Decisive Distinction*, a book devoted to a careful analysis of the questions of belief and unbelief, Ghazali asserts unequivocally that there can be no questioning of the religious teachings about bodily resurrection. To deny it is to become an unbeliever.[4] Furthermore, the fact that Ghazali identifies himself with the mystics and praises their methods does not mean that he accepts everything they say. There are many things in which he does not agree with the mystics, and we have seen in his treatment of mystical virtues how he points out certain defects in the mystics and tries to correct them by introducing philosophic ideas. Thus, if he mentions in the *Criterion* that the mystics deny bodily resurrection, this does not necessarily mean that he himself denies it. However, Ghazali always points out when he discusses this question that the spiritual rewards and punishments of the soul in the hereafter are greater than the pleasures or pains of the body. This view underlies his discussion of man's end in the hereafter. His most decisive proof of bodily resurrection is that God is unquestionably omnipotent, and so it is clearly within His power to reconstitute the body and effect a reunion between it and the soul.[5]

Life after death is the permanent existence of the resurrected soul and body. There are no longer any "actions" for which man is responsible.

1. *C*, pp. 7-8.

2. *Munqidh*, p. 101; cf. Muḥammad Ibn 'Abd al-Malik Ibn Ṭufayl, *Hayy ben Yaqdhān* (*Ḥayy Ibn Yaqẓān*), ed. by Léon Gauthier (2d ed.; Beirut: Imprimerie Catholique, 1936), pp. 15-16.

3. If we assume that Ghazali accepts bodily resurrection, this will justify the structure and hierarchy of his theory of virtue. It will point out an end for the virtues of the many and how these virtues lead to the virtues of the few. If we assume that he rejects bodily resurrection and believes in the resurrection of the soul alone, this, again, will not radically change the structure of his theory of virtue. The virtues of the few will continue to be *the* virtues of serious moral refinement, and love of God will continue to be the highest possible virtue.

4. *Fayṣal*, p. 191.

5. *Tahāfut*, pp. 363-66; cf. Arberry, *Reason and Revelation*, p. 63.

Virtue (or its opposite, vice) ceases to exist at death and man faces the consequences of the virtues or vices he acquired during his life: either otherworldly happiness or otherworldly affliction. In his description of otherworldly happiness, Ghazali says that it consists of life without death, pleasure without pain, wealth without poverty, perfection without defect, joy without sorrow, glory without disgrace, and knowledge without ignorance—all these will be eternal and will never diminish.[1] In the *Criterion*, he does not discuss in detail this otherworldly happiness; he only points out that it is the end which man can attain through sound knowledge and good action.[2] His detailed discussion of this happiness occupies a large part of the second half of the concluding book of the *Revival*. He gives a highly rhetorical account of happiness in the hereafter and for the most part repeats the traditional religious accounts which describe this happiness.[3]

Ghazali regards the fulfillment of divine commandments, especially as expressed in the Islamic teachings, as a necessary requirement for deserving otherworldly happiness. However, he admits that God's mercy may bestow this happiness on any human being, whatever his past deeds. He points out that there is a hierarchy within otherworldly happiness in proportion to man's achievement of moral refinement. Otherworldly happiness can be divided into two broad categories. The lower and more general is what is generally known as Paradise (*jannah*), and the highest and most particular category is the vision (*ru'yah*) of God or encounter (*liqā'*) with Him. Ghazali enumerates in detail the pleasures of paradise, quoting Koranic virtues and prophetic traditions extensively. He mentions things such as the rivers of paradise, its sounds, foods, drinks, nymphs, servants, palaces, and colorful dresses.[4] Within paradise some pious men occupy so high a place that they appear to those who reside

1. *C*, pp. 3, 109.

2. At the beginning of the *Criterion*, Ghazali presents otherworldly happiness and defines it in order to introduce the theme of the book, namely, the action which leads to happiness (*al-'amal al-mus'id*); cf. *C*, pp. 3-5.

3. *R*, IV. 10. 2909-3025; cf. Arberry, *Reason and Revelation*, pp. 63-64. In the *Book of the Forty*, Ghazali does not give the same account of paradise as in the *Revival*; instead he discusses the more general characteristics of otherworldly affliction; and he seems to be more rationally inclined in his discussion of that question; see *Arba'īn*, pp. 250-64. In the *Alchemy of Happiness*, the subject of the second half of book 10 of Quarter IV of the *Revival* is not even mentioned. The *Alchemy of Happiness* ends exactly where the first half of Book 10 of Quarter IV of the *Revival* ends, that is, with the part which deals with death before resurrection; see *Kīmiyā-yi*, II. 978-98.

4. *R*, IV. 10. 3007-3024.

in lower ranks as though they are the most remote stars. This, Ghazali says, corresponds to differences among the men who obey the literal commandments.[1]

In contrast to his lengthy account of the pleasures of paradise, Ghazali discusses the vision of God, the highest category of otherworldly happiness, briefly and in one paragraph. He describes it as the greatest pleasure which makes man forget the other delights of paradise. It is the ultimate bounty compared to which all the splendid pleasures of paradise are nothing.[2] In concluding this brief account, Ghazali emphasizes that man must only seek to attain the encounter with God, because man shares the rest of the pleasures of paradise with beasts of the field.[3] Ghazali's reason for discussing the highest category of happiness in the hereafter so briefly is the fact that he has already dealt with it in detail in Book 6 of Quarter IV of the *Revival*, in the course of his treatment of love of God.[4] At that point Ghazali raised the question of the otherworldly end which corresponds to love of God as the highest possible human virtue and this, he says, is the vision of God: "Paradise is the place of the pleasures of the senses; as for the heart, its delight consists in the encounter of God alone."[5] The happiest man in the hereafter is the one who loves God most during this life.[6]

This view of an otherworldly happiness consisting of two major divisions constitutes the end towards which virtue is directed and thus determines the place of each virtue within the reconstructed theory of virtue. This can be seen in the broad distinction between virtues of the many and those of the few, or virtues resulting from literal fulfillment of divine commandments and those corresponding to the inner interpretation of the commandments. The former virtues lead the many to the attainment of paradise and the latter lead the few to the attainment of ultimate happiness which is the vision of God. The heirarchy among ends in the hereafter explains, further, the hierarchy of particular virtues within

1. *R*, IV. 10. 3008-3009, 3011-3012.

2. *R*, IV. 10. 3025; cf. Ghazali, *Mishkāt al-Anwār*, ed. by Abū al-ʿIlā ʿAfīfī (Cairo: al-Dār al-Qawmiyyah li al-Ṭibāʿah wa al-Nashr, 1964), pp. 47-48.

3. *R*, IV. 10. 3025; cf. Mubārak, *al-Akhlāq ʿind al-Ghazalī*, pp. 123-24, where he says that Ghazali preferred the encounter with God to the pleasures of paradise.

4. *R*, IV. 10. 3025. Ghazali twice cites this reason in an apparent attempt to make the reader reflect on the question of the vision of God in relation to knowledge of God and love of Him.

5. *R*, IV. 6. 2609.

6. *R*, IV. 6. 2616.

Ghazali's reconstructed whole and shows why he arranges them in this special way. In this composite theory of virtue, therefore, virtues are arranged in accordance with their efficacy in leading to the attainment of happiness. The highest is the love of God which leads to ultimate happiness or the vision of God which is direct knowledge of God in the hereafter. Love of God, however, is not itself a form of knowledge; rather, it is a positive disposition of a passion which results from the knowledge of God in this life. If man wants to attain ultimate happiness in the hereafter, according to Ghazali, every knowledge and every action during his life must be directed to acquiring the virtue of love of God. Thus, Ghazali's theory of virtue is not only the central theme of his ethics but also the central issue which gives unity to his thought.

Ghazali's theory of virtue is composite, structured, hierarchical, and individually oriented. It is composite in the sense that it is constructed of various and diverse elements which form its component parts. It is structured in the sense that these component parts are woven together according to their role in the reconstruction of a special concept of virtue. It is hierarchical because the particular virtues included in it are arranged according to a particular ranking: the virtues acquired through unaided reason are subordinated to those known through divine revelation, the external virtues are subordinated to the internal virtues, and those of the many are subordinated to those of the few. This effort to order the virtues can be seen especially in the highest group, namely the mystical virtues, where man can attain each virtue only after he masters the one which precedes it. Ghazali's theory of virtue, finally, is oriented toward the well-being of the individual. It concerns itself primarily with man's individual spiritual salvation, the attainment of ultimate happiness in the hereafter.

Appendix I / On the Authenticity of the "Criterion of Action"

THE *Criterion of Action* (*Mīzān al-'Amal*) is a work of moderate size, written by Ghazali sometime after his *Standard of Knowledge* (*Mi'yār al-'Ilm*). It is anticipated in the latter, and in its introduction it is said that it follows the *Standard*.[1] Although the *Criterion* has been published at least four times, there is as yet no critical edition of it.[2] There exist at least nine manuscripts, eight of which are listed by us in the Bibliography. One of these, namely, Asad Efendi MSS, 1759, was completed in 546/1151, forty years after Ghazali's death.[3] The *Criterion* was translated into Hebrew by Abrahamo bar-Chasdai Barcinonesi (ca. 1240). This translation was edited by J. Goldenthal and published under the title *Compendium Doctrinae Ethicae* in Leipzig in 1839.[4] There are also two recent translations, one into French (with an introduction and analysis) by Hikmat Hachem (Paris, 1945), and the other into Urdu by Nasr Ullah Khan, published in Pindi Bahauddin, West Pakistan, with no date.[5]

The *Criterion* is listed as a work by Ghazali by many early biographers, such as al-Subkī, al Zabīdī, al 'Aydarūs, Ṭāsh Kubrā Zādah, and Ḥājjī Khalīfah.[6] It is also accepted as an authentic work of Ghazali

1. *Mi'yār*, p. 348; *C*, p. 2.

2. The first of these editions is the one cited above as *C*. The second edition of *C* was published in Cairo: al-Maṭba'ah al-'Arabiyyah, 1342/1923. There are further the following two recent editions: Cairo: Maṭba'at Muḥammad 'Alī Ṣabīḥ, 1963; Cairo: Dār al-Ma'ārif, 1964. These are also reproductions of *C*.

3. Asad Efendi MSS. 1759, fol. 173a. For more information about these manuscripts see *GAL*, I. p. 540. No. 27; *GAL(S)*, I. p. 749; Badawī, *Mu'allafāt*, pp. 79-81. Dilve Tarih-Coğrafya Fakültesi Ankara, Ismail Saib Sancar MSS, I/4464, fols. 39-71b, however, is not mentioned in any of these works because it belongs to an uncatalogued collection. See Bibliography.

4. Leipzig: Gebhard & Reisland, 1839.

5. Pindi Bahauddin, West Pakistan: Sufi Printing and Publishing Company, n.d.

6. al-Subkī, *Tabaqāt*, IV, 116; al-Zabīdī, *Itḥāf*, I. 29; 'Abd al-Qādir Ibn Shaykh

by modern scholars, such as L. Massignon, Maurice Bouyges, G. F. Hourani, and 'Abd al-Raḥmān Badawī in their bibliographical studies of Ghazali's works.[1]

It has been mentioned above that the *Criterion* was written shortly after the *Standard.* This means that it must have been written before the *Revival.* Many passages and sections in it, and even the titles of some of its sections, bear close resemblance to certain parts of the *Revival,* particularly Quarter I, Book 1; Quarter III, Books 1, 2, 3, and 4; and Quarter IV, Books 2 and 10. The correspondence between the two works seems to result from the fact that both deal primarly with ethics and cover the same subject matter, but they stress different priorities according to the specific aim of each book. It is common knowledge that Ghazali repeats himself many times, especially when dealing with the same or similar questions. This is apparent in the *Revival* itself, which repeats a discussion of some points in Quarter IV which has already been handled in earlier Quarters. In most cases, however, whenever Ghazali repeats statements about some ideas, he has a special reason for such repetition. This can be seen in his analysis of the idea repeated. Therefore, we should not be surprised to see sections of the *Criterion* repeated in the *Revival* and the changes which Ghazali inserts in the repetition may explain some important issues in both books.

Besides corresponding to the *Revival,* a substantial part of the text of the *Criterion* parallels another work on ethics written by a contemporary of Ghazali, namely, *al-Dharī'ah ilā Makārim al-Sharī'ah* of al-Rāghib al-Iṣfahānī (d. 1108). The literal resemblance between certain sections of these two books is so obvious that some of the biographers of Ghazali, such as al-'Aydarūs, consider the latter book a work by Ghazali.[2] Yet it is clear from the accounts of Ghazali's early biographers that this book is not his. Ghazali himself does not mention it in any of his commonly known works, and the same biographers ascribe *al-Dharī'ah* to al-Rāghib

al-'Aydarūs, *Kitāb Ta'rīf al-Aḥyā' bi Faḍā'il al-Iḥyā'* in *Mulḥaq Iḥyā' 'Ulūm al-Dīn* (Cairo: al-Maktabah al-Tijāriyyah al-Kubrā, n.d.), p. 9; Aḥmad Ibn Muṣṭafā Ṭāsh Kubrā Zādah, *Miftāḥ al-Sa'ādah wa Miṣbāh al-Siyādah* (2 vols.; Hayderabad, India: Dā'irat al-Ma'ārif, 1329/1911), II, 208; Ḥājjī Khalīfah, *Kashf al-Ẓunūn* ("Lexicon bibliographicum et encyclopaedicum), ed. by Gustavus Fluegel (London: Oriental Translation Fund of Great Britain and Ireland, 1835-1858), VI, 285.

1. Massignon, *Recueil,* p. 93; Bouyges, *Essai,* pp. 25-28; Hourani, "Chronology," p. 228; Badawī, *Mu'allafāt,* pp. 79-81.

2. al-'Aydarūs, *Ta'rīf,* p. 9.

al-Iṣfahānī.[1] In addition to this, al-Rāghib al-Iṣfahānī himself claims *al-Dharī'ah* as his in the introduction of his work *al-Mufradāt fī Gharīb al-Qur'ān.*[2] Ḥājjī Khalīfah attributes *al-Dharī'ah* to al-Rāghib al-Iṣfahānī and adds that Ghazali used to carry it with him constantly.[3] It is notable, however, that although these two thinkers were contemporaries and probably were on occasion in the same place, neithei of them mentions the other. The problem of the relation between these two thinkers cannot be solved at this stage and must await further evidence and research. The only hint we have so far is the statement of Ḥājjī Khalīfah. There is no doubt that *al-Dharī'ah* is not Ghazali's, and the next question is how to explain the close textual resemblance between certain sections of the two books. Despite the similarities, the arguments of the two books are different and the material which is common to some sections of both books is introduced, arranged, and incorporated in each case for a different purpose governed by the particular aim of the book. Whether both authors borrowed from a third source, whether one or many, or one of them borrowed from the other, cannot be decided at this point, especially since the details of the reationship between the two men are not yet established.

The first serious question raised about the *Criterion* was by the Andalusian philosopher Abū Bakr Muḥammad Ibn Ṭufayl (d. 1185). In the introduction to his *Ḥayy, the Son of Yaqẓān* (*Ḥayy Ibn Yaqzān*), he noticed that Ghazali in his *Incoherence* charges the philosophers with unbelief (*kufr*) for their denial of the resurrection of the body and their affirmation that only souls receive rewards and punishements.[4] Then Ibn Ṭufayl points out that "at the beginning of his [Ghazali's] *Criterion,*

1. Ṭāsh Kubrā Zādah, *Miftāḥ*, I, 183; cf. Ẓahīr al-Dīn al-Bayhaqī, *Tārīkh Ḥukamā' al-Islām*, ed. Muḥammad Kurd 'Alī (Damascus: al-Majma' al-'Ilmī al-'Arabī Bi-Dimashq, 1946), p. 112, where he considers al-Rāghib al-Iṣfahānī as the author of *al-Dharī'ah* and describes him as a thinker who was a leading master in both theology and philosophy. Cf. Badawī, *Mu'allafāt*, p. 383; Bouyges, *Essai*, p. 150.

2. al-Rāghib al-Isfahānī, *al-Mufradāt fī Gharīb al-Qur'ān* (Cairo: Muṣṭafā al-Bābī al-Ḥalabī, 1961), p. 5.

3. Ḥājjī Khalīfah. *Kashf*, III, 334. Aside from Ḥājjī Khalīfah's comment, there is no evidence that Ghazali met al-Rāghib al-Iṣfahānī or was acquainted with such a book.

4. Ibn-Ṭufayl, *Ḥayy*, p. 15. This is one of the three major points in which, according to Ghazali, the philosophers must be reckoned infidels; see his *Tahāfut*, pp. 344, 354, 376, where he classifies this charge as the third one; see also his *Munqidh*, p. 88, where he classifies it as the first of the three.

he says that this very same tenet is definitely held by the mystics (*ṣūfīs*)."[1] Ibn Ṭufayl continues: "Then, in his *Deliverer from Error* . . . he says that he himself holds the same belief as the mystics and that he had arrived at this conviction after a long and detailed study."[2] In pointing out such an important problem in the *Criterion*, Ibn Ṭufayl's aim is not to discredit or doubt the authenticity of this book, but to argue that Ghazali's writings contain both exoteric and esoteric teachings. Ghazali, according to Ibn Ṭufayl, presents his esoteric teachings in the form of symbols and allusions, which are meant to be understood by those who are endowed with great intelligence and willing to listen to Ghazali's own explanations. Ibn Ṭufayl continues that the *Criterion* is not one of the esoteric works which are not supposed to fall into the hands of the multitude (*maḍnūn*), and that none of the so-called *maḍnūn* works have ever reached Andalusia. Ibn Ṭufayl further casts doubt on the existence of any *maḍnūn* book written by Ghazali and if this is the case, the esoteric teachings may have to be sought within the well-known works of Ghazali. The *Criterion* seems to contain some such esoteric teachings, for, at the end of it, Ghazali, explaining how to interpret opinions, divides opinion (*ra'y*) into three classes: (1) an opinion in which one agrees with the multitude; (2) an opinion that conforms to instruction of students and seekers of counsel; and (3) an opinion that one holds intimately within himself and does not disclose except to those who share his convictions.[3]

On the basis of Ghazali's statement on the resurrection of the soul without the body as given in the *Criterion*, Hikmat Hachem, the translator of the book into French, concludes that this work must have been written toward the end of Ghazali's life when he must have abandoned certain doctrines he had held in earlier works. L. Massignon, who wrote a preface to this translation, also states that the *Criterion* was written after the *Deliverer*, sometime after 500/1106.[4]

1. Ibn Ṭufayl, *Ḥayy*, p. 15; cf. *C*, pp. 7-8, where Ghazali makes this statement. The text is the same on this point in all the manuscripts mentioned above in the bibliography.

2. Ibn Ṭufayl, *Ḥayy*, pp. 15-16. A similar case can be found in Quarter IV of the *Revival* where Ghazali maintains that the "only" thing which returns to God is the "restful soul" (*al-nafs al-muṭma'innah*) (*R*, IV. 2. 2305). Then in *al-Risālah al-Laduniyyah* (which was written sometime after the *Revival*) he says that men of wisdom call the essence of man the rational soul (*al-nafs al-nāṭiqah*); whereas in the Koran it is called the "restful soul" (*al-nafs al-muṭma'innah*), and the mystics call it the "heart"; all of these terms refer to the same substance. *Laduniyyah*, pp. 23-24; cf. *R*, III. 1. 1350.

3. *C*, pp. 212-216.

4. Hikmat Hachem, *Critère*, p. xi.

On the basis of this latter date, W. Montgomery Watt argues in his article on "The Authenticity of the Works Attributed to al-Ghazālī"[1] that the *Criterion* is unauthentic. Watt's argument against the authenticity of the *Criterion* is based on the general principles he uses in the examination of all of Ghazali's works. He uses three criteria. The first is the place assigned to reason in the work, and according to this criterion any work which considers reason the highest faculty is not written after the *Deliverer* and the *Niche* (*Mishkāt*). The second criterion is consistency and clarity of purpose. Books which are collections of disparate materials put together without any clear principle cannot have been composed by Ghazali. The third criterion is the attitude towards orthodox dogma and practice. Any work in which the author criticizes the Ash'arites or is not orthodox cannot belong to Ghazali's last period.[2] By applying these criteria to Ghazali's works Watt presents a provisional list of unauthentic works, including the *Criterion.*[3] Then, in a special appendix, he uses these three criteria as well as an analysis of some textual problems in the *Criterion* to prove it lacks authenticity and adds: "If anyone wants to make statements about al-Ghazali on the basis of these [spurious] works, he must first do something to justify his use of such material."[4] We are therefore compelled to discuss Watt's arguments. He asserts that the *Criterion* cannot have been given its present form by Ghazali, although there may be Ghazalian material in it.[5] By applying his three criteria Watt reaches the following conclusions. (1) In most of the book the primacy of reason seems to be accepted without question; the *Criterion*, therefore, cannot belong to the closing stages of Ghazali's life. (2) The argument of the book is extremely confused and full of contradictions; therefore, the book falls under suspicion.[6] This suspicion, according to Watt, will ripen into certainty that the *Criterion* is not an authentic work when two passages in it are compared with two parallel passages of the

1. *JRAS*, 1952, pp. 24-45. Although this article aims at establishing a basis for judging all the works of Ghazali, the discussion of the authenticity of the *Criterion* seems to be the major outcome of the entire article. Indeed, in a lengthy appendix devoted solely to this book, Watt says: "This is perhaps the most important book to be discussed." *Ibid.*, p. 38.

2. *Ibid.*, pp. 27-29.

3. *Ibid.*, p. 30.

4. *Ibid.*, p. 31.

5. *Ibid.*, p. 38.

6. *Ibid.*

Revival: "indeed, it will become clear, I hope, that the *Mīzān* [*Criterion*] is an unintelligent compilation from very varied sources."[1]

The first of these passages is the allegory of the slave performing the pilgrimage in the section of the *Criterion* which deals with the duties of the pupil and this parallels a similar section in the first book of Quarter I of the *Revival*. Watt points out that the lessons drawn from this allegory differ in these two books, and that while they are excellent in the *Revival*, they are clusmy in the *Criterion*. He concludes that on the basis of this comparison the interpretation of the allegory in the *Criterion* "is spurious, the work of a forger who objected to something in the interpretation of the allegory in the *Iḥyā'* [*Revival*]; the passage must therefore be subsequent to the *Iḥyā'* [*Revival*]."[2] We cannot accept this argument since we have shown that the *Criterion* must have been written before the *Revival*. Furthermore, the presence of two different interpretations of the same allegory in these two books does not necessarily mean that one of them must be unauthentic. Indeed, Ghazali repeats some allegories, stories, and sayings in different parts of the *Revival* over and over again, and draws different lessons from them. Yet the *Revival* is unanimously accepted as authentic.

The second passage is an autobiographical one in the *Criterion*. Watt says, "pp. 44-48 of the *Mīzān* [*Criterion*] is closely parallel to *Iḥyā'* [*Revival*], III. Book 2 *bayān* 8 f."[3] He shows that these two passages are not identical. For the most part they have the same wordings with only slight grammatical changes, such as the use of the third or the second or the first person. According to him, the most important difference is that the words whose form tends to make the passage autobiographical (i.e., which are in the first person) do not occur in the *Revival*. Then he proposes various possible theories about the relation between these two passages. The most plausible theory in Watt's view is that the existing autobiographical form is a fraudulent invention and that the whole passage was copied from the *Revival* with slight modifications. "In view of what the rest of the *Mīzān* [*Criterion*] is, I think this is most probably the case."[4] We, on our part, do not see why the reshaping which gives certain related passages a different form should make any of these passages spurious.

1. *Ibid.*, p. 39.
2. *Ibid.*
3. *Ibid.*
4. *Ibid.*, p. 40.

Watt's final conclusion is that the *Criterion* as it stands "cannot have received its form from al-Ghazālī himself, and it contains much material that cannot be his."[1] We have already argued that none of the steps leading to this conclusion can be defended.

In a later article on "al-Ghazālī," Watt makes the following comment about the *Criterion*: "Since al-Ghazālī does not appear to refer to the *Mīzān* [*Criterion*] in his later works, and since he became very critical of philosophic ethics, it is possible that, as his enthusiasm waned, he rejected much of what he had written in this work."[2] (He makes the same point in his book, *Muslim Intellectual.*)[3] This position is certainly different from the one Watt took in his earlier article, "The Authenticity of the Works Attributed to al-Ghazālī." Watt's new argument is that the book as it exists belongs to Ghazali. However, because Ghazali criticized philosophic ethics in the *Deliverer*, certain sections of it must still be rejected as not representing Ghazali's mature views. The argument has, therefore, shifted from the authenticity of the book itself to the place of the ideas expressed in it within the totality of Ghazalian thought.

1. *Ibid.*
2. Watt, "al-Ghazālī," p. 1040.
3. Watt, *Muslim Intellectual*, p. 150.

Appendix II / Subdivisions of the Four Principal Virtues

The following four tables cover Ghazali's lists of virtues in the *Criterion* and in the *Revival*, as well as those of Miskawayh and Avicenna. The aim of these tables is to enable the reader to compare the two lists of Ghazali, and to compare Ghazali's lists with those of Miskawayh and Avicenna.[1]

The rest of this Appendix deals with Ghazali's accounts of those subdivisions of the four principal virtues which are not discussed in the text of Chapter II, taking into consideration the slight modifications of the philosophic tradition he introduces in them.[2] The subdivisions are presented here for the sake of completeness.

1. *R*, III. 2. 1443; *C*, pp. 92, 94, 96-97; Miskawayh, *Tahdhīb*, pp. 19-24; Avicenna, *Akhlāq*, pp. 152-54.

2. This modification is particularly apparent in Ghazali's discussions of virtues under temperance, especially wit, joy, and cheerfulness.

TABLE 4

GHAZALI'S LIST OF VIRTUES IN THE *Criterion*

WISDOM	COURAGE	TEMPERANCE	JUSTICE
Discretion	Magnificence	Modesty	......
Excellence of discernement	Intrepidity	Shame	......
Penetration of idea	Greatness of soul	Remission	......
Correctness of opinion	Endurance	Patience	......
	Gentleness	Liberality	......
	Fortitude	Good calculation	......
	Nobility	Joy	......
	Manliness	Tenderness of character	......
	Correct evaluation of self	Self-discipline	......
		Good appearance	......
		Contentment	......
		Tranquility	......
		Abstinence	......
		Cheerfulness	......
		Honest dealing	......
		Righteous indignation	......
		Wit	......

TABLE 5

GHAZALI'S LIST OF VIRTUES IN THE *Revival*

WISDOM	COURAGE	TEMPERANCE	JUSTICE
Discretion	Magnificence	Liberality	......
Excellence of discernement	Intrepidity	Modesty	......
Penetration of idea	Manliness	Patience	......
Correctness of opinion	Greatness of soul	Remission	......
Awareness of subtle actions and mysteries of the evils of soul	Endurance	Contentment	......
	Gentleness	Abstinence	......
	Fortitude	Cheerfulness	......
	Suppression of anger	Honest dealing	......
	Correct evaluation of self	Wit	......
	Amiability, etc.	Righteous indignation	......

TABLE 6
MISKAWAYH'S LIST OF VIRTUES

WISDOM	TEMPERANCE		COURAGE	JUSTICE
Intelligence	Modesty		Greatness of soul	Friendship
Retention	Sedateness		Bravery	Concord
Prudence	Liberality	Liberality	Composure	Family fellowship
Quickness and soundness of understanding	Integrity	Magnificence	Fortitude	Recompense
Clarity of mind	Contentment	Altruism	Patience	Fair play
Capacity for learning easily	Mildness	Nobility	Gentleness	Honest dealing
	Self-discipline	Clarity	Self-possession	Amiability
	Good appearance	Open-handedness	Manliness	
	Leniency	Remission	Endurance	
	Correct evaluation of self			
	Abstinence			

TABLE 7
AVICENNA'S LIST OF VIRTUES

TEMPERANCE	COURAGE	WISDOM	JUSTICE
Liberality	Patience	Eloquence	......
Contentment	Gentleness	Sagacity	......
	Generosity	Firmness of opinion	......
	Forgiveness	Determination	......
	Pardon	Truthfulness	......
	Relinquishment	Faithfulness	......
	Open-handedness	Amity	......
	Keeping secret	Mercy	......
		Composure	......
		Excellence of commitment	......
		Humility	......

Divisions of Wisdom

Although Ghazali mentions five of these, he only discusses four of them. They are as follows:

1. "Discretion" (*ḥusn al-tadbīr*) is the excellence of deliberation in deducing what is best and finest for the attainment of great goods and noble things. It is employed by man for himself or in giving advice to another, in the management of the household or the city, or to resist the enemy and to ward off an evil, and in general, in every important and grave matter. If the matter is insignificant and inconsiderable, then it is called cleverness, but not discretion.[1] The definition is closely related to the definition of al-Fārābī, and corresponds to Aristotle's minor intellectual virtue of deliberative excellence.[2]

2. "Excellence of discernment" (*jaudat al-dhihn*) is the power of finding the true judgment when opinions are obscured, and controversy arises about them.[3] Ghazali's description of this virtue has much in common

1. *C*, p. 92; cf. al-Fārābī, *Fuṣūl*, pp. 130-31. There is a rather close textual resemblance between Ghazali's accounts of the virtue of "discretion" and the rest of the virtues under wisdom, and those which correspond to them in al-Fārābī's *Fuṣūl*.

2. Aristotle *Nicomachean Ehtics* 6. 9. 1142b24-26.

3. *C*, p. 29; cf. al-Fārābī, *Fuṣūl*, p. 131; Avicenna, *'Ahd*, p. 143.

with Muslim philosophers, particularly al-Fārābī and Avicenna, as well as with Aristotle's virtue of understanding.[1]

3. "Penetration of thought" (*thaqābat ar-ra'y*) is quickness of conjecture about the means which lead from things to their commendable consequences. This corresponds to what Miskawayh and al-Fārābī call intelligence.[2]

4. "Correctness of opinion" (*ṣawāb aẓ-ẓann*) is hitting on what appears to be the truth, without reasoned proof. Al-Fārābī gives a similar definition which may also be traced, although not directly, to Aristotle's minor intellectual virtue of judgment.[3]

For Ghazali, these virtues are means between two extremes. He does not specify the relevant extremes for each virtue; rather he lists those extremes as divisions of the vices of wisdom. Under deceit, which is the extreme of excess, he lists astuteness (*dahā'*), slyness (*jarbazah*), and cunning (*makr*); stupidity, which is the extreme of defect, includes inexperience (*ghamārah*), foolishness (*ḥumq*), and insanity (*junūn*).[4] Ghazali does not discuss the vices of excess in the *Revival* and only gives a brief account of them in the *Criterion*. The vices of defect, however, receive somewhat more attention:

"Astuteness" is excellence in producing what is useful for attaining what the person regards as good but which is in truth not good in itself. This is the same definition which al-Fārābī gives to this vice; the vice of slyness differs from astuteness only in that slyness aims at base gains.[5]

"Inexperience" implies the lack of experience in practical things in general and, at the same time, unsoundness of imagination. A man may be inexperienced in one class of things and not in another.[6]

"Foolishness" is the impairment of deliberation on what leads to the desired end so that one seeks the wrong means. Thus the fool has a sound

1. Aristotle *Nicomachean Ethics* 6. 10. 1143a12-14.

2. *C*, p. 92, where the Arabic term for this virtue is *naqāyat ar-ra'y* ("purity of idea"). But in Asad Efendi MSS, 1759, fol. 74b, the Arabic term for this virtue is *thaqābat ar-ra'y*, which makes more sense and agrees with *R*, III. 2. 1443; cf. al-Fārābī, *Fuṣūl*, p. 133; Miskawayh, *Tahdhīb*.

3. *C*, p. 92; cf. al-Fārābī, *Fuṣūl*, p. 131; Aristotle *Nicomachean Ethics* 6. 11. 1143a19-24.

4. *C*, p. 93; *R*, III. 2. 1443, where Ghazali calls deceit *khidā'* instead of *khibb*. Furthermore, the vice of cunning is only mentioned in the *Revival*.

5. *C*, p. 93; al-Fārābī, *Fuṣūl*, p. 129.

6. *C*, p. 93; *R*, III. 2. 1443; al-Fārābī, *Fuṣūl*, p. 132.

purpose but his method is unsound. Foolishness can be natural or caused by sickness.[1]

"Insanity" is foolishness as well as unsoundness of purpose. The insane, besides following the wrong means, aim at the wrong end; they choose that which should not be chosen.[2]

Divisions of Courage

Only those which are not discussed in the text of Chapter II are mentioned here:

1. "Manliness" (*shahāmah*) is defined as the aspiration to perform deeds in expectation of goodness. No extremes of excess or defect are mentioned here.[3]

2. "Nobility" (*nubl*) is defined as the soul's rejoicing in great deeds and its constant delight in this.[4]

3. "Endurance" (*iḥtimāl*) is a virtue between undue daring (*jasārah*) and restless fear (*hala'*). Ghazali defines it as restraining the soul from accepting harmful things. He regards it as a kind of patience (*ṣabr*), a virtue which he lists under temperance. Although there is no virtue called endurance in Avicenna or Miskawayh, the latter mentions two virtues which are indirectly related to this virtue, namely, composure (*'iẓam al-himmah*) and enduring hard work (*iḥtimāl al-kadd*). The former is a virtue of the soul which causes it to sustain calmly both the happiness of good fortune and its opposites, including the distress which accompanies death. The latter is a power of the soul which uses the organs of the body for what is good through practice and proper habits.[5] Ghazali's virtue of endurance is distinguished from those of Miskawayh in that it is primarily concerned with resisting harmful things. In this way, it is a form of patience.

   While Ghazali does not have any reservations in calling endurance a virtue, Aristotle considers it as neither identical with virtue or wickedness, nor as a different genus. For Aristotle endurance is fundamentally the same as continence, except that it is in relation to pain. It corresponds to courage, and has one opposing vice, namely

1. *C*, p. 93; *R*, III. 2. 1443; al-Fārābī, *Fuṣūl*, pp. 132-33.

2. *C*, p. 93; R, III. 2. 1443.

3. *C*, p. 95; *R*, III. 2. 1443, where this virtue is mentioned by name only but not defined; cf. Miskawayh, *Tahdhīb*, p. 22; Aristotle *Nicomachean Ethics* 4. 5. 1126b1, where he does not list it as one of the virtues, but as a quality praised in men: "sometimes we call angry people manly."

4. *C*, p. 95; *R*, III. 2. 1443; cf. Miskawayh, *Tahdhīb*, p. 22, where he classifies it under liberality, which is in turn under temperance.

5. *C*, pp. 94, 134; *R*, III. 2. 1443; Miskawayh, *Tahdhīb*, pp. 21-22.

softness or effeminacy. Aristotle considers endurance as good and softness as bad, but it is not as radically good as courage.[1] Ghazali is aware of continence and places it on a lower rank than virtue proper. It does not enable man to attain perfection but saves him from becoming vicious.[2] Endurance, however, is what is expected of a virtuous man in relation to pain.

4. "Intrepidity" (*najdah*) is defined as confidence of the soul in facing death, when necessary, without fear. It is the mean between insolence (*jasārah*) and desertion (*inkhidhāl*). Insolence, the extreme of excess, means recklessness in facing death when it is not right to do so. Desertion is retreating for fear of destruction when it is not right to do so.[3] Intrepidity is a virtue which corresponds to courage in the sense of bravery in the battlefield. Aristotle discusses it in his account of courage.

5. "Fortitude" (*thabāt*) is defined briefly as the strength of the soul and its being free from weakness.[4]

6. "Amiability" (*tawaddud*) is a virtue which is mentioned in the *Revival* only. It is listed as the last of the virtues subordinated to courage without being specifically discussed.[5] In the *Supreme Purpose*, however, Ghazali defines the amiable person (*wadūd*) as one who wants for all men what he wants for himself. This is the application of the divine attribute "Amiable" (*Wadūd*) to man.[6]

Divisions of Temperance

In the text of Chapter II four virtues were discussed under temperance, namely, modesty, shame, liberality, and contentment. Following are the rest of the virtues subordinated to temperance.

1. "Remission" (*musāmaḥah*) is defined as the canceling of part of what is due to one voluntarily and gladly. It is the mean between excessive insistence upon one's right (*munāqashah*) and carelessness (*ihmāl*). Ghazali here reproduces Miskawayh's definition of this virtue, listed under liberality.[7] Ghazali's apparent approval of this virtue, as well

1. Aristotle *Nicomachean Ethics* 7. 1. 1145b1-2.

2. *C*, pp. 74-75.

3. *C*, p. 94; *R*, III. 2. 1443, where the virtue and its two extremes are mentioned by name only. Cf. Miskawayh, *Tahdhīb*, p. 21.

4. *C*, p. 95; *R*, III. 2. 1443; cf. Miskawayh, *Tahdīb*, p. 21.

5. *R*, III. 2. 1443.

6. *Maqṣad*, p. 78.

7. *C*, pp. 96, 98; *R*, III. 2. 1443; cf. Miskawayh, *Tahdhīb*, p. 23: "Remission is the cancellation of part of what is due to one. All of this should be the result of volition and choice."

as some other philosophic virtues, is accompanied by his conviction that such virtues are not directly relevant to the higher levels of moral refinement. A man who acquires the virtue of remission, for example, is a good man, yet he is still restricted by his involvement in worldly affairs; when such a man discovers the right path, remission will cease to be crucial for his character training.

2. "Good calculation" (*ḥusn al-taqdīr*) is defined as spending for one's own needs moderately. It is the mean between prodigality and meanness which are also the extremes of the virtue of liberality.[1]

3. "Self discipline" (*intiẓām*) is a virtue which is primarily concerned with regulating the different aspects of one's necessary expenditures.[2]

4. "Patience" (*ṣabr*), for Ghazali, is a virtue which is related to endurance, a virtue he lists under courage. In his view endurance is in reality nothing but "learning how to be patient." Thus as a virtue, patience is more comprehensive and important. He defines it as the resistance of the soul to passion and avoidance of vile pleasures. This definition corresponds to that of Miskawayh and Avicenna.[3] His brief discussion of patience in the context of philosophic virtues and his reliance in this discussion on the Muslim philosophers suggest that Ghazali does not want to elaborate on this virtue further here. He postpones his detailed treatment of it to his discussion of the qualities of salvation.[4]

5. "Abstinence" (*wara'*) is defined by Ghazali as adorning the soul with good and virtuous deeds for the sake of its perfection and for the attainment of nearness to God. It is a mean between dissimulation (*riyā'*) and insolence (*hutkah*). The former, the extreme of excess, is the imitation of virtuous people for sake of fame and boasting, while the latter is avoidance of adorning the soul with good deeds and openly committing vile things.[5] Ghazali's definition of abstinence resembles that of Miskawayh except that Miskawayh does not discuss its extreme of excess with the same detail as Ghazali. Indeed, Ghazali makes dissimulation the subject of half of Book 8 of Quarter III of the *Revival*.[6]

6-8. "Wit" (*ṭalāqah* or *laṭāfah*), "joy" (*inbisāṭ*), and "cheerfulness" (*ẓarf*) are three social virtues which are associated with social gatherings

1. *C*, p. 98.

2. *C*, p. 98; cf. Miskawayh, *Tahdhīb*, p. 20, where he extends this virtue to mean the management of all things related to one's interests, not only expenditures.

3. *C*, p. 98; *R*, III. 2. 1443; cf. Miskawayh, *Tahdhīb*, p. 20; Avicenna, *'Ahd*, p. 145, where he classifies it under courage.

4. *R*, IV. 2. 2177-2209.

5. *R*, III. 2. 1443; *C*, pp. 99, 101.

6. *R*, III. 8. 1865-1935; cf. Miskawayh, *Tahdhīb*, p. 21.

devoted primarily to amusement and enjoyment.[1] They seem to correspond to Aristotle's virtues concerning social life and the interchange of words and deeds, although Ghazali does not include the latter in his account of these virtues.[2] He defines wit as respectable jesting without any obscenity (*fuḥsh*) or spiritlessness (*infirāk*). It is the mean between frowning (*taqṭīb*) and excessive seriousness (*jidd*), and play (*hazal*). Wit, therefore, is a virtue in respect to jesting in the widest sense.[3] For Ghazali jesting as such is blameworthy because it implies indulgence in play, amusement, and wasting valuable time. Although he admits that proper jesting is needed for relaxation, Ghazali maintains that jesting may lead to excessive laughter which weakens the spirit and is the sign of an empty heart. In order to show that excessive laughter is bad, Ghazali points out that the Prophet "laughed without bursting out into laughter." One should emulate the Prophet who preferred smiling to laughter.[4] Ghazali is convinced that a person who laughs excessively reveals his ignorance of the dangers of this life and the affliction which may await him in the hereafter, citing the example of al-Ḥasan al-Baṣrī, who did not laugh for thirty years, as the proper attitude toward jesting.[5]

Moreover, jesting is harmful because it can easily lead to falsehood. Therefore, according to Ghazali, telling the truth is an essential consideration in relation to jesting. He supports this with a tradition about the Prophet which reports that "He jested but only spoke the truth."[6]

In addition to laughter and falsehood as dangers of jesting, there is yet a more important consideration which controls the virtue of wit. This is Ghazali's attitude toward speech as a whole. He names twenty evils of speech, or, as he prefers to call them, evils of the tongue. He regards silence (*ṣamt*) as a virtue because people waste their time talking instead of utilizing it for more important ends, such as invoking the names of God. To follow the right way one must say only what is necessary in the shortest possible phrases.[7] This

1. It is important to point out here that I have taken the liberty of rearranging the Arabic terms Ghazali uses for the first and third of these three virtues. There seems to be a confusion between *ṭalaqah* and *ẓarf*. The latter term is used by the translators of the *Nicomachean Ethics* to render "wittiness"; see Aristotle, *Akhlāq*, fol. 31b; cf. Aristotle *Nicomachean Ethics* 2. 7. 1108a23. It is also used in this sense by Muslim philosophers such as al-Fārābī; see his *Fuṣūl*, p. 113.

2. Aristotle *Nicomachean Ethics* 4. 6. 1126b11-1128b9.

3. *C*, pp. 99, 101; cf. al-Fārābī, *Fuṣūl*, p. 113: "Wit (*ẓarf*) is a mean in jesting, play, and so forth, between impudence and folly, and dullness." Cf. Aristotle *Nicomachean Ethics* 4. 8. 1127b35-1128b9.

4. *R*, II. 10. 1297; III. 4. 1577-78.

5. *R*, III. 4. 1578.

6. *R*, II. 10. 1297; III. 4. 1578.

7. *R*, III. 4. 1547-53; II. 10. 1306.

restriction makes proper jesting difficult if not impossible, and almost suggests that jesting is essentially undesirable. Although Ghazali agrees with Aristotle that relaxation and amusement are necessary, he favors only limited participation in jesting so that wit approaches the extreme of defect, which is only perfunctorily mentioned in the definition of this virtue.[1] Ghazali's attitude toward jesting seems to be further affected by his view of social intercourse which is the subject of the next two virtues.

"Joy" (*inbisāṭ*) is listed as one of the virtues subordinate to temperance, but is never mentioned or defined after that. Ghazali seems to consider it as part of cheerfulness.[2] Indeed, some aspects of wit are included in cheerfulness which appears to be a general virtue in relation to social gatherings dedicated to amusement. Ghazali regards "cheerfulness" (*ẓarf*) as a mean between frowning (*taqṭīb*), which is excessive avoidance, and play (*hazal* or *'abath*), which is excessive admiration of a companion or a participant in a social gathering. He describes it as recognizing the class of those people one meets socially, fulfilling one's social commitments, and behaving appropriately in social situations.[3] Since relaxation refreshes one's mind, some kind of intimate association becomes necessary, during which man leaves solitude and departs from the way of life of brutish people without violating the conditions of proper jesting. In a special chapter on the account of the "Prophet's speech and laughter," Ghazali states that the Prophet used to pass time with his companions, "admiring what they said, and smiling with them."[4]

The virtue of cheerfulness resembles Aristotle's virtue of friendliness or friendship without affection, whose end is being together for social amusement. According to Ghazali man must associate properly with those who are his intimates and those who are not. In being cheerful to all men, however, the friendly man associates differently with people of high rank and with ordinary people, rendering to each class what is befitting.[5] He mentions that the Prophet used to be intimate with people of high station, giving them a special regard, while at the same time he used to associate with the poor and loved them.[6] In spite of this favorable attitude toward companionship, Ghazali still teaches that seclusion (*'uzlah*) is better for those who seek the higher levels of morality, the levels of mystical experience, and even makes seclusion the subject of Book 6 of Quarter II of the *Revival*. There he tries to maintain a balance between the

1. *C*, p. 99; cf. Aristotle *Nicomachean Ethics* 4. 8. 1128b2.
2. *C*, pp. 96, 99.
3. *C*, p. 99.
4. *R*, II. 10. 1307.
5. *R*, II. 5. 1003; cf. Aristotle *Nicomachean Ethics* 4. 6. 1126b35-1127a2.
6. *R*, II. 10. 1295-96.

advantages and disadvantages of both seclusion and association.[1] Gathering for the sake of amusement and enjoyment, however, is not sufficiently rewarding according to him to make a man seriously engaged in purifying his character prefer companionship. The key to all social virtues is the idea that the individual's life is crucial for his salvation. It is important that he spend every minute of it in a way which brings about that salvation. This may include some relaxation for the refreshment of the soul, but it considerably restricts the virtues of wittiness, joy, and cheerfulness, and suggests that they are closely related to the excess of defect.

9. "Honest dealing" (*musā'adah*) is another virtue which deals with social gatherings, and is thus related in a way to the preceding three virtues of wit, joy, and cheerfulness.[2] Ghazali defines it as renouncing differences of opinion and arguments with companions about ordinary matters for the sake of enjoying society. It is the mean between peevishness (*shakāsah*) and flattery (*malaq*); the former is the extreme of excess and it signifies differing with companions about the conditions of sociability, whereas the latter is the extreme of defect which reveals one's affection to companions without attention to the disdain that may be incurred.[3] Since the end of honest dealing is enjoying society, the emphasis here is on moderation in dealing with one's social companions.

10. "Tenderness of character" (*damāthah*) is the right disposition of the concupiscent faculty to what is desired. This definition corresponds to Miskawayh's account of the same virtue[4] and, consequently, is another instance of Ghazali's acceptance of a philosophic virtue without elaboration.

11. "Tranquility" (*hudū'*) is a virtue which is defined as the calmness of the soul when it attains beautiful pleasures.[5] Ghazali mentions no extremes of this virtue or the one before it nor does Miskawayh.[6]

12. "Good appearance" (*ḥusn al-hay'ah*) is the desire of necessary attire without any frivolity. Although this virtue is also discussed by philosophers such as Miskawayh and Ibn 'Adī,[7] Ghazali forms his own

1. *R*, II. 6. 1081.

2. This term occurs in Esad Efendi MSS, 1759, fol. 80b; it is preferred to the term *musāmaḥah*, which occurs in *C*, p. 99. where it is obviously a misprint because Ghazali lists it as *musā'adah* in *C*, p. 97. On the other hand, there is another virtue called *musāmaḥah* (remission) in *C*, pp. 96, 98; cf. *R*, III. 2. 1443.

3. *C*, pp. 99, 101; *R*, III. 2. 1443; cf. Ibn 'Adī, *Tahdhīb*, p. 99.

4. *C*, p. 98; cf. Miskawayh, *Tahdhīb*, p. 20, "tenderness of character (*damāthah*) is the disposition of the soul to what is praiseworthy, and its zeal to accomplish the good."

5. *C*, p. 99.

6. *C*, pp. 98-99; cf. Miskawayh, *Tahdhīb*, p. 20.

7. *C*, p. 98; cf. Miskawayh, *Tahdhīb*, p. 21; Ibn 'Adī, *Tahdhīb*, p. 99, where he

opinion about it. In a special chapter on "The account of the Prophet's Character and Manner in regard to Dress," Ghazali states that the Prophet used to wear whatever was at hand. "He had a padded garment which he used to wear, saying, 'I am only a slave, I dress as the slave dresses...'."[1] Ghazali's preference for a minimum of adornment is further reflected in his enumeration of three types of dress which are permissible. The cheapest type is a garment made from a rough material meant to cover necessary parts of the body and to last for one day and one night. This is, according to Ghazali the dress most preferred by people who are seeking otherworldly ends. The most expensive kind of dress is the type of clothes used by the multitude who seek the enjoyment of worldly things. Between these two there is a middle type which is permissible for people of moral refinement as long as they do not seek enjoyment or softness.[2] Thus, while accepting good appearance as a virtue, Ghazali obviously prefers that the practice of this virtue be limited.

13. "Righteous indignation" (*tasakhkhuṭ*) is the last of the virtues subordinate to temperance. Ghazali defines it as being grieved at undeserved good fortune and undeserved bad fortune. It is the mean between envy (*ḥasad*) and spite (*shamātah*).[3] Envy is being grieved at good fortune which comes to a deserving person known to the envious man, and spite is being delighted by bad fortune afflicting undeserving persons known to the spiteful man.[4]

In dealing with this virtue Ghazali seems to be in almost complete agreement with Aristotle. This is especially important because Muslim philosophers such as Avicenna and Miskawayh, with whose doctrines Ghazali is familiar, do not mention righteous indignation. Ghazali, however, differs from Aristotle in regarding this virtue in terms of being grieved at both undeserved good fortune and undeserved bad fortune, whereas Aristotle maintains that the righteously indignant man is pained by undeserved good fortune only. On the other hand, both agree that the three dispositions of this virtue and its extremes are related to the fortunes of people we know or with whom we have something in common.[5]

calls it "love of adornment" (*ḥubb al-zīnah*)and regards it as a virtue for kings and princes etc., but a vice for monks, ascetics, and men of learning.

1. *R*, II. 10. 1320.

2. *C*, p. 186.

3. *C*, pp. 99-100. Ghazali here uses a special Arabic term which means "righteous indignation." In *R*, III. 2. 1443, he calls this virtue *qillat al-ṭama'*, which literally means "uncovetousness." The terms for the extremes are used by the translators of the *Nicomachean Ethics*, Aristotle, *Akhlāq*, fol. 31b; cf. Aristotle *Nicomachean Ethics* 2. 7. 1108a35-1108b1.

4. *C*, p. 101; *R*, III. 2. 1443, where envy is mentioned by name only; cf. p. 135, where he defines envy as wishing the disappearance of fortune from those who deserve it.

5. *R*, III. 4. 1695-96; *C*, p. 135; cf. Aristotle *Nicomachean Ethics*, 2. 7. 1108b2-3.

Ghazali inquires into the vice of envy in detail. He regards it as a by-product of anger and a strictly forbidden (*ḥarām*) and blameworthy quality. The proper attitude toward such an evil is to know it, especially since envy is easily confused with other habits of character from which it should be distinguished. These are admiration (*ghibṭah*) and competition (*munāfasah*). They are commendable and can even be obligatory if they are related to religious duties such as prayer or almsgiving.[1]

According to Ghazali there are many reasons which bring about envy, but the one which underlies them all is "love of this life," because there cannot be enough worldly goods for all those who are seeking them. Thus, as long as men continue to seek worldly things, there will be envy among them; even learned men will envy each other if they seek wealth and fame.[2] It is only when men seek the hereafter that they can cease to envy each other.

In suggesting methods of avoiding and curing the vice of envy, Ghazali points to the correct attitude which is the state of righteous indignation. But by making righteous indignation conditional on seeking the goods of the hereafter, he seems to extend this virtue beyond its philosophic bounds and certainly beyond the understanding set forth by Aristotle.

1. *C*, p. 134; *R*, III. 4. 1689; cf. al-Rāghib al-Iṣfahānī, *Dharī'ah*, p. 135.
2. *R*, III. 4. 1996-97.

SELECTED BIBLIOGRAPHY

This is a bibliography of works cited. For a bibliography of Ghazali, see Badawī, *Mu'allafāt al-Ghazālī*; Bouyges, *Essai de chronologie des œuvres d'al-Ghazali*; Hourani, "The Chronology of Ghazali's Writings"; MacDonald "The Life of al-Ghazali"; and al-'Uthmān, *Sīrat al-Ghazālī*.

Ghazali's Works

C: *Mīzān al-'Amal* ("Criterion of Action"). Cairo: Maṭba'at Kurdistān al-'Ilmiyyah, 1328/1910.

The following manuscripts of *C* have been consulted:

Ankara. Dilve Tarih-Coğrafya Fakültesi. Ismail Saib Sancar MSS. 1/4464.

Istanbul. Millet Kütüphanesi. Feyzullah MSS. 1279.

Istanbul. Süleymaniye Kütüphanesi. Asad Efendi MSS. 1759.

Istanbul. Süleymaniye Kütüphanesi. Fatih Camii Kütüphanesi MSS. 2877.

Madrid. San Lorenzo de El Escorial MSS. 1130.

Madrid. San Lorenzo de El Escorial MSS. 875.

Madrid. Biblioteca Nacional de Madrid MSS. 59.

Rabat. Bibliothèque Général. Maktabat 'Abd al-Ḥayy al-Kattānī MSS. 251.

R: *Iḥyā' 'Ulūm al-Dīn* ("The Revival of the Religious Sciences"). 15 vols. Cairo: Lajnat Nashr al-Thaqāfah al-Islāmiyyah, 1356/1937-1357/1938.

RB: *Iḥyā' 'Ulūm al-Dīn*. 4 vols. Cairo: Būlāq, 1289/1872.

RM: *Iḥyā' 'Ulūm al-Dīn*. Harvard University. Semitic Museum MSS. 76 (2280).

Arba'īn: *Kitāb al-Arba'īn fī Uṣūl al-Dīn*. Cairo: Maktabat al-Jundī 1383/1963.

Fayṣal: *Fayṣal-al-Tafriqah bayn al-Islām wa al-Zandaqah*. Edited by Sulaymān Dunyā. Cairo: 'Īsā al-Bābī al-Ḥalabī, 1961.

Imlā': *al-Imlā' 'alā Ishkālāt al-Iḥyā'* in *Mulḥaq Iḥyā' 'Ulūm al-Dīn*. Cairo: al-Maktabah al-Tijāriyyah al-Kubrā, n.d.

Iqtiṣād: *al-Iqtiṣād fī al-I'tiqād*. Edited by I. A. Čubukču and Hüseyn Atay. Ankara: Nur Matbaasi, 1962.

Kīmiyā-yi: *Kīmiyā-yi Sa'ādat*. 2 vols. 2d ed. Tehran: Kitāb-furūshī va Chāpkhāne-yi Markazī, 1333/1954.

Laduniyyah: *al-Risālah al-Laduniyyah*. In *al-Jawāhir al-Ghazālī*. Cairo: Maṭba'at al-Sa'ādah, 1934.

Maqāṣid: *Maqāṣid al-Falāsifah*. Edited by Sulaymān Dunyā. Cairo: Dār al-Ma'ārif, 1961.

Maqṣad: *al-Maqṣad al-Asnā Sharḥ Asmā' Allāh al-Ḥusnā*. Cairo: Maṭba'at al-Kulliyyāt al-Azhariyyah, n.d.

Mishkāt: *Mishkāt al-Anwār*. Edited by Abū al-'Ilā 'Afīfī. Cairo: al-Dār al-Qawmiyyah li al-Ṭibā'ah wa al-Nashr, 1964.

Mi'yār: *Mi'yār al-'Ilm*. Edited by Sulaymān Dunyā. Cairo: Dār al-Ma'ārif, 1964.

Munqidh: *al-Munqidh min al-Ḍalāl*. Edited by Jamīl Ṣalībā and Kāmil 'Ayyād. 5th ed. Damascus: Maṭba'at al-Jāmi'ah al-Sūriyyah, 1956.

Qudsiyyah: *al-Risālah al-Qudsiyyah* ("The Jerusalem Tract"). Translated and edited by A. L. Tibawi in "Al-Ghazali's Tract on Dogmatic Theology," *Islamic Quarterly*, IX (1965), 65-122.

Tahāfut: *Tahāfut al-Falāsifah* (Incohérence des philosophes). Edited by Maurice Bouyges (Bibliotheca arabica scholasticorum, série arabe, t. II), Beirut: Imprimerie Catholique, 1927.

Walad: *Ayyuhā al-Walad*. In *al-Jawāhir al-Ghazālī*. Cairo: Maṭba'at al-Sa'ādah, 1934.

Arabic Primary Sources

ABŪ DĀWŪD, IBN AL-ASH'ATH AS-SIJISTĀNĪ.

Sunan: *Sunan*. 2 vols. Cairo: al-Maktabah al-Tijāriyyah, 1935.

ARISTOTLE.

Nafs: *Kitāb al-Nafs*. Translated by Ḥunayn Ibn Isḥāq. Edited by 'Abd al-Raḥmān Badawī. Cairo: Maktabat al-Nahḍah al-Miṣriyyah, 1954.

Akhlāq: *Kitāb Arisṭū fī al-Akhlāq* ("Nicomachean Ethics"). Rabat: Bibliothèque Centrale MSS. 2508/80.

ARISṬŪṬĀLĪS. *See* ARISTOTLE.

AL-ASH'ARĪ, ABŪ AL-ḤASAN 'ALĪ IBN ISMĀ'ĪL.

Ibānah: *al-Ibānah 'an Uṣūl al-Diyānah*. Hyderabad: Majlis Dā'irat al-Ma'ārif, n.d.

Luma' : *Kitāb al-Luma' fī al-Radd 'alā Ahl al-Zaygh wa al-Bida'*. Edited by Richard J. McCarthy. Beirut: al-Maktabah al-Sharqiyyah, 1952.

Maqālāt : *Maqālāt al-Islāmiyyīn* (Die Dogmatischen Lehren der Anhanger des Islam). Edited by Helmut Ritter (Bibliotheca Islamica, 1). 2d ed. Wiesbaden: Franz Steiner Verlag. 1963.

Averroes

Tahāfut : *Tahāfut al-Tahāfut* (Incohérence de l'incohérence). Edited by Maurice Bouyges. (Bibliotheca arabica scholasticorum, série arabe III). Beirut: Imprimerie Catholique, 1930.

Avicenna

'Ahd : *Fī al-'Ahd*. In *Tis' Rasā'il*. Pp. 142-51.

Aḥwāl : *Aḥwāl al-Nafs*. Edited by Aḥmad Fu'ād al-Ahwānī. Cairo: 'Isā al-Bābī al-Ḥalabī, 1952.

Akhlāq : *Fī 'Ilm al-Akhlāq*. In *Tis' Rasā'il*. Pp. 152-56.

Fī al-Akhlāq wa al-Infi'ālāt al-Nafsāniyyah : *Fī al-Akhlāq wa al-Infi'ālāt al-Nafsāniyyah*. In *Memorial Avicenne* IV *Miscellanea*. Contribution de M. Luis Massignon, Mme. Denise Remondon et M. G. Vatom. Cairo: Publications de l'Institut Français d'Archéologie Orientale, 1954.

Ishārāt : *al-Ishārāt wa al-Tanbīhāt*. Edited by Sulaymān Dunyā. 4 parts in 3 vols. Cairo: Dār al-Ma'ārif, 1958.

Nafs : *Kitāb al-Nafs* (*al-Shifā'* : *Physics* VI). In *Avicenna's De Anima*. Edited by F. Rahman. London: Oxford University Press, 1959.

Najāt : *al-Najāt*. 2d ed. Cairo: Muḥy al-Dīn Ṣabrī al-Kurdī, 1936.

Shifā' : *al-Manṭiq* : *Shifā'* : *al-Manṭiq*, Vol. VIII, *al-Khaṭābah*. Edited by Muḥammad Salīm Sālim. Cairo: Wizārat al-Ma'ārif al-'Umūmiyyah, 1954.

Shifā' : *Metaphysics* : *al-Shifā'* : *Metaphysics*. Vol. II. Edited by Muḥammad Yūsuf Mūsā *et al.* Cairo: U.A.R. Wizārat al-Thaqāfah wa al-Irshād al-Qawmī, 1960.

Tis' Rasā'il : *Tis' Rasā'il fī al-Ḥikmah wa al-Ṭabī'iyyāt*. Cairo: Amīn Hindiyyah, 1326/1908.

al-'Aydarūs, 'Abd al-Qādir Ibn Shaykh.

Ta'rīf : *Kitāb Ta'rīf al-Aḥyā' bi Faḍā'il al-Iḥyā'*. In *Mulḥaq Iḥyā' 'Ulūm al-Dīn*. Cairo: al-Maktabah al-Tijāriyyah al-Kubrā, n.d.

AL-BĀQILLĀNĪ, ABŪ BAKR.

Tamhīd : *Kitāb al-Tamhīd*. Edited by Richard J. McCarthy. Beirut: al-Maktabah al-Sharqiyyah, 1957.

AL-FĀRĀBĪ, ABŪ NAṢR MUḤAMMAD.

Fuṣūl : *Fuṣūl al-Madanī* ("Aphorisms of the Statesman"). Edited by D. M. Dunlop. Cambridge: Cambridge University Press, 1961.

Iḥṣā' : *Iḥṣā' al-'Ulūm*. Edited by 'Uthmān Amīn. 2d ed. Cairo: Dār al-Fikr al-'Arābī, 1949.

Millah : *Kitāb al-Millah wa Nuṣūs Ukhrā* ("Book of Religion and Related Texts"). Edited by Muhsin Mahdi. Beirut: Dār al-Mashriq, 1968.

AL-FĪRŪZĀBĀDĪ, MUḤAMMAD IBN YA'QŪB.

Qāmūs : *al-Qāmūs al-Muḥīṭ*. 4 vols. 3d ed. Cairo: Būlāq, 1344/1925.

ḤĀJJĪ KHALĪFAH.

Kashf : *Kashf al-Ẓunūn* (Lexicon bibliographicum et encyclopaedicum). Edited by Gustavus Fluegel. London: Oriental Translation Fund of Great Britain and Ireland, 1835-58.

AL-HARAWĪ, 'ABD ALLĀH AL-ANṢĀRĪ.

Manāzil : *Manāzil al-Sā'irīn*. Edited by S. de Laugier de Beaurecueil. Cairo: Imprimerie de l'Institut Français d'Archéologie Orientale, 1962.

AL-ḤARBĪ, IBRĀHĪM IBN ISḤĀQ.

Ikrām : *Ikrām al-Ḍayf*. Cairo: Maṭba'at al-Manār, 1349/1930.

IBN ABĪ AL-DUNYĀ, ABŪ BAKR 'ALĪ.

Makārim : *Makārim al-Akhlāq*. Berlin: Staatsbibliothek, Preussischer Kulturbesitz MSS. 5388.

IBN 'ADĪ, YAḤYĀ.

Tahdhīb : *Tahdhīb al-Akhlāq*. Edited by Mar Severius Afram Barṣaum. In "Jahja ibn-'Adi's Treatise on Character-Training," *American Journal of Semitic Languages and Literatures, XLV* (1928-1929), 1-34, 94-129.

IBN AL-ḤAJJĀJ, MUSLIM.

Ṣaḥīḥ : *Ṣaḥīḥ*. 16 vols. Cairo: al-Maṭba'ah al-Amīriyyah, 1929.

IBN ḤANBAL, AḤMAD.

Musnad: al-Musnad. 6 vols. Cairo: Būlāq, n.d.

IBN MĀJAH, MUḤAMMAD IBN YAZĪD AL-QAZWĪNĪ.

Sunan: Sunan. 2 vols. Edited by Muḥammad Fu'ād 'Abd al-Bāqī. Cairo: Dār Iḥyā' al-Kutub al-'Arabiyyah, 1952-1953.

IBN MANẒŪR, JAMĀL AL-DĪN MUḤAMMAD B. MUKARRAM AL-ANṢĀRĪ.

Lisān: Lisān al-'Arab. 20 vols. Cairo: Būlāq, 1308/1901.

IBN RUSHD. *See* AVERROES.

IBN SĪNĀ. *See* AVICENNA.

IBN TAYMIYYAH, TAQIYY AL-DĪN AḤMAD.

Muwāfaqat: Muwāfaqat Ṣaḥīḥ al-Manqūl li-Ṣarīḥ al-Ma'qūl. 2 vols. Edited by Muḥammad Muḥy al-Dīn 'Abd al-Ḥamīd and Muḥammad Ḥāmid al-Faqī. Cairo: Maṭba'at al-Sunnah al-Muḥammadiyyah, 1951.

Naqḍ: Naqḍ al-Manṭiq. Edited by Muḥammad 'Abd al-Razzāq Ḥamzah and Sulaymān b. 'Abd al-Raḥmān al-Ṣāni'. Cairo: Maṭba'at al-Sunnah al-Muḥammadiyyah, 1951.

Radd: al-Radd 'alā al-Manṭiqiyyīn. Edited by 'Abduṣ-Ṣamad Sharafud-Dīn al-Kutubī. Bombay: Qayyimah Press, 1949.

IBN ṬUFAYL, MUḤAMMAD IBN 'ABD AL-MALIK.

Ḥayy: Ḥayy ben Yaqdhān (Ḥayy Ibn Yaqẓān). Edited by Léon Gauthier. 2d ed. Beirut: Imprimerie Catholique, 1936.

AL-'IRĀQĪ, 'ABD AL-RAḤĪM, AL-ḤĀFIẒ.

Mughnī: al-Mughnī 'an Ḥaml al-Asfār fī al-Asfār fī Takhrīj mā fī al-Iḥyā' min al-Akhbār. On the margin of *R*.

JĀLĪNŪS (GALEN).

Akhlāq: Mukhtaṣar Kitāb al-Akhlāq. Edited by Paul Kraus. In "Mukhtaṣar Kitāb al-Akhlāq," *Bulletin of the Faculty of Arts of the University of Egypt*, V (1937), 25-51.

AL-JUWAYNĪ, IMĀM AL-ḤARAMAYN.

Irshād: al-Irshād. Cairo: Maktabat al-Khānjī, 1950.

AL-KALĀBĀDHĪ, ABŪ BAKR MUḤAMMAD.

Ta'arruf: al-Ta'arruf li-Madhhab Ahl al-Taṣawwuf. Edited by Ṭāha 'Abd al-Bāqī Surūr. Cairo: 'Īsā al-Bābī al-Ḥalabī, 1966.

AL-KHARRĀZ, ABŪ SA'ĪD AḤMAD IBN 'ISĀ.

Ṣidq: Kitāb al-Ṣidq. Edited by 'Abd al-Ḥalīm Maḥmūd. Cairo: Dār al-Kutub al-Ḥadīthah, n.d.

AL-KINDĪ, ABŪ YŪSUF YA'QŪB IBN ISḤĀQ.

Ḥīlah: Risālah fī al-Ḥīlah li Daf' al-Aḥzān. Edited by H. Ritter and R. Walzer. In "Studi su al-Kindi II, uno scritto morale inedito di al-Kindi," *Memorie della Reale Academia Nazionale dei Lincei,* Ser. VI, Vol. VIII, Fasc. 1 (1938), pp. 1-38.

AL-MAKKĪ, ABŪ ṬĀLIB.

Qūt: Qūt al-Qulūb. 2 vols. Cairo: Muṣṭafā al-Bābī al-Ḥalabī, 1961.

MISKAWAYH, ABŪ 'ALĪ AḤMAD IBN MUḤAMMAD.

Tahdhīb: Tahdhīb al-Akhlāq ("The Refinement of Character"). Edited by Constantine K. Zurayk. Beirut: American University of Beirut, 1968.

AL-QUSHAYRĪ, ABŪ AL-QĀSIM 'ABD AL-KARĪM.

Risālah: al-Risālah. 2 vols Edited by 'Abd al-Ḥalīm Maḥmūd and Maḥmūd ibn al-Sharīf. Cairo: Dār al-Kutub al Ḥadīthah, 1966.

AL-RĀGHIB AL-IṢFAHĀNĪ, ABŪ AL-QĀSIM AL-ḤUSAYN.

Dharī'ah: al-Dharī'ah ilā Makārim al-Sharī'ah. Cairo: Maṭba'at Idārat al-Waṭan, 1299/1882.

Mufradāt: al-Mufradāt fī Gharīb al-Qur'ān. Cairo: Muṣṭafā al-Bābī al-Ḥalabī, 1961.

AL-RĀZĪ, ABŪ BAKR MUḤAMMAD IBN ZAKARIYYĀ.

Sīrah: al-Sīrah al-Falsafiyyah. In *Opera Philosophica.* I, 99-111.

Ṭibb: al-Ṭibb al-Rūḥānī in *Opera Philosophica.* I, 15-96.

Nafs: al-Qawl fī al-Nafs wa al-'Ālam. In *Opera Philosophica.* I, 281-90.

Opera Philosophica: Opera Philosophica I. Edited by Paul Kraus. Cairo: University of Fu'ād I, 1939.

AL-RĀZĪ, FAKHR AL-DĪN.

Nafs: Kitāb al-Nafs wa al-Rūḥ. Edited by Muḥammad Ṣaghīr Ḥasan al-Ma'ṣūmī. Islamabad, Pakistan: Islamic Research Institute, 1968.

AL-SARRĀJ, ABŪ NAṢR.

Luma': Kitāb al-Luma'. Edited by 'Abd al-Ḥalīm Maḥmūd and Ṭāha 'Abd al-Bāqī Surūr. Cairo: Dār al-Kutub al-Ḥadīthah, 1960.

AL-SUBKĪ, TĀJ AL-DĪN.

Ṭabaqāt: Ṭabaqāt al-Shāfi'iyyah al-Kubrā. 6 vols. Cairo: al-Maṭba'ah al-Ḥusayniyyah, 1323/1905-1324/1906.

AL-SUHRAWARDĪ, SHIHĀB AL-DĪN.

'Awārif: 'Awārif al-Ma'ārif: In *Mulḥaq Iḥyā' 'Ulūm al-Dīn*. Cairo: al-Maktabah al-Tijāriyyah al-Kubrā, n.d.

AL-ṬABARĪ, MUḤAMMAD IBN JARĪR.

Jāmi': Jāmi' al-Bayān 'an Ta'wīl al-Qur'ān. Edited by Maḥmūd Muḥammad Shākir. Cairo: Dār al-Ma'ārif, n.d.

ṬĀSH KUPRĀ ZĀDAH, AḤMAD IBN MUṢṬAFĀ.

Miftāḥ: Miftāḥ al-Sa'ādah wa Miṣbāḥ al-Siyādah. 2 vols. Hyderabad, India: Dā'irat al-Ma'ārif, 1329/1911.

AL-ZABĪDĪ, MUḤAMMAD IBN MUḤAMMAD AL-ḤUSAYNĪ AL-MURTAḌĀ.

Itḥāf: Itḥāf al-Sādah al-Muttaqīn bi Sharḥ Iḥyā' 'Ulūm al-Dīn. 10 vols. Cairo: al-Maṭba'ah al-Maymūniyyah, 1311/1893.

Other Sources

Abdel-Kader, Ali Hasan. *The Life, Personality and Writings of al-Junayd*. London: Luzac & Co., Ltd., 1962.

Ali, Abdulla Yūsuf. *The Translation of the Meanings of the Holy Koran*. 2 vols. 3rd ed. Beirut: Khalil al-Rawaf, 1965.

Arberry, A. J. *The Koran Interpreted*. New York: MacMillan Co., 1955.

———. "The Nicomachean Ethics in Arabic," *BSOAS*, XVII (1955), 1-9.

———. *Revelation and Reason in Islam*. London: George Allen & Unwin, 1965.

———. *Sufism: An Account of the Mystics of Islam*. London: George Allen & Unwin, 1950.

Aristotle. *Metaphysics*. Translated by Hippocrates G. Apostle. Bloomington, Indiana: Indiana University Press, 1966.

———. *Nicomachean Ethics*. Translated by H. Rackham. (The Loeb Classical Library). London: William Heinemann Ltd., 1962.

———. *Nicomachean Ethics*. Translated by S. D. Ross. New York: Oxford University Press, 1942.

———. *Politics*. Translated by H. Rackham. (The Loeb Classical Library). London: William Heinemann Ltd., 1962.

Badawī, ʻAbd al-Raḥmān. *Dawr al-ʻArab fī Takwīn al- Fikr al-Awrubbī*. Beirut: Dār al-Ādāb, 1965.

———. "al-Ghazālī wa-Maṣādiruhu al-Yūnāniyyah." *Abū Ḥāmid al-Ghazālī fī al-Dhikrā al-Miʼawiyyah al-Tāsiʻah li-Mīlādihi*. Edited by Zakī Najīb Maḥmūd. Cairo: al-Majlis al-Aʻlā li-Riʻāyāt al-Funūn wa al-Ādāb wa al-ʻUlūm al-Ijtimāʻiyyah, 1961.

———. *Shaṭaḥāt al-Ṣūfiyyah. I. Abū Yazīd al-Bisṭāmī*. Cairo: Maktabat al-Nahḍah al-Miṣriyyah, 1949.

———. *Rasāʼil Ibn Sabʻīn*. Cairo: al-Dār al-Qawmiyyah li al-Ṭibāʻah wa al-Nashr, 1964.

Bellamy, James A. "The Makārim al-Akhlāq by Ibn Abī ʼl-Dunyā." *Muslim World*, LIII (1963), 106-119.

Boer, T. J. de. "Ethics and Morality (Muslim)." *ERE*, V, 501-513.

Bousquet, G. H. *Iḥʼyaʼ ʻOuloum ed-Din ou Vivification des Sciences de la foi*. Paris: Librairie Besson, 1955.

Bouyges, Maurice. *Essai de chronologie des œuvres d'al-Ghazali (Algazel)*. Édité et mis à jour par Michel Allard. Beirut: Imprimerie Catholique, 1959.

Dunlop, D. M. "The Nicomachean Ethics in Arabic, Books I-VI." *Oriens*, XV (1962), 18-34.

Fāris, Bishr. *Mabāḥith ʻArabiyyah*. Cairo: Maṭbaʻat al-Maʻārif, 1939.

Fāris, Nabih Amin. "The Iḥyāʼ ʻUlūm al-Dīn of al-Ghazzālī." *Proceedings of the American Philosophical Society* LXXI (1939), 15-19.

Gardet, L. "Ḥāl". *EI*², III, 83-84.

Hachem, Hikmat, trans. *Critère de l'action: traité d'éthique psychologique et mystique d'Abū-Hāmid al-Ghazzālī*. Version française et étude analytique. Paris: Librairie Orientale et Américaine, 1945.

Hourani, George F. "The Chronology of Ghazali's Writings." *JAOS*, LXXIX (1959), 225-33.

al-Hujwīrī. *The Kashf al-Maḥjūb*. Translated by Reynold A. Nicholson. Leyden: E. J. Brill, 1911.

Jabre, Farid. *La notion de la maʻrifa chez Ghazali*. (Recherches VIII.) Beirut: Les Lettres Orientales, 1958.

Jadaane, Fehme. *L'influence du stoïcisme sur la pensée musulmane*. Beirut: Dār al-Mashriq, 1968.

Lerner, Ralph, and Mahdi, Muhsin, eds., *Medieval Political Philosophy: A Sourcebook*. New York: MacMillan, 1963.

MacDonald, Duncan B. "The Life of al-Ghazali, with Especial Reference to His Religious Experiences and Opinions." *JAOS*, XX (1899), 71-132.

Mahdi, Muhsin. *Ibn Khaldūn's Philosophy of History*. Chicago: University of Chicago Press, 1964.

Marmura, Michael. "Ghazali on Ethical Premises." *The Philosophic Forum* (New Series) I (1969), 393-403.

Massignon, L. "al-Makkī." *EI*, III, 174.

———. *Recueil de textes inédits concernant l'histoire de la mystique en pays d'Islam*. Paris: Librairie Orientaliste Paul Geuthner, 1929.

Mubārak, Zakī. *al-Akhlāq 'ind al-Ghazālī*. Cairo: al-Maktabah al-Tijāriyyah, n.d.

al-Nashshār, 'Alī Sāmī. *Nash'at al-Fikr al-Falsafī fī al-Islām*. 3rd ed. Alexandria: Dār al-Ma'ārif, 1965.

Pickthall, Muhammad Marmaduke. *The Meaning of the Glorious Koran*. New York: New American Library, n.d.

Plato. *Republic*. Translated by Francis MacDonald Cornford. New York: Oxford University Press, 1965.

———. *Republic*. Translated by Paul Shorey. 2 vols. London: William Heinemann Ltd., 1956.

———. *Laws*. Translated by A.E. Taylor. In Plato, *The Collected Dialogues*. Edited by Edith Hamilton and Huntington Cairns. New York: Bollingen Foundation, 1965.

Rahman, F. *Avicenna's Psychology*. London: Oxford University Press, 1952.

Umaruddin, M. *The Ethical Philosophy of Al-Ghazzali*. Aligarh, India: Aligarh Muslim University Press, 1962.

al-'Uthmān, 'Abd al-Karīm. *al-Dirāsāt al-Nafsiyyah 'ind al-Muslimīn*. Cairo: Maktabat Wahbah, 1963.

———. *Sīrat al-Ghazālī wa Aqwāl al-Mutaqddimīn fīh*. Damascus: Dār al-Fikr, n.d.

Van den Bergh, Simon. "Ghazali on 'Gratitude Toward God' and Its Greek Sources." *Studia Islamica*, VII (1957), 77-98.

———. "The 'Love of God' in Ghazali's Vivification of Theology." *Journal of Semitic Studies*, I (1956), 299-308.

Van Ess, Josef. *Die Gedankenwelt des Ḥārit al-Muḥāsibī*. Bonn: Das Orientalische Seminar der Universität Bonn, 1961.

Walzer, R., and Gibb, H. A. R. "*Akhlāḳ*." *EI*², I, 325-29.

Watt, W. Montgomery. "The Authenticity of the Works Attributed to al-Ghazali." *JRAS* (1952), pp. 24-45.

———. "Ghazālī." *EI*², II, 1038-1041.

———. *Muslim Intellectual: A study of al-Ghazali*. Edinburgh: University Press, 1963.

Zaehner, R. C. *Hindu and Muslim Mysticism*. New York: Shocken Books, 1969.

Journals and Encyclopedias

(Only journals that are cited more than once in the bibliography are abbreviated here).

BSOAS: *Bulletin of the School of Oriental and African Studies* (London, 1917-).

EI: *The Encyclopedia of Islam*. Edited by M. Th. Houtsma *et al.* 4 vols. Leiden: E. J. Brill, 1943-49.

*EI*²: *The Encyclopedia of Islam*. Edited by Bernard Lewis *et al.* Leiden: E. J. Brill, 1960- .

ERE: *Encyclopedia of Religion and Ethics*. Edited by J. Hastings. 12 vols. New York, 1908-22.

JAOS: *Journal of the American Oriental Society* (New Haven, 1860-).

JRAS: *Journal of the Royal Asiatic Society* (London, 1834-).

Other Reference Works

GAL: Brockelmann, Karl. *Geschichte der arabischen Litteratur*. 2 vols. 2nd ed. Leiden: E. J. Brill, 1943-49.

GAL(S) *Ibidem. Supplement*. 3 vols. Leiden: E. J. Brill, 1937-42.

INDEX

Philosophy, 1, 2, 4, 5, 6, 8, 13, 17, 20, 21
Physics, 4, 5, 13, 16, 17
Pilgrimage, 90, 175
Plato, 24, 25n, 38, 39, 67, 72n, 73
Politics, 4, 5, 7, 8, 17, 18, 162
Poverty, 48, 69, 71, 113, 139, 140, 141, 161, 167
Prayer and ritual purity, 88, 89, 116, 189

al-Qushayrī, 107, 109, 112, 138n, 141n, 142, 149, 150, 154n

al-Rāghib al-Iṣfahānī, 24n, 52n, 55n, 66n, 67n, 77n, 81n, 171, 172, 189n
Rahman, F., 26n, 27n
al-Rāzī, Abū Bakr, 25n, 28n, 60, 61, 62n, 63n
Religious formula, 87, 88, 142
Remission, 183, 184
Repentance, 113, 114, 118, 124-127, 132, 145, 158
Resolve, 114, 115, 116, 117, 123
Revelation, 3, 10, 11, 13, 16, 25, 81, 85, 86, 102, 104, 108, 149, 162, 164, 169

Ṣafā, 90
al-Sarrāj, 107, 109, 113, 154n
Satisfaction, 113, 118, 145, 153, 154, 155, 156
Science: philosophical, 4, 7, 13, 14, 17; practical, 4, 5, 7, 8, 11, 14, 15, 16; rational (non-religious), 8, 12, 14, 15, 16, 17, 107; religious, 8, 12, 13, 14, 15, 16, 17; theoretical, 4, 5, 7, 11, 16
Self-discipline, 184
Self-examination, 114, 115, 119, 120, 121, 123
Shāfi'ite school, 1n
Shame, 65, 66, 67, 183
al-Shiblī, 105
Sincerity, 114, 115, 117, 118, 123
Singing, 101
Smith, M., 15n
Soul: 3, 7, 8, 11, 13, 14, 15, 16, 17, 23, 24, 25, 26, 27, 28, 29, 30, 32, 33, 34, 35, 40, 45, 47, 50n, 51, 53, 56, 63, 64, 72, 74, 77, 78, 79, 80, 83, 93, 101, 107, 111, 112, 113, 115, 116, 119, 120, 121, 123, 126, 128, 135, 156, 161, 162, 165, 166, 172, 173, 182, 183, 184, 187; animal, 25, 26, 29, 35, 47, 63, 161; greatness of, 47, 49, 51, 54, 74; powers or faculties of, 25, 38, 115, 119, 121, 123, 129, 162
Stoics, 54, 83n, 108n
al-Subkī, Tāj al-Dīn, 1n, 2n, 106n, 170
al-Suhrawardī, Shihāb al-Dīn, 113n

al-Ṭabarī, 45n
Ṭāsh Kubrā Zādah, Aḥmad ibn Muṣṭafā, 170, 171n
Temperance: 24, 29, 38, 39, 42, 46, 56-72, 74, 75, 77, 96, 97, 98, 136, 177n, 182, 183, 186, 188; regarding food, 36, 56, 57-60, 61, 63, 64; regarding sex, 56, 60-63, 64
Theology, dialectical, 1, 2n, 9, 12, 13, 17, 79, 126
Tranquility, 187
Travel, 92, 98, 100
Trust, 111, 113, 114, 118, 142, 143, 144, 145, 154
Truthfulness, 114, 115, 117, 118, 119, 123, 136
Ṭūs, 1n

Uḥud, 45
Umaruddin, M., 19n
al-'Uthmān, 'Abd al-Karīm, 28n

Van den Bergh, S., 83n, 108n, 147n
Van Ess, J., 120n
Vice, 23, 27, 29, 32, 33, 35, 43, 54, 56, 62, 70, 72, 73, 79, 88, 167, 181, 182, 188, 189
Vigilance, 114, 115, 119, 120, 121, 123
Virtue: acquisition of, 3, 31, 32, 33, 74, 85, 115; as the mean, 24, 33, 34, 35, 36, 37, 38, 42, 43, 47, 49, 51, 52, 53, 55, 56, 57, 58, 60, 62, 65, 66, 68, 70, 73, 74, 96, 134, 135, 181, 183, 184, 185, 186, 187, 188; key to ethics, 23, 108; moral, 30; practical, 26, 27, 29, 30;

DATE DUE

DEC 1 7 1982			